The Military Legacy of the Civil War

The
Military Legacy
of the Civil War

THE EUROPEAN INHERITANCE

By

Jay Luvaas

THE UNIVERSITY OF CHICAGO PRESS

Library of Congress Catalog Number: 59-12288

THE UNIVERSITY OF CHICAGO PRESS, CHICAGO 37
Cambridge University Press, London, N.W. 1, England
The University of Toronto Press, Toronto 5, Canada

To My Mother and Father

Preface

Few wars have so fired the popular imagination as the American Civil War. Scarcely a week goes by without the appearance of another biography of a Union or Confederate leader, a battle study written especially for this generation, or an attractive reprint of some scarce diary or memoir. Since World War II especially, the ranks of the Civil War enthusiasts in this country have swelled until they now represent a formidable cult.

There have been times, too, when the Civil War was a popular subject among foreign military circles. A surprising number of European soldiers traveled to America to observe the conflict, and periodically since 1865 the Civil War has been the object of special study in the major armies of Europe. Exactly what was learned, how much military doctrine actually was influenced by the Civil War, is not easy to determine. Manifestly it has varied from country to country and from time to time, but nobody today doubts that the Civil War is an important chapter in military history. The late Field Marshal Erwin Rommel, it is rumored, gained much useful knowledge from a visit he is supposed to have made to the Civil War battlefields twenty years ago, and although he did not actually make such a trip, there are a great many European soldiers who have done so. Only recently Field Marshal Montgomery made news by his blunt criticisms while visiting the national shrine at Gettysburg.

In this book I have attempted to determine the reasons why European soldiers have studied and written about the Civil War and what military lessons they have learned—or thought they could learn—from it. Each writer is portrayed against a background of ideas and doctrines prevalent in his own army, for in no other way is it possible to understand a man's views and measure his influence. Particular attention has been paid to the British, German, and French students of the Civil War, partly because they were by far the most prolific of all European historians of the conflict and also because their armies were the most influential and would typify the reaction to the Civil War found elsewhere. I suspect that a study of the Russian military literature of the period would lead to some interesting facts about cavalry, but linguistic barriers unfortunately make such a study impossible.

It is intended that this be the first of three volumes on the military legacy of the Civil War. A second volume will be devoted to "The American Inheritance," and a third will examine the legacy insofar as naval warfare is concerned.

I am indebted to many people for help given along the way. Theodore Ropp of Duke University conceived the project and has given constant and much needed encouragement and advice; he is very much a part of this book. Captain B. H. Liddell Hart has in generous measure answered my questions about his ideas and writings and has similarly approached others on my behalf. Harold T. Parker, Robert H. Woody, E. Malcolm Carroll, and J. Wesley Williams of Duke University, Jeremy North, a friend to all book collectors, and Wilbor Kraft of Allegheny College read most of the manuscript in various stages of preparation and made many helpful suggestions. The late Mr. L. S. Amery generously presented the first volume of his *Memoirs*, and the late Dr. Douglas Southall Freeman graciously took time from his busy schedule to answer questions. Charles Scott Sullivan of Durham loaned several important volumes from his library, Frederick B. M. Hollyday of Duke shared his extensive knowledge of German military history, and Paul V. Reslink of Allegheny drew the sketches found in chapter ii. I also owe much to Duke University and Allegheny College for financial assistance while the book was in progress, and I wish to acknowledge the special privileges allowed by the librarians of both institutions and of the Royal Military College of Canada. Anne Risher and Marie Stellato typed the manuscript under difficult circumstances, and Roberta Heller and Barbara Lazuka did their teacher a favor by assisting with the proofreading. Above all, I owe an immeasurable debt to my wife both for valuable assistance in preparing the manuscript and also for tolerating me in the process. The only thing in this book for which I can claim sole responsibility is the errors.

I wish, too, to acknowledge those who have helpfully responded to my requests for information. General Friedrich von Boetticher, Lieutenant Colonel Alfred H. Burne, Generalleutnant Kurt Dittmar, Lieutenant Colonel Pierre Evrard, Major General J. F. C. Fuller, Lieutenant Colonel G. A. Rimbault, Major E. W. Sheppard, Major General Arthur G. Trudeau, and Lieutenant Colonel F. W. Young have all supplied facts not available elsewhere. General Gunther Blumentritt volunteered many worthwhile suggestions, and the novelist John Masters elaborated upon his introduction, as an officer of the 4th Prince of Wales Own Gurkha Rifles, to the study of the Civil War.

I wish especially to thank Captain B. H. Liddell Hart for permission to include his "Analysis of Cavalry Operations" as Appendix B and also for permission to quote passages from *Thoughts on War*, *The Ghost of Napoleon*, and *The British Way in Warfare* (Faber & Faber, Ltd.) and *The Remaking of Modern Armies* (John Murray, Ltd.). I should like further to quote from the following: Major General J. F. C. Fuller, *Grant and Lee* (Eyre & Spottiswoode, Ltd.), *The Army in My Time* (Rich & Cowan, Ltd.), and *War and Western Civilization* (Gerald Duckworth & Co., Ltd.); Alan Moorehead, *Montgomery* (Hamish Hamilton, Ltd.); G. F. R. Henderson, *The Science of War* (Longmans, Green & Co., Ltd.); and the Earl of Dundonald, *My Army Life* (Edward Arnold, Ltd.; quoted with permission of the publisher and the author's representatives).

I am indebted to the Controller of Her Majesty's Stationery Office for permission to reproduce the sketches found in chapter ii and to Captain Victor Gondos, Jr., editor of *Military Affairs*, for permission to use my earlier articles on G. F. R. Henderson and Justus Scheibert and also to quote from Professor R. A. Preston's "Letter from a British Military Observer of the American Civil War," which appeared in *Military Affairs*, Vol. XVI (1952).

Contents

Contents

1

The Fog of War

On April 12, 1861, Confederate guns fired upon Fort Sumter. The ensuing bombardment lasted a scant two days and caused no casualties to either side, but the Civil War that followed lasted four years and ended only after frightful destruction and loss of life. Some two thousand distinct battles were fought, and more than half a million Americans died in combat or as a direct result of the war. Wars of this scope and intensity had not been known in Europe since the days of the French Revolution and Napoleon.

In many respects this was a unique war. It was a civil war between two sections of the country, but it also manifested many traits of a total war between nations. Each block of states had its own government, its own army; each could claim the loyal support of the overwhelming majority of its citizens. Most civil wars do not alter the geography of a country even though control of the central government may change hands, but a Confederate victory in 1865 would have confirmed the establishment of an independent nation south of the Mason-Dixon Line.

It was a war of improvisation. Whole new armies had to be created, weapons produced, equipment found. Few of those who clashed in battle in 1861 had seen previous active service, for the newly formed Confederate States had no regular army, and that of the United States, numbering only about sixteen thousand, was to a large extent absorbed by the frontier and hence was not available to enforce Lincoln's policies in the South. Militia and volunteers rushed to fill the ranks, both North and South, but after the initial enthusiasm had waned and the rigorous campaigns had begun to take their toll, replacements no longer could be obtained in sufficient number from these groups and it was necessary to resort to conscription. Hardened though the Civil War soldier became from a dozen battles, he remained essentially a citizen at war, in outlook and appearance quite different from professional soldiers in most European armies.

The Civil War differed from previous wars in other respects as well. The enormous distances involved posed new problems in logistics and increased the importance of river transportation. Railroads, used here for the first time to transport troops in war, became vital supply arteries and offered far-reaching possibilities to the strategist. Because the success or failure of a campaign often rested upon a single-line track and overworked rolling stock, railroads became prime targets for fast-moving cavalry, while the maintenance, defense, and repair of railroad lines required special techniques and organizations. New weapons also were introduced or used on a large scale for the first time in war. Breech-loading rifles, rifled artillery, land mines, hand grenades, even "stink shells," added to the destructive power of Civil War armies. The field telegraph, lamp and flag signaling, and the captive observation balloon helped overcome some of the problems in communication created by distance and the undeveloped countryside. The ironclad and corresponding developments in coast defense altered traditional concepts of warfare. Like most American wars, the Civil War was a war of extraordinary engineering feats (Union army engineers once built a railroad bridge 414 feet long in forty hours),[1] a war in which significant advances were made in military hygiene and medicine. It was, in short, a total war, the first great war fought with the tools and weapons of the Industrial Revolution.

Although the recruits of 1861 learned the rudiments of drill and elementary tactics from manuals based largely upon existing French regulations, the Civil War also represented a prophetic departure from tactics recently employed in Europe. This was especially true of infantry and cavalry. Following the example of Napoleon, nearly every European army except the British (who adhered to the linear tactics of the Duke of Wellington) had adapted some type of column formation for infantry, stressing in various degrees the development of musketry fire by skirmishers and the action of massed batteries of artillery as preparation for the decisive bayonet attack. The line met the column in the Crimea in 1854–56, where it became apparent that both systems, carried to excess, had grievous shortcomings. The Russians had relied too much upon bayonet attacks by heavy columns, formations that took long to deploy and offered a vulnerable target. The British line, on the other hand, while superb in defense, in attack had deteriorated into "an irreg-

---

[1] Francis Trevelyan Miller (editor-in-chief), *The Photographic History of the Civil War* (New York, 1911), V, 273.

ular chain of skirmishers, in which the men . . . got so mixed up together that it became no longer possible to fire volleys, or to make regular movements."

The French and the Prussians already had developed their own answer to the tactical problem—light columns that could either deploy in line or else attack in formation, whichever was required. The French regulations of 1831 rejected both big columns and linear formations by systematizing the action of skirmishers and recommending an attack by columns nine ranks deep once the fire fight had been developed. The Prussian regulations of 1847 likewise stressed the importance of skirmishers but stipulated columns of companies rather than battalions. In 1859 the favorite attack formation of the French had consisted of two lines of battalions en masse separated by a distance of five hundred to a thousand yards and preceded by a thick line of skirmishers. Frequently French infantry also resorted to bayonet charges, obeying the spirit of an order issued by the Emperor Napoleon III before the campaign, that new firearms were dangerous only at a distance and would not prevent the bayonet from being, as in the past, *l'arme terrible* of French infantry. According to one French marshal, in a battle where his forces had been greatly outnumbered "we won back with the bayonet more than we had lost with the fusillade," and near the end of the war the emperor decreed that when on the defensive, "the lines of infantry will be disposed . . . alternately in battalions deployed and in battalions in double columns; useless skirmishing will be avoided, and while the deployed battalions engage in firing by files the others will repulse the charge and attack . . . with the bayonet."[2]

Such was the nature of battle anticipated by many Americans two years later, and the volunteers of 1861 spent countless hours learning the use of the bayonet and drilling in maneuvers few of them realized soon would become obsolete. French tactics had succeeded in Italy because the French were veteran soldiers—many of them having served in the African campaigns—and could adapt their tactics to the terrain; but for the Civil War soldiers marching naïvely off to their first battle the outcome was to be quite dif-

[2] Captain A. F. Becke, *An Introduction to the History of Tactics 1740–1905* (London, 1909), pp. 39–41; Commandant J. Colin, *The Transformations of War* (London, 1912), pp. 27–29; E. M. Lloyd, *A Review of the History of Infantry* (London, 1908), pp. 241–44; Général Thoumas, *Les transformations de l'armée française: Essais d'histoire et de critique* (Paris, 1887), II, 449–55.

ferent. They soon discovered that much of their training, scanty though it was, was of no use to them in a war fought under totally new conditions. Why continue to drill with the bayonet when, more often that not, "an outburst of flame and smoke" was all that could be seen of the enemy? "No thought now of manual of arms, but only of celerity of movement and rapidity of fire." By the time the Civil War soldier grew accustomed to battle conditions, the Springfield and Enfield rifles had largely replaced the obsolete muskets, giving him killing power at ranges exceeding half a mile. Unless surprise could be achieved, massed infantry attacks no longer were feasible against an enemy armed with such a weapon, and the column yielded to looser and more extended fighting formations and advance by rushes. Gradually the Civil War soldier learned also to seek shelter in trenches or behind breastworks, until by late 1863 battlefields were honeycombed with defense lines. This, too, was something new to warfare. The siege of Sevastopol (1854-55) had anticipated the siege of Vicksburg, but never before had improvised intrenchments dominated a battlefield as in the Wilderness or the fighting for Atlanta. Under these conditions flexible formations and swift outflanking maneuvers offered practically the only chance for success.[3]

The transformation in cavalry tactics was no less striking. In 1861 European cavalry still relied upon the lance and saber and fought primarily by what were known as shock tactics. Massed into dense formations, cavalry was literally hurled at the enemy in an effort to crush his forces by the sheer impact of the mounted charge. In the melee that followed, the sword and saber—"cold steel" was the phrase preferred by advocates of shock tactics—were effective weapons, far handier than firearms at close range.

But conditions did not favor shock tactics in America. Traditionally, most American cavalry were either dragoons or mounted rifles, armed with carbines and Colt revolvers. As a matter of fact, cavalry dependent upon shock action had never existed in the United States Army. In the Civil War the new regiments scarcely

[3] Bruce Catton, *America Goes to War* (Middletown, Conn., 1958), pp. 14 ff.; Fenwick Y. Hedley, "The School of the Soldier," in Miller, *Photographic History of the Civil War*, VIII, 179-88; Lloyd, *History of Infantry*, pp. 244-50; Major Arthur L. Wagner, "Hasty Intrenchments in the War of Secession," *Papers of the Military Historical Society of Massachusetts*, XIII (Boston, 1913), 127-54 *passim*. Hereafter cited as *M.H.S.P.*

had time to train, and the rough and thickly wooded terrain rarely permitted the old-style cavalry charge. As firepower increased, moreover, the chances for the success of massed cavalry formations decreased correspondingly. The Confederate General Nathan Bedford Forrest recognized early in the war that the day of saber charges against infantry was over, and after Shiloh, his biographer tells us, he generally fought on foot, using the horse chiefly as a means of conveyance.[4] If Forrest attached greater value to dismounted tactics than some of his contemporaries, it is a fact that most Civil War cavalry preferred firearms to the sword even when fighting mounted. A well-known Union cavalryman has testified:

Not until the closing days of the war did we wake up to what our experience . . . ought to have taught us. My division was the first . . . in the Army of the Potomac that had first-class repeating arms. Green regiments, that you couldn't have driven into a fight with old arms, became invincible the very moment that good arms were placed in their hands. . . . There are only two arms that cavalry should use in modern warfare,—the repeating magazine gun, either rifle or carbine, and the revolver.[5]

Dismounted tactics were not new, for dragoons had existed since the sixteenth century, but never before had mounted infantry, as the Civil War cavalry was called, been employed on such a large scale—to the incidental bewilderment of most foreign military observers.

The Civil War also saw the first extensive use of rifled field artillery. Rifled artillery had actually been employed by the French in Italy two years previously, but while it had clearly demonstrated its superiority to the smoothbore, the evidence was far from complete. The next test came in America, but this too was a period of transition. Some artillerists preferred the three-inch rifle for its greater accuracy and range; others remained faithful to the twelve-pounder Napoleon smoothbore because it carried heavier charges and was better suited for canister. Much of the fighting took place in woods where the superior range of the

[4] Colonel George T. Denison, *A History of Cavalry from the Earliest Times with Lessons for the Future* (2d ed.; London, 1913), pp. 316-95 *passim*; Major General John K. Herr and Edward S. Wallace, *The Story of the U.S. Cavalry, 1775-1942* (Boston, 1953), pp. 60-142; John Allan Wyeth, *Life of Lieutenant-General Nathan Bedford Forrest* (New York, 1908), pp. 36, 648.

[5] Major General James H. Wilson, "The Cavalry of the Army of the Potomac," *M.H.S.P.*, XIII, 85.

rifled gun was no real advantage, and so both armies tried to maintain a more or less equal balance of rifled guns and smoothbores, and both, apparently, disregarded at first the lessons of the Napoleonic wars and had to learn for themselves the advantages of massed artillery.[6]

In Europe, and especially in the three great military and industrial powers of England, Prussia, and France, the American campaigns attracted considerable attention. This was an era of international tension and consequently of intensified interest in military affairs. Englishmen sought to remedy the military weaknesses exposed in the Crimean War and the Indian Mutiny. Prussia instituted a series of military reforms intended to make good Bismarck's threat to unify the German states "with blood and iron." France, universally regarded as the leading military power in Europe after two successful wars, pursued foreign policies that might give rise to still another conflict along the Rhine or in Mexico.

Each nation, moreover, had a special stake in the Civil War. England had strong cultural and linguistic ties with America; Englishmen in general were concerned over slavery; within the army there was strong sympathy for the Confederates; and the "Trent" incident in 1861 made war with the United States a distinct possibility. Personal rather than political or diplomatic considerations explain the interest of most Germans in the sectional conflict. Thousands of families in Prussia and the other German states had close friends or relatives fighting with the Union army. Undoubtedly many letters from Americans were received, letters like those from a young German with the Union cavalry to his uncle, the famous Prussian cavalry general Karl von Schmidt, describing the military events of the war.[7] Nor could France view the war with detached interest. Aside from the question of diplomatic recognition of the Confederacy, which in itself would require some appraisal of the military situation, Napoleon III's continued support of Maximilian in Mexico in all probability would have precipitated a crisis with the United States. For this reason

6 Major General Henry J. Hunt, "Artillery," *M.H.S.P.*, pp. 89–125; Major E. S. May, *Achievements of Field Artillery* (Woolwich, 1893), pp. 49–75; Jennings Cropper Wise, *The Long Arm of Lee or The History of the Artillery of the Army of Northern Virginia* (Lynchburg, Va., 1915), I, 149–55.

7 Franz von Schmidt, *Avantgarde: Weg und Welt eines preussischen Reitergenerals* (Berlin, 1941), pp. 166–67.

alone there must have been many French officers who were anxious to learn what they could about the Union army.[8]

European soldiers desiring to learn something about the military operations of the Civil War could derive information from three types of eyewitness accounts. Their most convenient source obviously was the newspaper, for war correspondents, first seen in the Mexican (1846–47) and Crimean wars, contributed frequent articles on the main events of the war. This was particularly true in England, where public interest was greatest and where Sir William Howard Russell's forceful and controversial dispatches appeared frequently in the *Times*.[9] *Le Moniteur* maintained a regular correspondent in America, and Georges Clemenceau, the stormy French political leader of the First World War, recorded the fall of Richmond for *Le Temps*.[10] The war was also given adequate coverage in Germany, particularly in the military journals. But most war correspondents were not military men, and, like the majority of their readers, they were concerned primarily with general conditions and broad issues. The military reader looking for technical data was forced to turn elsewhere.

Occasionally a second source, the published narrative of someone who had visited America during the war, contained such information. Many European soldiers actually served in the Union or the Confederate army. The Prussian Heros von Borcke, for instance, was a member of Major General J. E. B. Stuart's staff, and a fellow Prussian, Viktor von Scheliha, became chief engineer for the Confederate army in the department of the Gulf. There were also many soldiers who, like Lieutenant Colonel James Arthur Lyon Fremantle, visited the seat of war in an unofficial capacity. Informed civilians interested in military science—the Comte de Paris

[8] The standard works on the diplomatic relations between Europe and America during this period are Donaldson Jordan and Edwin J. Pratt, *Europe and the American Civil War* (Boston and New York, 1931), and Frank L. Owsley, *King Cotton Diplomacy: Foreign Relations of the Confederate States of America* (Chicago, 1931; rev. ed., 1959).

[9] Russell was the most celebrated war correspondent of his day, having originally made his reputation reporting the Crimean War. *My Diary North and South* (Boston, 1863) remains one of the best foreign accounts of America during this period. (Unfortunately Russell left for England in April, 1862.) Frederick Milnes Edge, a "Special Correspondent of the Morning Star with the Armies of the United States," was less famous, but he saw more of the war. Cf. Edge, *Major-General McClellan and the Campaign on the Yorktown Peninsula* (London, 1865). Frank Lawley was a special correspondent representing the London *Telegraph*.

[10] *Le spectateur militaire*, XXXIX (1862), 209; Wythe Williams, *The Tiger of France: Conversations with Clemenceau* (New York, 1949), p. 17.

and the Marquis of Hartington are obvious examples—and immigrants who had participated in the war likewise wrote of their experiences in America. But with the notable exception of Von Scheliha's *Treatise on Coast-Defence*,[11] most of the books written by unofficial observers were only of limited use as a source of military information. Their chief significance is that they were published while the war was still in progress or shortly thereafter, and hence were available during the years when European interest in the Civil War was at its peak.

Reports and other writings of official military observers constituted the third and by far the richest source of information. Curiously enough, no regular apparatus for securing technical military information existed in the mid-nineteenth century. Occasionally officers were exchanged between two armies by temporary agreement, but the practice of sending military attachés was still in its infancy, and no such officers were stationed in either capital during the Civil War.[12] Nevertheless, authentic information could be acquired in several ways. The Austrians obtained much of their technical data from a "detailed report" sent by a soldier of fortune and former officer in the Austrian army.[13] The British War Office received "frequent reports" from Lord Lyons, Her Majesty's Ambassador to the United States. When this source failed to supply "such correct detailed information as appeared to be necessary,"[14] various teams of military observers were sent to the war zone with minute instructions to guide their investigations.

[11] See below, pp. 75–78.

[12] Even in Europe the practice of exchanging military attachés was not yet universal. A French military attaché was appointed to Berlin in 1851, but not until 1860 did France make similar appointments to the other Continental powers. In England there had been talk of sending a military attaché to Prussia in 1860, but no action was taken until 1864, when the government became alarmed over the "disturbed state" of Europe. Information obtained in correspondence with Lieutenant Colonel Pierre Evrard, French Army, Assistant Military Attaché in Washington in 1955, and Major General Arthur G. Trudeau, U.S. Army, Assistant Chief of Staff. See also Colonel Willoughby Verner, *The Military Life of H.R.H. George, Duke of Cambridge* (London, 1905), I, 361–62; and the *Almanach de Gotha: Annuaire diplomatique et statistique* for this period.

[13] Captain Boleslawsky, who later served in Mexico, submitted this report in September, 1864. It apparently contained data on the military use of railroads and communications, artillery and other military equipment in use during the Civil War. Excerpts from this report are printed in Wendelin von Boeheim, "Das Eisenbahnbau-Versuche und seine Leistungen im letzten Kriege," *Oesterreichische militärische Zeitschrift*, VII Jg. (1866), II, 1–27. Cited hereafter as Von Boeheim, "Das Eisenbahnbau-Corps."

[14] *Hansard's Parliamentary Debates*, 3d ser., CLXXIII (London, 1864), 564.

France, Prussia, and Switzerland also had official observers in America, just as the United States had been represented by a military commission in Europe at the time of the Crimean War.[15] Most of these observers were from the technical services, the artillery or the engineers, and their reports contain a wealth of information about the organization, arms, and equipment of the Civil War armies. The British probably were the best informed, having observers with both armies in addition to official missions sent to the North in 1862, 1863, and 1864. Major Justus Scheibert, the Prussian observer, participated in several campaigns with the Army of Northern Virginia. A French military mission, headed by a colonel who could not speak English, spent the better part of one year observing the Union forces. Even Switzerland was officially represented at the headquarters of the Army of the Potomac in 1862.

Many of these official reports are available. Two official British reports were printed at the War Office, the contents of each being considered at the time confidential. Major portions of the reports of the French and Swiss observers have also been published, and Scheibert summarized his own findings in a book written for popular consumption soon after the war. From these as well as from the unofficial writings of other observers, it is evident that the European armies hoped to acquire much useful knowledge about the war then being fought on the far side of the Atlantic.

In this day of super-spies, the Central Intelligence Agency, and rigid security restrictions, it is difficult to conceive the elementary nature of military intelligence in the 1860's. Field Marshal Sir John Burgoyne, Inspector General of Fortifications of the British army, corresponded frankly with his counterparts in Belgium, Russia, and the United States about recent technical developments. He apparently felt no reluctance in asking Brigadier General Joseph G. Totten, Chief of Engineers in the Union army, to provide an official British observer with a plan of

. . . a fort or part of one, showing your most modern improved system of construction, application of materials, interior arrangements for the convenience and efficiency of the service, etc.; in short, a good understanding of the progress in the service and art of military engineering that your countrymen are so likely to have produced at this eventful period of the general introduction of rifle guns, armour plating, etc.

[15] Captain George B. McClellan, later general-in-chief of the Union army, was a member of this commission.

As Sir John candidly admitted:

After all, though we are bound to respect the desires of those whom we visit, you and I, General, know very well that for any *sinister* object we might have, we can obtain all that is most important by cursory view as ordinary passers by, and by open ordinary conversation; and on that principle, as well as for the duty of being courteous to strangers, I have myself constantly advocated the opening of all our sources of military engineering information to all the world.[16]

To the officer in question, Lieutenant Colonel T. L. Gallwey, Sir John gave the following instructions:

Your object will be to study rather general systems and principles, such as are usually considered open to all the world, and in which nations take a pride in offering their improvements to others; and to avoid prying into any details in which the authorities desire to maintain any degree of mystery or reserve. You will make all the authorities fully acquainted with your course of proceedings and researches, courting from them all details and particulars that you desire, but dropping at once, and *bona fide*, any to which they shall offer objection; that is, so far as distinct researches are concerned, for of course you are not required to shut your eyes to what passes under ordinary observation. You will be able to show by a free offer of communicating to the officers of the United States Army all the information regarding the practices in our Service, which we are so unreservedly willing to afford to foreigners, your reasons for not considering the extent of your inquiries unreasonable.[17]

The orders of the officer of the Royal Artillery who accompanied Gallwey reveal a similar attitude:

You will bear in mind that although you are sent to the United States for a specific purpose, you do not go in any strictly official character. You will prosecute your inquiries quite openly, asking freely for information that you may feel would be interesting in a scientific or professional point of view, and which you believe is of a character that would not be kept secret in England from any officer accredited by a friendly nation. In any case where your demand shall be met by hesitation or refusal, you will at once abstain from any further inquiries in that direction, relinquishing any attempt to investigate points which the authorites may show a wish to conceal.[18]

16 Lieut. Col. The Hon. George Wrottesley, *Life and Correspondence of Field Marshal Sir John Burgoyne, Bart.* (London, 1873), II, 412–13.

17 Lieutenant Colonel T. L. Gallwey and Captain H. J. Alderson, *Report upon the Military Affairs of the United States of America* (London: War Office, 1864), p. 76.

18 *Ibid.*, p. 75.

Neither the Union nor the Confederate army seems to have been afraid to give foreign observers access to technical information. General Totten himself forwarded two copies of a document on permanent fortifications and seacoast defenses to General Burgoyne, and observers with the Confederate armies likewise were intrusted with technical data. Scheibert was shown secret plans of the Confederate defenses in Charleston Harbor, although, like a British observer who visited Petersburg, he was not permitted to take away with him "any description whatever, on paper."[19]

As a rule, foreign observers were well received by both belligerents. This was particularly true in the South, perhaps because the Confederate officials were anxious to win friends and, if possible, recognition in Europe. Although at the time of the "Trent" incident the United States "was more than usually careful to guard her forts and military buildings from the inquisitive eye of the foreigner,"[20] military visitors were welcome in the North as well. Most foreign officers were invited to inspect the forts around Washington, and usually they received cordial treatment from Union officers; even General W. T. Sherman, whose dislike for visitors of any kind amounted almost to an obsession, behaved "most courteously" toward a British officer who visited his headquarters.[21] One British officer was harshly criticized for publishing snatches from conversations with Union generals supposedly conducted in confidence, and another, who happened to be out of uniform, was "insulted and knocked down" by a Union officer in the heat of a political argument,[22] but these cases were exceptional.

English newspapers occasionally complained that the civilian authorities in Washington were not as co-operative as they might be ("No one who wishes to avoid contact with a man of boorish

---

[19] Justus Scheibert, *Mit Schwert und Feder, Erinnerungen aus meinen Leben* (Berlin, 1902), pp. 55, 155; Lieut. Featherstonhaugh, "Notes on the Defences of Petersburg," Corps of Royal Engineers, *Professional Papers,* XIV (1865), 190. This important publication will be cited hereafter as R.E. *Professional Papers.*

[20] General Sir Richard Harrison, *Recollections of a Life in the British Army* (London, 1908), p. 107.

[21] *Ibid.,* p. 110. Lieutenant Colonel Fletcher, *History of the American War* (London, 1864–65), III, 104. See also Ella Lonn, *Foreigners in the Union Army and Navy* (Baton Rouge, 1951), pp. 273–308.

[22] Captain Richard Harrison was the officer attacked for his indiscreet though harmless article in *Blackwood's Edinburgh Magazine.* See below, p. 28. The name of the second officer is unknown. The *Army and Navy Journal,* August 6, September 10, December 3, 1864.

manners and a coarse vulgar nature will go near Mr. Stanton"),[23] but as a rule the army treated its foreign visitors well. In 1864 several of the observers seem to have had difficulty obtaining permission to visit the Army of the Potomac; however, denial or deferment of such permission was in each case a decision of some civilian official and does not appear to have been motivated by the desire to withhold military information. The United States government usually objected to foreign officers' entering Confederate lines—again, not so much for fear that they would reveal military secrets but because most foreign officers were suspected of being "rebel sympathizers."[24] Hence most foreign officers who visited the Confederacy had to do so surreptitiously. Lieutenant Colonel Fremantle entered by way of Texas; Lieutenant Colonel Garnet Wolseley was smuggled via the "underground route" across the lower Potomac;[25] and Justus Scheibert sailed from Nassau on a blockade runner, landing at Charleston as an "unofficial" visitor. An official mission to the Confederacy was likely to involve the touchy question of diplomatic recognition, and the Prussian government was anxious to avoid this issue.[26]

Finally, it may be noted that the Civil War presented unique difficulties for the foreign observer. It was a new kind of war, one which he could not always understand. Improved weapons, new tactics, and complex problems of communication and supply made it difficult for him to appreciate the significance of the American campaigns and the lessons they might hold for the future. Moreover, the vast distances involved made it almost impossible for him to visit the armies in the West, where the character of the war differed somewhat from that in Virginia. Because he was apt to be either an engineer or an artillery officer, he was not always aware of the more general problems of morale, the raising of volunteer armies, conscription, and the relationship between statesman and soldier in a democracy at war. As a career soldier, the foreign

[23] Quoted in the *Army and Navy Journal*, December 3, 1864.

[24] This attitude was not without precedent. French officials did not permit the Delafield Commission to visit their lines during the Crimean War after the Americans had signified their intention of also visiting the Russians. Colonel R. Delafield, *Report on the Art of War in Europe in 1854, 1855, and 1856 ...* (House Ex. Doc., 36th Cong., 2d sess. [Washington, 1861]), p. xv.

[25] Ella Lonn, *Foreigners in the Confederacy* (Chapel Hill, 1940), pp. 348–51; Field Marshall Viscount Wolseley, *The Story of a Soldier's Life* (Westminster, 1903), II, 119–26.

[26] Scheibert, *Mit Schwert und Feder,* pp. 43–45.

observer often found it difficult to understand the American armies, and if—like most European soldiers—he sympathized with one side or the other, he found it difficult to be objective.

It is understandable, then, that the proverbial "fog of war" settled over the Civil War battlefields, obscuring certain lessons and distorting others, and that undue attention consequently was devoted to those military and geographical areas where the visibility seemed clearest.

What information did these observers take back with them? How was this information utilized? What lessons, if any, did later soldiers claim to have learned from studying what the observers and others had written about the Civil War? Were the armies of Europe ever influenced by the American campaigns, and if so, how? Or if not, why?

Many clues can be found in the literature written by European soldiers about the Civil War. Quite possibly the archives of the various war offices and ministries would yield additional information on the subject, but it seems reasonable to assume that the published memoirs, official reports, tactical and strategical studies, and military journals would reveal any substantial doctrinal changes brought about by the Civil War. Certainly these sources would present an accurate image of the Civil War as it appeared through foreign eyes.

The trail of ideas at times is faint and difficult to follow. In places it is but lightly traveled, and often it is obscured by signs of more recent conflict or lost in a maze of conflicting evidence and opinion. Yet along the way are signposts, soldiers and military writers who were able to discern some of the military lessons of the Civil War. A few of these signposts are boldly placed, others are only faintly visible, but, looking back from the vantage point of nearly a century, one can retrace many of the steps taken along the way.

2

The English Observers

The Civil War was followed closely in England. At first many professional soldiers were inclined to regard it strictly as an affair between amateurs,[1] but eventually even the skeptics came to view the American campaigns seriously. Lord Wolseley, then a young officer, later recalled "the breathless interest and excitement with which from month to month, almost from day to day, we English soldiers read and studied every report that could be obtained of the war as it proceeded."[2]

Soon after the outbreak of war, English officers began to arrive at the scene of hostilities. Some journeyed all the way from England to "see something of this wonderful struggle," while others managed a visit from nearby Canada, where the British garrison had been strengthened recently as a result of the "Trent" crisis. How many English officers came to this country during 1861–65 is not known, but there must have been a considerable number. While most official observers remained in the north, many British officers went south, either because they sympathized with the Confederacy or because most of their intelligence came from Northern sources and there was no other way in which they could obtain "trustworthy information regarding the Southern plans, or operations, or mode of fighting."[3] The English thus were able to observe the war from both sides, and, in this respect at least, their coverage of the military operations was more complete than that of the other European armies.

Interest in the Civil War doubtless was related to the army re-

[1] Alexander Innis Shand, *The Life of General Sir Edward Bruce Hamley* (Edinburgh and London, 1895), I, 135; R. A. Preston, "Military Lessons of the American Civil War: The Influence of Observers from the British Army in Canada on Training the British Army," *Army Quarterly*, LXV, No. 2 (January, 1953), 230. Cited hereafter as Preston, "Military Lessons of the Civil War."

[2] Viscount Wolseley, "An English View of the Civil War," *North American Review*, CXLIX (September, 1889), 725. Cited hereafter as Wolseley, "English View of the Civil War."

[3] Lieut. Col. Fremantle, *Three Months in the Southern States: April–June, 1863* (New York, 1864), Preface, p. 3; Wolseley, *Story of a Soldier's Life*, II, 119-20.

form movement in the 1860's. Both the Crimean War and the Indian Mutiny had exposed glaring weaknesses in the British military structure, and public concern had been further accelerated in 1859 by a French invasion scare. To meet this "threat," hundreds of Volunteer Rifle Corps were formed. "Fiery meetings were held all over the country at which militant patriots let off steam against the French." Even General Sir William Napier, author of the renowned *History of the Peninsular War*, raised himself in his death-bed to bombard his friends and the *Times* with elaborate plans for the use of the Volunteers against Britain's traditional enemy. Within one year the Volunteer Corps swelled from 15,000 to nearly 160,000 members. This invasion scare had scarcely subsided before war broke out in America,[4] and the military observers reflect this agitation for army reform. The Volunteer Movement drew their attention to the performance of the American volunteers. The mismanagement of the Crimean War taught the necessity of adequate training and good leadership. And with the campaigns of the great Napoleon as interpreted by Jomini forming the basis of their formal education, they were also interested in seeing to what extent the American campaigns conformed to generally accepted doctrines of war.

Probably the first British soldier to reach America was Major General Sir George Bell, a retired veteran of the Peninsular and Crimean wars. Sir George arrived in Washington in September, 1861, while Major General George B. McClellan was rebuilding the Union army after its recent defeat at the first battle of Bull Run. Sir George did not witness any actual fighting, but he did see enough of McClellan's army to form a definite opinion of its worth:

The Federal army is increasing every day in strength and discipline, the men are strong, stout and healthy, in fine feather, and ready to prime and load. McClellan is the very man to lead them. . . . He has thrown up a great many strong redoubts in the most commanding positions, covering the country for many miles. . . . From all I can see and learn, the Federal army are now in the ascendant, and will win the day. There is money at command, the capital secure, an increasing army and good commissariat. . . . General McClellan . . . learned something in the Crimea.[5]

[4] F. W. Hurst, *The Six Panics and Other Essays* (London, 1913), p. 37; H. A. Bruce, *Life of General Sir William Napier* (London, 1864), II, 447–48, 465–74; Fortescue, *History of the British Army*, XIII, 527–33.

[5] Sir George Bell, *Soldier's Glory: Being Rough Notes of an Old Soldier*, arranged and edited by Brian Stuart (London, 1956), pp. 309–10.

Another prominent English officer to visit the Civil War armies was Lieutenant Colonel Henry Charles Fletcher of the Scots Guards, or Scots Fusilier Guards, as they were known at the time. Fletcher accompanied the Union army in the Peninsular campaign (1862), and later he visited both the Union and Confederate armies in the West. Although he wrote more to acquaint his countrymen with details of the war than to point out specific military lessons, his professional views occasionally colored the pages of his three-volume *History of the American War*.

Fletcher's writings show the influence of the Volunteer Movement. Unlike many English officers at the beginning of the Civil War, he did not scoff at the apparent ineptness of the American volunteers. He observed that inexperienced troops often behaved surprisingly well under cover but were difficult to manage when in the open or exposed to enemy fire: "Like all young and undisciplined troops, the men were fond of using their rifles but careful not to expose themselves"; therefore "much powder was wasted at long ranges" and "little harm was done." Fletcher considered the rank and file of the Army of the Potomac "half disciplined" and the officers "unpractised" in 1862, but he felt that by the following year this army had vastly improved. Given capable leadership, the American soldier was "equal to any task which might reasonably be required."[6]

Later, in his *Report on the Military Academy at West Point*, Fletcher elaborated upon the importance of good leadership to a hastily raised volunteer army. In the Civil War "the value of previous [military] education became felt, and as the war progressed, the West Point officers more and more came to the front, until at its termination with scarcely an exception on both sides, those who have left a name in its history had previously received their training at the Academy." The historical accuracy of this statement may be questioned, but Fletcher's meaning is clear: he saw a "considerable analogy" between the needs of the United States and Canada with respect to military education, and he recommended the establishment of a military academy "somewhat on the model of West Point" whenever Canada should attempt to train her own officers. It may be added that when the Royal Military College of Canada

---

[6] *History of the American War*, I, 84–87; II, 33 n., 284–85, 437; III, 118–19. Like many European soldiers, Fletcher believed in the natural superiority of the Southern soldier because of his background and lifelong familiarity with horse and rifle.

was established in 1876, it did in fact borrow many of its features from West Point, including a four-year curriculum rather than the two-year courses of Sandhurst and Woolwich.[7]

In his *History* Fletcher paid little attention to tactics. Evidently he did not comprehend that modern firepower rather than American temperament was the basis for the change in infantry tactics:

The rapid, well sustained attack, which in many of the great European combats has led to important successes, *does not appear adapted to the qualities of the Federal soldiery*. Indomitable perseverance, cheerfulness under fatigue and hardship, diligence in entrenching, and stubbornness in defending these entrenchments, seem to be especial characteristics which render them, when well-armed and skilled in the use of their weapons, most formidable opponents.[8]

At first Fletcher failed also to appreciate the importance of firepower to cavalry. In his view "the nature of the country and the absence of the requisite military training" had prevented cavalry "from performing the duties usually assigned to that arm in European armies." He did not believe that the rifle had replaced the lance and saber, for while he could see the advantages of dismounted fighting in reconnaissance, he remained at first a loyal advocate of shock tactics in combat. "Neither at Gettysburg, nor indeed at any of the great battles of the war, had cavalry borne a conspicuous part," and the reason for this, according to Fletcher, was because cavalry in both armies had failed to master the technique of shock tactics. He claimed that "Jeb" Stuart, the famous Confederate cavalry leader, had "admired the *arme blanche* [shock tactics] as the true weapon for a horseman, but unfortunately, neither time nor means were at hand to organise and discipline a force on the model of European cavalry."[9]

Ten years later, however, Fletcher showed a greater appreciation for the value of mounted infantry, particularly in the rough and heavily wooded terrain of North America:

In the greater portion of Canada there is little ground for the action of Cavalry organized similarly to that of European armies, although

[7] Lieut. Col. Henry Charles Fletcher, *Report on the Military Academy at West Point, U.S.* (n.p., n.d.), pp. 20, 24. The first commandant at R.M.C. was Lieutenant Colonel E. O. Hewett, an English observer with the Union army in 1862. George F. G. Stanley, *Canada's Soldiers, 1604–1954: The Military History of an Unmilitary People* (Toronto, 1954), p. 244.

[8] *History of the American War*, III, 366. Italics mine. See also p. 87.

[9] *Ibid.*, I, 256; II, 432; III, 222–23.

for mounted infantry there might be considerable scope, and this question of the best method of organizing and arming horsemen requires deep consideration and a careful study of recent campaigns, especially those of the great American Civil War. It is, I believe, the opinion of General [Philip H.] Sheridan . . . that the teachings of modern campaigns show the desirability of augmenting the mounted infantry, or cavalry armed with good rifles and taught to fight on foot, at the expense of the artillery. No doubt there is much that may be urged on the other side, but this instance is given with the view of showing that modern military history together with a just estimate of the probable theatre of war, should influence the decision of those whose duty it is to organize an army.[10]

Although Fletcher witnessed a major campaign and was personally acquainted with generals in both armies, his writings are disappointing. For all practical purposes, his *History* must be regarded as a secondary source, since he wrote about battles he did not see and leaned heavily upon the published works of others. In so doing, he deprived posterity of an eyewitness account, for instead of recording the impressions of a military observer, he often echoed the statements of others. Although he appreciated the qualities of the Civil War volunteers, he did not understand the real meaning of Civil War tactics. And despite his knowledge of the western campaigns, Fletcher stressed the war in the East, which "gradually assumed the characteristics of the more regular operations conducted by European armies."[11]

The Marquis of Hartington, a prominent young Liberal member of Parliament with an interest in military affairs, was another who observed both the Union and the Confederate armies. Landing in New York in August, 1862, he spent several weeks touring the North with his brother, Lord Edward Cavendish, an officer stationed at the time in Canada. These two young representatives of the great house of Cavendish inspected the Washington defenses ("some of the forts . . . looked very strong"), met McClellan and President Lincoln ("a very well-meaning sort of man, but . . . about as fit for his position now as a fire-shovel"), and rode over the Antietam battlefield. Writing ten days after the battle, Lord Hartington was astounded by what he had seen: ". . . in about seven or eight acres of wood there is not a tree which is not full of bullets and bits of shell. It is impossible to understand how anyone could

10 Fletcher, *A Lecture Delivered at the Literary and Scientific Institute Ottawa* . . . (Ottawa, 1875), p. 10.

11 *History of the American War,* II, 185.

live in such a fire as there must have been there." Failing to obtain permission from the Washington authorities to pass through the Union lines, Lord Hartington and his brother were smuggled across the Potomac at night by Confederate sympathizers. They visited Richmond, met Secretary of War James A. Seddon and President Jefferson Davis, and spent a week with the Army of Northern Virginia, then encamped on the heights above Fredericksburg, before sailing from Charleston on a blockade runner. Shortly after his return to England, Lord Hartington was named Under Secretary at the War Office, in which capacity he soon became involved in proposed legislation to regulate the Volunteer forces.

Like Sir George Bell, Lord Hartington never saw the American soldier in combat. The two were agreed that the new regiments comprised good soldier material, and Lord Hartington shared Fletcher's conviction that trained officers were essential to a volunteer army. He described a regiment of New York Volunteers as

. . . a very fine-looking lot of men indeed, mostly farmers and country people from Western New York, quite as respectable a looking lot as any of our volunteers. They seemed very jolly and in good spirits, but they had had no drill whatever, and I don't see who is to give it to them. The sentry at the Colonel's tent was sitting on a camp-stool and reading the newspaper. I believe a few of the officers have been in other volunteer regiments, but I could not make out that they had a single regular officer among them. It seems a great pity that such fine material should be thrown away, as they very likely may be, by having utterly incompetent officers.

He also wrote critically of the Union replacement system. Not only were there many regiments no better trained and disciplined than the regiment described above, but even worse was the fact that "all this time there were old regiments which are reduced to seventy or eighty men, but they [the United States government] will not fill them up, but go on raising new ones from some rotten reasons about bounties and length of service and that sort of thing; but really because the State Governors like to have the appointment of the new officers."[12] Here indeed he touched upon a tender issue, for the replacement system allowing veteran regiments to be depleted while new regiments were being raised was both foolish and inefficient. Writing after the war, Sherman described this mode of recruitment and promotion as "the greatest mistake in our Civil

[12] Bernard Holland, *The Life of Spencer Compton, Eighth Duke of Devonshire* (London, 1911), I, 39–46.

War." Sherman himself would have preferred the German method whereby each regiment in the field had a depot from which to draw trained replacements—a system somewhat similar to that adopted by the British army in 1870.[13]

Evidently what he saw in America made a lasting impression upon Lord Hartington. In the Parliamentary debates over the Volunteer Act of 1863, regulating the organization and discipline of the various Rifle Corps that had sprung up since 1859, he frequently underlined his arguments by references to the Civil War. "Military men say that we have not acquired much additional information about any scientific point in the art of war from the contest now raging in the United States," Lord Hartington told the Commons in 1863. However, he hoped that

. . . from that war we might learn many very useful things in connection with the services of Volunteers. The army of the North, which seemed to be imperfect in discipline, and which was wanting in esprit de corps, had not been found efficient in aggressive warfare; but the army of the Southern states was composed of men animated by very much the same feeling, and drawn from the same class as our Volunteer force.

He believed that the English Volunteers would compare favorably with the Confederate soldiers and that, if the proposed Volunteer Act were passed, 150,000 such men would be available "if the soil of England should be invaded."[14]

For the purposes of this study it is unfortunate that Lord Hartington did not see more of the Civil War, for he was one of the most prominent of all foreign visitors to the American armies. Appointed Secretary of State for War for a brief time in 1866 and again in 1882, he was named in 1888 chairman of the Hartington Commission, whose purpose was to inquire into the "civil and professional administration of the Naval and Military Departments and their relations to each other and to the Treasury." The work of this famous commission is not pertinent, and in fact many of its recommendations were never adopted;[15] but because Lord Hartington left an enduring mark upon the British army, his impressions of the Civil War are of unusual significance.

[13] W. T. Sherman, *Memoirs of Gen. W. T. Sherman, Written by Himself* (New York, 1891), II, 387–88.

[14] *Parliamentary Debates*, 3d ser., CLXX (1863), 1698–99. The Volunteer Bill (Bill 108) was passed as amended June 16, 1863. *Ibid.*, CLXXI, 964.

[15] Colonel John K. Dunlop, *The Development of the British Army 1899–1914 . . . with Special Reference to the Territorial Force* (London, 1938), pp. 19–22.

Another prominent unofficial observer was Lieutenant Colonel James Arthur Lyon Fremantle of the celebrated Coldstream Guards. Fremantle was on leave from the British army when he entered Texas in the spring of 1863. He spent three fascinating months traveling through the Confederacy, his wanderings taking him to every Confederate state east of the Mississippi except Florida. He visited many of the South's leading generals—Joseph E. Johnston in Mississippi, Leonidas Polk in Tennessee, P. G. T. Beauregard in South Carolina—and he viewed the battle of Gettysburg from the headquarters of Robert E. Lee. After the battle Fremantle entered the Union lines and made his way to New York, but before sailing for England he witnessed still another scene in the great American drama—the New York Draft Riots. Upon his return to England, Fremantle wrote a narrative of his trip entitled *Three Months in the Southern States*. He was an observant traveler, and his recorded impressions present a vivid, detailed, and sympathetic picture of conditions in the Confederacy. Since his book was of a popular nature, it is difficult to determine Fremantle's professional views of the military events he observed, but perhaps his comments on the tactics of Civil War cavalry provide a clue.

Like many other observers, Fremantle was frankly puzzled by Civil War cavalry:

Every impartial man confesses that these cavalry fights are miserable affairs. Neither party has any idea of serious charging with the sabre. They approach one another with considerable boldness, until they get to within about forty yards, and then, at the very moment when a dash is necessary, and the sword alone should be used, they hesitate, halt, and commence a desultory fire with carbines and revolvers. . . . Stuart's cavalry can hardly be called cavalry in the European sense of the word.[16]

Like Fletcher, Fremantle recognized the special advantages of mounted infantry in rough and wooded terrain, but he did not believe that it could stand a "fair charge of regular cavalry" in the open. And he doubted whether Stuart's troopers in their turn were capable of charging infantry.[17]

Fremantle had a higher regard for the Civil War infantry. At

16 *Three Months in the Southern States*, pp. 284–85.

17 *Ibid.*, pp. 158, 251. Captain Fitzgerald Ross, an officer in the Austrian Hussars who was also with the Confederate army at Gettysburg, recorded similar observations about Civil War cavalry, but he showed a better understanding of the special problems of the Confederates. See Fitzgerald Ross, *A Visit to the Cities and Camps of the Confederate States* (London, 1865), p. 31.

Gettysburg, for example, he was amazed by the conduct of the veteran Confederates who went under fire "with the most perfect nonchalance. They show no enthusiasm or excitement, but the most complete indifference." This he attributed to the experience of two years' almost uninterrupted fighting. Fremantle considered the American troops fairly well disciplined although poor marchers, and what seems to have impressed him most about the leadership of the Confederate army was the way in which the men would follow only those officers who were conspicuous in battle, thus making "every atom of authority . . . purchased by a drop of . . . blood."[18]

Fremantle noticed still another peculiarity of the Civil War: battles tended to grow beyond the immediate control of field commanders. At Gettysburg, for example, he was astonished to learn that Lee "during the whole time the firing continued . . . only sent one message and only received one report. It is evidently his system," Fremantle concluded, "to arrange the plan thoroughly with the three corps commanders, and then leave to them the duty of modifying and carrying it out to the best of their abilities." This, as other observers and later studies would show, was the essence of Lee's system of command.[19]

Whether Fremantle actually observed more than his book indicates will never be known. Probably he did, for there is some evidence to suggest that he deliberately withheld certain types of information in order not to betray a confidence or reveal a military secret.[20] What little Fremantle did devote to military subjects indicates that he was an alert observer, but unaware of any fundamental changes in the mode of conducting war. He mentioned the occasional use of intrenchments (had Fremantle visited Virginia one year later he conceivably would have given this subject more attention), and he described Fort Sumter in technical detail; but nowhere did he attempt to evaluate what he had seen. This was the task of the official observers, who had already begun to flock to the scene.

The first official British military observers arrived in 1862. They

[18] *Three Months in the Southern States*, pp. 159, 226, 253, 289.

[19] *Ibid.*, p. 260. For confirmation of this observation, see Major General Sir Frederick Maurice, *Robert E. Lee the Soldier* (Boston, 1925), p. 144.

[20] "As Fort Sumter must be in a very different state now to what it was when I saw it, I think there can be no harm in describing the fort as it then stood" (*Three Months in the Southern States*, p. 180 n.). "I have omitted a description of this little gunboat, as she is still doing good service in Charleston harbor" (*ibid.*, p. 192 n.).

came, for the most part, from the British garrison in Canada, and because the War Office was interested primarily in the technical aspects of the war, nearly all official observers belonged to either the Corps of Royal Engineers or the Royal Artillery. A few army doctors made the trip to study medical techniques in the Union army, and a military commission especially appointed to survey the defenses of Canada also visited the Northern states to learn more about the military capabilities of a potential enemy.[21]

The Peninsular campaign was especially well covered. Captain F. Beaumont, Royal Engineers, accompanied McClellan's army, made several ascents in Professor Lowe's famous observation balloon, and returned to England with news that the captive balloon "is capable of being turned to practical account" for military purposes. Convinced that little actually was known about the subject, Beaumont wrote an article about his observations. He subsequently became an advocate of military ballooning in the British army, serving as an associate member of a committee which conducted experimental balloon ascents for reconnaissance purposes at Aldershot and at Woolwich in 1863. But faith in the observation balloon eventually waned in the Union army, and, despite Beaumont's enthusiasm, military ballooning remained "almost dormant" in the British army until the time of the Ashanti War in 1873.[22]

McClellan's army was visited by three other junior officers, these being sent by order of General Sir W. F. Williams, Commander of Her Majesty's Forces in British North America. Reaching the Union army in the Peninsula in late May, 1862, this mission was "cordially welcomed by General McClellan, and granted every facility for seeing the disposition and organization of the army." It remained with the Union army for nearly two weeks, when, "having gained as much information as we could on artillery subjects," it returned to Canada, looking over as many factories and military installations as possible on the way. The three officers promptly submitted a detailed report of their findings.[23]

[21] R. A. Preston, "A Letter from a British Military Observer of the American Civil War," *Military Affairs*, XVI (Summer, 1952), 49. Cited hereafter as Preston, "British Military Observer." See also *Parliamentary Debates*, CLXXIII (1864), 83–84.

[22] Captain F. Beaumont, "On Balloon Reconnaissances as Practised by the American Army," R.E. *Professional Papers*, XII (1863), 94–103; Whitworth Porter, *History of the Corps of Royal Engineers* (London, 1889), II, 190–91. Also see below, pp. 26, 41–42.

[23] This confidential report, which has no published title, was submitted to Lieutenant General Sir W. F. Williams August 1, 1862. It was signed by Captain Thomas

The contents of this *Report* reflect an honest concern over recent developments in artillery. The rifled field piece was not new; it had been used sparingly by the French in their campaign against the Austrians in 1859 and by the British in the Arrow War of 1860, and most European armies had conducted experiments with the weapon. But never before had rifled artillery been used on so extensive a scale. Rumors of its destructive power soon reached Europe, and the British, engaged in building new fortifications, were anxious to use this opportunity to benefit from the experiences of the Civil War armies. This explains why these observers "embraced every opportunity of witnessing the artillery practice, being present at every action or skirmish along the entire line of the Federal

Twelve-pounder boat howitzer on an iron field carriage. (From sketch appended to unpublished official report by Captain Thomas Mahon and others, 1862, in Public Record Office, London.)

army that occurred during our stay,"[24] and why their *Report* contained detailed information on the construction of ordnance, particularly the three-inch and Parrott rifled guns, projectiles for rifled artillery, and the manufacture of ammunition and gunpowder.

It would be futile to attempt to describe most of the technical data treated in the *Report* of the military mission of 1862, but the conclusions and the general observations are of interest. The three officers found it difficult to judge the effects of the artillery fire because of the wooded nature of the country around Richmond.

Mahon, Royal Artillery, Inspector of Warlike Stores in Canada; Captain R. Grant, Royal Engineers, and Lieutenant T. C. Price, Royal Artillery. A printed copy of the report is preserved in the Public Record Office. Cited hereafter as Mahon, *Report*.

[24] *Ibid.*, p. 3.

They reported that there was nothing faulty with the quality of Union artillery matériel but that often the guns were manned by men "who were but little versed in the principles of gunnery. . . . All the field batteries which came under our observation were well horsed, and the simple manoeuvres required in taking up a position in the field were performed with facility: but their general efficiency as artillery was not good, and the firing made by them was generally inferior." These officers discussed the relative merits of the different types of artillery. Rifled guns had greater range, they reported, but smoothbores supposedly gave the greatest promise of endurance. Rifled guns were the more accurate, but the time fuses for the round projectile of the smoothbores seemed to be more dependable. Curiously enough, these officers discovered that

a very high opinion was entertained of the "Napoleon" [smoothbore] as a field gun, from its mobility and effectiveness as a shell gun; it has been more used than any rifled field gun, from the fact that the principal amount of work required from the artillery was in the shelling of woods . . . as there, the accuracy and range of rifled guns are comparatively useless, while the destructive effect of shells and spherical case are considered much superior.[25]

The Civil War, then, demonstrated the need of retaining some smoothbore field pieces, despite the obvious advantages of the new rifled guns.

These observers reported that the wrought-iron gun carriages that had replaced the old wooden carriages of the siege artillery made it possible for fewer men to handle the guns with greater speed and efficiency than before, and they also mentioned a repeating gun found in McClellan's army:

We saw some practice at 250 yards range against a target, with this gun, which was very bad; this appeared to be the fault of the ammunition, as the bullets were too small, and few of them took the rifling. It fired with great rapidity, but soon got out of order, and would not be likely to remain long in proper trim, without being served by a mechanic . . . who understood the working of the machinery. It might be useful in the defence of a narrow passage or bridge, but it is questionable whether it would be of any great practical utility in the open field of battle.[26]

[25] *Ibid.*, pp. 10–11, 14, 19. Brigadier General W. F. Barry, McClellan's chief of artillery, willingly furnished the British observers with information about artillery in the various other Union armies.

[26] *Ibid.*, p. 43.

Unlike Beaumont, these officers had genuine doubts about the military value of balloons:

The practical advantages of the balloon seem hardly commensurate with the expense, but they are enabled to get from it a general notion of the position of the enemy, especially at night, when camp fires are plainly seen, and by comparing the number of fires on both sides, they are enabled to form an estimate of the comparative numbers. It has also been found useful in noting the effect and range of artillery when firing over intervening obstacles, such as woods, etc.[27]

In accordance with instructions, the three observers inspected all ironclad ships under construction in the various ports they visited.

Union repeating gun attached to the Army of the Potomac. (From sketch appended to Mahon Report, 1862.)

They also studied the Washington defenses, which they decided "would require a large number . . . to . . . man efficiently." It was characteristic of the time that they should be furnished "a reliable plan of Washington, showing the position of the works of defence."[28] In fact, they were able to glean much of their information from published documents, many of which, along with specimens of shells, were forwarded to England to accompany their report.

Still another British observer visited the Union army in 1862. Captain Edward Hewett, Royal Engineers, had been among those sent to reinforce the British garrison in Canada as a result of the "Trent" incident. In the fall of 1862 he made a trip to Washington

[27] *Ibid.*, p. 51.   [28] *Ibid.*, pp. 45, 58.

and spent some time with McClellan's army on the upper Potomac, after which he traveled to the western theater, returning to Canada late in November. "Official reports which Hewett is known to have made on his return to Canada cannot now be located,"[29] but a lengthy letter that he wrote to his mother reveals some of his impressions of the Union army.

Hewett's comments closely resemble those of Fletcher and Lord Hartington. He described the soldiers as "splendid looking and intelligent fellows," well-equipped but poorly disciplined, whose shortcomings could be blamed on incompetent leadership.[30] Unless better officers were developed soon, he predicted, "all the arms, clothing material and harness, and guns of these insane armies will be unserviceable in a year or so." Nothing but the hard school of experience "will create the spirit of order and discipline which will at last work its own cure and gradually reform the army."[31]

We do not know what technical developments Hewett reported to his superiors, but his findings could not have differed significantly from those of the mission that had preceded him by only a few months. His letter clearly implies that he did not comprehend the influence of the new weapons upon tactics. Like Fletcher, he noticed the tendency of American troops to utilize cover:

Neither side can be manoeuvred under fire, and this is about the secret of the whole present American War, the men on either side can be brought under fire, and when there will stand well: but they are not good enough either in morale or field movements to advance, change position, or retire—The moment they have to manoeuvre, they get into confusion and break, this their own officers admit and also that the charges either of Cavalry or Infantry are purely imaginary; they may and have occasionally made a rush; but never get within 300 yards of one another; but normally wavered, halted, and fired irregularly and when one side or the other get tired first bolts, led by their officers almost invariably on the Northern side.[32]

29 Preston, "British Military Observer," p. 49.

30 Hewett was one of the few European soldiers who did not consider the Confederate soldier the better fighter. "You must not," he cautioned his mother, "think that there is any want of courage on either side, for there is not, nor must you think that the Southern soldiers are much better than the Northern, for they are not, only the courage of them is better directed and applied in earnest" (ibid., p. 56).

31 Ibid., pp. 53–54. Hewett's comments on the inefficiency of Union officers may well be justified, for in 1862, 131 Union officers were dismissed, most of them because they were regarded as unfit. The following year only 17 officers were dismissed on the same grounds, and of these, 8 had their dismissals revoked. Kenneth P. Williams, Lincoln Finds a General (New York, 1949), II, 544–45, 828.

32 Preston, "British Military Observer," p. 56.

Hewett's comments on cavalry are still more revealing:

The Southern cavalry are the better than the Northern but still as cavalry they are poor enough. The cavalry on both sides, but more especially the Northerns, are merely mounted infantry. They are not taught to use the sword at all, and indeed several regiments can muster but few swords anyway. They are armed with rifles and revolvers, the consequence is that they never charge or get well amongst the infantry, (the only chance for cavalry) but dismount and skirmish, and of course get beaten as all cavalry must, in that sort of work against Infantry.

Manifestly Hewett was an adherent of shock tactics—so much so that when he personally charged the empty line of forts around Cincinnati in the best quixotic tradition to demonstrate the merits of a "sudden dash of *well mounted cavalry*," he could not understand why the Union troops who witnessed the spectacle "were absolutely aghast at the idea of cavalry charging even the slightest obstacle."[33]

Hewett's impressions of Civil War cavalry were shared by another officer of the Royal Engineers, who visited the Army of the Potomac in late 1863. Captain (later General Sir Richard) Harrison[34] had a low opinion of the Union cavalry, which he thought

would disgrace some of our wildest Irregulars raised in the north of India at the time of the mutinies. . . . Their horses were poor and ill kept, their equipment ragged, and their discipline bad, and they looked more like a disorganised mob of infantry on horseback, than the cavalry they were intended to represent. They were, however, well armed with swords, revolvers, and breech-loading carbines, which latter, by a Yankee device, fire seven rounds without reloading, and may with ease be discharged by one hand.

As for the infantry, he witnessed a "crack regiment" at drill and judged its performance as "certainly not better, if as good as one of our moderate County Volunteer Regiments in England." Like most foreign military observers, Harrison also visited the Washington

[33] *Ibid.*, pp. 51–52.

[34] By an officer of the Royal Engineers, "A Trip to Meade's Army on the Rappahannock," *United Service Journal*, CV (May–August, 1864). Although this article was unsigned, years later in his memoirs General Harrison described his visit to Meade's headquarters in November, 1863 (*Recollections of a Life in the British Army during the Latter Half of the 19th Century* [London, 1908], pp. 109–11). The incidents described in both accounts are so similar that there can be no doubt that Harrison wrote the article for the *United Service Journal*, even though he later claimed to have sent the article to *Blackwood's Edinburgh Magazine*.

defenses, which he did not describe except to state that he "would rather have to defend than attack them."[35]

Harrison accompanied Lieutenant Colonel W. F. Drummond Jervois, then Deputy Director of Fortifications, "on a special service tour" to Canada and the United States. Their immediate objective was to report and make recommendations on the defenses of Canada, but both officers took advantage of every opportunity to observe military installations while traveling in the North. According to Harrison, Jervois was anxious to see "everything possible wherever we went. . . . I had not only to go and look about, but also to take notes and drawings of all I saw." Upon their return to England, Harrison compiled a report containing such observations as might be useful "if at any time we went to war with our American cousins."[36] This report unfortunately cannot be located, but Jervois evidently learned something from these observations. In his *Report of the Defence of Canada*, he recommended that "the vital points of the country should be protected by works of fortification, chiefly earthworks."[37] A previous report, submitted in 1862, had declared the strategic city of Toronto too extensive to cover with adequate defenses,[38] but Jervois, recalling "that the earthworks in the vicinity of Washington occupy 35 miles . . . in length," recommended the construction of similar works to protect Toronto. Assuming the use of intrenchments by a British-Canadian field army in the event of war, he pointed out what he considered to be the inherent weakness of temporary works—they required a much larger and better-disciplined force for defense than permanent fortifications.[39] Jervois also recommended that British naval bases be defended by fortifications combined with "permanent obstacles

---

[35] "A Trip to Meade's Army," pp. 333, 337-38.

[36] Harrison, *Recollections*, p. 107.

[37] *Report on the Defence of Canada, Made to the Provincial Government on the 10th November 1864, and of the British Naval Stations in the North Atlantic: Together with Observations on the Defence of New Brunswick, etc.* (London, 1865), p. 15.

[38] *Report of the Commissioners Appointed To Consider the Defences of Canada* (War Office, January 27, 1862), pp. 16-17. So far as can be determined, none of the five officers who compiled this report ever visited the American armies, although as early as January, 1862, it was recognized that "The United States of America are now a military power, and have demonstrated their capability of raising and equipping in a short . . . time an enormous mass of troops. . . . And late operations in the western rivers . . . have shown that they also possess the power of rapidly extemporizing a formidable fleet, adapted for lake warfare" (*ibid.*, p. 5).

[39] Jervois, *Report on the Defence of Canada*, pp. 16-23 *passim*, 39, 44.

and extemporized submarine and floating obstructions," constructed along principles which "have long been acted upon by all other naval powers, [and] by none to a greater extent than the United States."[40]

Jervois made a second trip to the United States in 1865, when he had occasion to visit the captured Confederate works at Richmond and Petersburg. He concluded that the importance of these works often had been overrated. At the Petersburg crater the Union Forces

would probably have succeeded in storming the breach . . . if the assaulting party had been sufficiently game to go in after the crater was formed. But failing to do so, they got rather sick of regular attack, and they took to working round the flank of the Confederates; Richmond was captured by the defeat of the Confederate army on the right flank of the Petersburg entrenchments and not by the taking of these works.[41]

Jervois was especially interested in problems relating to coast defense, and in his reports upon fortifications and the defense of Canada he made several significant references to the Civil War. He mentioned the "great strides" that the Americans had made in the construction of armor-plated ships and rifled ordnance. He wrote of "the great value of submarine mines" as employed in the defense of Confederate coastal works. With the help of data contained in "the confidential report which was made by the Confederate office of engineers on the subject," Jervois made specific recommendations for the construction of sea fortifications in England.[42]

Although their writings are but little known, probably more British officers visited both armies in 1864 than in any previous year. By this time it had become apparent that great strides had been made in certain technical areas, and that Lord Lyons, the British ambassador, was no longer able to furnish the War Office sufficient information on these improvements. It was necessary, therefore, to send new observers to supplement what was already known about the Civil War armies and their mode of fighting. One such mission,

[40] *Ibid.*, p. 36.

[41] These views were expounded in a discussion following a lecture before the United Service Institution on the subject of modern fortifications. Cf. *Journal of the Royal United Service Institutions*, X (1867), 459–60. This publication is cited hereafter as *R.U.S.I. Journal*.

[42] *Ibid.*, p. 460; (Jervois), *Report with Reference to the Progress Made in the Construction of the Fortifications for the Defence of the Dockyards and Naval Arsenals, etc., of the United Kingdom* (London, [1867]), pp. 9, 10 n.

comprising an officer each from the Corps of Royal Engineers, the Royal Artillery, and the Royal Navy, was ordered to "report professionally" upon the most recent developments in their respective fields. These officers were not expected to accompany the Union army and report upon the military operations, but rather to collect "facts bearing on the *matériel* of war." Because most war industries were situated in the North and also for obvious diplomatic reasons, this mission was instructed to remain within the Union states.[43] This did not deter other British officers from stealing a visit south, for at least two officers of the Royal Engineers visited the besieged lines at Richmond and Charleston, although whether they did so in an official capacity is not clear.

Operations in Virginia in 1864 were covered from both sides. One enterprising observer, a Lieutenant Featherstonhaugh, was able to slip into Petersburg while that city was still in Confederate hands. Writing "entirely from memory," the route by which he left the Confederacy not permitting him to take any written description of the defense of Petersburg, Featherstonhaugh's report was considered of such significance that the 1865 issue of the *Professional Papers* of the Corps of Royal Engineers was delayed until it had been received. Like Jervois, Featherstonhaugh regarded the Confederate works "by no means formidable, either in trace or profile"; but he attached greater importance than Jervois to the "extensive use made of bomb-proofs," and he placed great value in the use of land mines in the defense of fortified places.[44]

Three British officers, one of them a general, viewed the siege of Richmond from the Union lines. Major General Hastings Doyle, commander of British forces in Nova Scotia, paid a visit to the Army of the James. Accompanied by Major General B. F. Butler and his staff, General Doyle was "escorted round the lines . . . and introduced to the leading officers of the several corps."[45] An un-

[43] *Parliamentary Debates*, CLXXIII, 857. The full instructions given the army officers are to be found below, pp. 35–38. The report by Lieutenant Colonel Gallwey and Captain Alderson mentions a Captain Goodenough, who had submitted a separate report to the Admirality. *Report upon the Military Affairs of the United States of America* (War Office, 1864), p. 58. A copy of this confidential report is preserved at the Public Record Office.

[44] Lieutenant Featherstonhaugh, "Notes on the Defenses of Petersburg," R.E. *Professional Papers*, XIV (1865), 190–94; Captain H. Schaw, "The Present State of the Question of Fortification," *R.U.S.I. Journal*, X, 447.

[45] A few of General Doyle's opinions of his visit are found in the *Army and Navy Journal*, December 3, 1864. They appeared originally in the London *Army and Navy Gazette*.

identified British field officer was the second to visit the Union lines. Writing to a member of Parliament, this officer described the forts around Washington as being so extensive that they would require a large army to defend them. The arrangements at a military hospital he inspected were "strikingly complete." At the front he was met cordially by General U. S. Grant, who apparently discussed freely with him the problems of the campaign.[46]

What most impressed this officer was "the deadly character" of Civil War firearms, the technical advances of the Americans, and the new type of warfare. He admired the ingenuity of the "labor-saving contrivances" he saw; he visited gun foundries and factories and queried front-line soldiers about the performance of their weapons. He learned, for example, that while the new seven-shot carbine in the hands of raw troops led to a waste of ammunition, it was "very destructive when entrusted to known cool shots and would enable a very few men to defend a narrow pass, a gateway, etc." Every soldier he met looked well clothed and fed, if not well drilled, and the North appeared to have unlimited resources. By 1864 it was obvious that improvised earthworks were "the marked feature" of the Civil War; to this observer it also seemed evident that the armies were too large and bulky "to move about or work expeditiously" and that the habit of intrenching made the Civil War troops "reluctant to break up 'a home!'" After traveling three thousand miles in the North, this military visitor saw enough of the war to predict that before "this struggle closes there will be so great a development and improvement in all kinds of arms, both for military and naval warfare, that the world will act wisely in leaving itself open to profit by American ingenuity."[47]

The third British officer to view the fighting around Richmond and Petersburg was Major H. A. Smyth, of the Royal Artillery. Smyth lived so near to Grant's headquarters that "many of the dispatches were read, and most matters openly discussed" in his hearing. He had the good fortune to witness the final assault against

---

[46] "Here I had opportunity of witnessing the display of his [Grant's] very remarkable facility for the dispatch of business, which alone could prevent a person in his position from being overwhelmed. We were incessantly interrupted by messengers bringing letters, messages, etc. Without being in the least disconcerted, he at once attended to the matter before him, wrote the necessary instructions, and then resumed his conversation." Quoted from a letter which appeared originally in the London *Star* and was reprinted in the *Army and Navy Journal*, January 14, 1865.

[47] Quoted in *ibid*.

Lee's lines which took place on April 2, 1865.[48] Smyth was greatly interested in the progress of field intrenchments during the later stages of the war. He was astonished to see "a breastwork, perfectly efficient against musketry fire, thrown up along the entire front of a brigade, in forty minutes," and he appreciated the need for flank attacks against a position thus fortified. Because of the heavily wooded terrain, Smyth did not believe that the new rifled artillery would render obsolete the old twelve-pound brass Napoleon field gun. He agreed with the other observers who had commented on the Confederate earthworks at Petersburg, maintaining that they had been taken primarily by what he called an "old-fashioned" infantry assault against the center rather than directly by Sheridan's successful outflanking movement, as Jervois had stated. Like most British observers, Smyth questioned the value of dismounted cavalry. The battle of Five Forks (April 1, 1865) went far "to modify the novel opinions expressed . . . by Federal cavalry officers . . . that 'their cavalry was a self-supporting institution,' and was, besides being good cavalry, as efficient on foot as most infantry." Admitting that such cavalry was "very effective" in corralling prisoners, he pointed out that this was accomplished generally by "pursuing mounted *when organized resistance was at an end*."[49]

British observers likewise witnessed some part of the military operations at Charleston from both sides. A Lieutenant Innes, of the Corps of Royal Engineers, visited the Confederate forces defending Charleston in 1864. He suffered the same handicap as Featherstonhaugh: the notes he took were "necessarily rather meagre" because he was "unable to take anything bulky in the way of drawings" out of Charleston. Also, "the publication of more detailed plans" would obviously have been "unjustifiable under the circumstances." He forwarded copies of Union General Q. A. Gillmore's *Official Reports* to England,[50] and when he reached Halifax he prepared a technical paper on the defenses of Charleston Harbor. Innes was especially interested in artillery. The light guns of the Confederates, he reported, were "almost worthless," and most of the damage to Union warships was being done by the ten-inch Columbiads and the seven-inch rifles. Fort Sumter had "suffered no injury of any

[48] H. A. Smyth, "Account of the Final Attack and Capture of Richmond, by the Federal Army, Commanded by General Grant," *Minutes of Proceedings of the Royal Artillery Institute*, IV (1865), 363. Major Smyth was later sent to France as an observer with the Prussian army in 1870. *Ibid.*, VII (1871), 184–202.

[49] *Ibid.*, IV, 365–67, 370.   [50] See below, p. 44.

consequence" from naval attacks alone, but heavy destruction had been caused by the Union siege guns on Morris Island. Innes concluded that rifled guns were "much more effectual . . . than smooth bores" and that earthworks were more effective against modern artillery fire than forts constructed of brick and masonry.[51]

Two months previously another British officer who had visited Fort Sumter had arrived at substantially the same conclusion. Describing a Union shelling of the fort, this observer testified that

once inside the place, and in the bomb-proofs, we were perfectly safe. The bomb-proofs are lofty and spacious, and well ventilated. The last bombardment has not injured them in the slightest degree; indeed, they are, if anything really stronger than before, from the amount of *debris* knocked down upon them. . . . The place is undoubtedly very much injured; indeed, it is hardly possible to do the walls any further damage. The sea front is almost entirely knocked in the area, and you can now walk up from the sea to the top of the walls.[52]

The Union forces before Charleston likewise entertained British visitors. Lieutenant Colonel T. L. Gallwey and Captain H. J. Alderson had left England on January 30, 1864, on an official tour of inspection. Secretary of State William H. Seward had promptly provided the necessary passes to enable them to visit the army in the field as well as government arsenals and armories, but because the Army of the Potomac was then in winter quarters, Gallwey and Alderson decided that after seeing the Washington defenses "and the various Government establishments from which we could gain any information bearing on the subject of our mission," they would defer their visit to Grant's army until spring, "when we could better judge of the condition and equipment of the Federal forces." They went instead to South Carolina, where they could observe the siege of Charleston and obtain "valuable information as to the efficiency and endurance of the Parrott rifled ordnance."[53] They also attempted to board the Union fleet, "to ascertain how the monitors had stood the battering they endured during the bombardment of Fort Sumter," but were refused permission.

Returning to New York in early April, Gallwey and Alderson proceeded to Washington with the intention of accompanying the

[51] Lieutenant Innes, "Notes on the Defences of Charleston, South Carolina," R.E. *Professional Papers*, XIII (1864), 16–24 *passim*.

[52] Quoted in the *Army and Navy Journal*, January 23, 1864.

[53] Gallwey and Alderson, *Report upon the Military Affairs of the United States of America*, Preface.

Army of the Potomac on active service. Much to their surprise, they were informed that the Secretary of War, Edwin M. Stanton, had withdrawn all passes and would not grant them special permission to visit the front. Disappointed, the two officers continued their tour, observing the casting of heavy ordnance at the Pittsburgh foundry and inspecting permanent defenses at four key ports along the Atlantic seaboard. Returning to England in mid-June, they submitted a lengthy report to the Under Secretary of State for War.

The Gallwey *Report* contains detailed answers to a series of specific questions framed by the Royal Artillery and the Corps of Royal Engineers. Alderson, for example, received the following instructions from the Director of Ordnance:

The subject to which your attention will naturally be first directed, is the system which is adopted in the United States of employing guns of very large calibre of cast iron. Accurate information will be valuable as to the preparation and character of the metal, the method of casting in their foundries, the mode of finishing and rifling, with drawings of each of the processes. . . . You will ascertain what reasons have led to the disuse of some of the guns which were employed till lately, what guns are most used now, and what is the opinion of the Artillery generally as to their respective advantages.

Alderson was expected to supply the details in construction and the relative consumption of round shot, common shells, shrapnel, and grapeshot. He was also asked to investigate the following:

Which of the systems of rifling lately in use are preferred? Has experience led to the abandonment of any of them?
Has any experience been had of either polygonal or oval boring?
Is any system of breech-loading in use for cannon of any calibre?
Are any lead-coated projectiles, either for breech or muzzle-loaders, employed, and with what result?
What is the composition of a field battery, number of carriages, horses, men, rounds carried, etc.?
Are any rifled guns used also for firing round shot?
Has any, and what, method been adopted of strengthening cast-iron guns, and with what result?

With regard to any "novel contrivances" that had seen use, Alderson was asked to find out which had been successful, particularly—

What is now the general opinion of the value of balloons in war?
What is thought of the value of small-arm rifle shells or explosive bullets?

Is steam traction employed for military transport over heavy ground, and, if so, how is it made available?

What has been the success of the Union repeating gun, and other machines for mounting a large number of rifle barrels, which are said to have been issued for use in the field?

You will inquire whether the large number and diversity of calibres, and systems of artillery, have led to much confusion in supply.

It is understood that the Americans make use of iron carriages occasionally for both field and heavy artillery.

You will ascertain if any such carriages have been under fire, and whether they are found strong and repairable, and generally whether the American experience is encouraging for the introduction of wrought iron in heavy constructions for which we now use wood exclusively.

The question of small arms will also come under your observation, and you will ascertain the description and merits of the arm generally in use with the infantry, its range and accuracy, and what is the opinion entertained with regard to the universal or partial adoption of breech-loaders for rifles.

You will make similar inquiries regarding the carbine of the cavalry.[54]

From Gallwey's instructions we learn specifically what the Corps of Royal Engineers was anxious to learn:

The first object of research to you . . . will naturally be fortifications, and the attack and defence of them.

Alterations may have arisen, or have been adopted by so ingenious a people as the Americans, in the ordinary arrangements and constructions in fortifying, from their great recent practice, which may be worthy of notice; but where the most important changes are to be looked for will be those connected with the effect of the employment of rifled cannon, which have in no other war been brought into use on any extended scale.

In permanent fortifications great efforts have, no doubt, been made in the application of iron for cover to embrasures, as well as to parapets in general; what has been proved to be the most effective, most simple, and cheapest preparation, form, and manner of putting together the material in open batteries or in casemates? If it be thought advisable to apply iron to land defences, in what respect does it differ from its use for sea batteries?

How far have any alterations been made in the construction of field or siege works, arising from the effect of rifled cannon upon them?

As in the United States they are constructing considerable permanent defensive works in various parts, it would be of much interest to ascertain their general *principles* of construction, showing their interior arrangements and details. You do not require the plan and details of any specific fort . . . but of a fort which will exhibit their

[54] *Ibid.*, pp. 75-76.

most approved general system, from which we might perhaps imbibe useful lessons for ourselves in fortification.

Many expedients in pontooning, bridging, rafts, temporary stagings for wharfage etc. may have originated during this war; as well as practices for establishing and improving the military communications.

How railroads have been most effectually destroyed, and how reinstated and repaired according to circumstances—measures which are quite novel as connected with warfare.

Also how navigations have been improved, or obstructed. . . .

A most important subject will be that of military transport when

By hoisting shells in the manner indicated and elevating the heavy fortress artillery with metal elevating screws, the Parrott guns were "very easy to work." (From sketch included in the Gallwey and Alderson confidential official Report upon the Military Affairs of the U.S.A., 1864, Public Record Office, London.)

not afloat; the nature of the means employed, description of carriages or pack-saddles, as applied for the different services; the proportions allotted to each under different circumstances, with the organization for its management.

The field equipment, nature, and quantity of tools and materials for the Engineer service, will, of course, form a leading feature with you in this part of the inquiry.

Amidst the existing contest among nations for superiority in construction of rifled cannon, and armour plating to resist it, the citizens of the United States have the repute of having made much progress, the extent of which it will be of great interest to ascertain, so far as may be allowed.

The requisite being, as regards the guns, what will best combine the several high qualities that have been found singly in many. They are

1. Great endurance, without any but the slightest liability to burst or to be rendered unserviceable. In addition to the number of rounds fired from them as usually recorded, there should be a considerable number of rounds fired rapidly at full charges, and with the piece consequently much heated, which is very trying on many guns, while it may frequently be required in action, particularly on board ship.

2. Simplicity in construction of gun, shot, and shell; that is, not complicated, nor liable to be put out of order by the effect of weather, or of such accidents and ill-usage as must occur in service.

3. Accuracy of fire, with length of range and low trajectories, and a capability of obtaining from the guns high initial velocities.

After the guns themselves, will be of interest the construction of their carriages of different kinds, and the means of working them.

The organization and equipments of the troops will be worthy of attention; and, in particular, in those matters that simplify or facilitate movements in the field.

Any other subject of military interest which falls under your notice will be reported upon, and those in most detail for which your opportunities may happen to be most favorable.[55]

Significantly, neither Alderson nor Gallwey was asked to report on any innovations in tactics or strategy that might have occurred. Indeed, these officers had very little opportunity to obtain firsthand information from the battlefields, for while they enjoyed "ample means of inspecting everything connected with the war equipment of the Federal army," Stanton's refusal to allow them to visit the Army of the Potomac deprived them of "any personal opinion" of this equipment during active operations. This did not prevent them, however, from answering the greater part of the questions they had been sent to investigate. If their report did not yield information that was startlingly new, it at least corroborated and in most instances supplemented what others had observed before them.

Gallwey and Alderson both had been ordered to observe the progress of artillery, especially the new rifled guns, so it is scarcely surprising that a large portion of their *Report* should be devoted to this subject. Amid the many pages of charts, illustrations, and statistics can be found information that even the layman can appreciate. Evidently as late as 1864, the artillery of the Army of the Potomac consisted of two-thirds smoothbores, principally because this was the best type of gun for canister "and therefore better adapted to the nature of the country in which the fighting was carried on."

55 *Ibid.*, pp. 76–77.

The *Report* stated that "great progress" had been made in heavy cast-iron guns of ten- and fifteen-inch caliber. Rifled Parrott guns were fairly inexpensive and easy to produce, but had little endurance.[56] The Whitworth rifle, a breech-loading field piece of English make, likewise had a serious weakness. Federal officers told Gallwey and Alderson that the breech-closing mechanism "was found very liable to clog from dirt," although they had no gun that could rival it for accuracy or range.[57]

Gallwey and Alderson examined fragments of burst guns for indications of weaknesses; they reported at length upon the various manufacturing processes of artillery; and they studied the loading of heavy siege and coast artillery guns. They were astonished to discover that the big fifteen-inch Columbiads were handled by but one noncommissioned officer and six gunners, while to work a gun of nearly the same weight in England no less than twenty-four well-drilled men were required, and they could not load and aim the piece "nearly as fast" as the American gun crews. They attributed this entirely to two causes: the greater facility of working wrought-iron carriages over wooden ones and "the ease and quickness with which the gun is elevated or depressed." The new wrought-iron carriages, whose introduction was stimulated by favorable reports on Russian experiments brought back by the American observers sent to the Crimean War, had "stood the test of actual service" and had the practical advantage of interchangeable parts. As for the elevating screws, they were likely to become damaged by flying splinters or stones, but Gallwey and Alderson heard of no cases where any had been broken or damaged by the recoil.[58]

Gallwey and Alderson also learned something about how such artillery should be used. Whenever guns were mounted *en barbette* —that is, on the top tier of a fortification and exposed to enemy fire—their inefficiency had been "strongly demonstrated." Guns so

[56] At the battle of Fredericksburg the Confederates "lost both their 30-pounder Parrotts by explosion . . . after most effective use" (Jennings Cropper Wise, *The Long Arm of Lee or the History of the Artillery of the Army of Northern Virginia with a Brief Account of the Confederate Bureau of Ordnance* [Lynchburg, 1915], I, 388). Gallwey and Alderson, *Report upon the Military Affairs of the United States*, pp. 34–35.

[57] *Ibid.,* 69. "There were various types of breech-loading cannon in existence or being experimented with at the time of the Civil War. None of them, however, were very successful, with the possible exception of the Whitworth gun" (Fred Albert Shannon, *The Organization and Administration of the Union Army, 1861–1865* [Cleveland, 1928], I, 127).

[58] *Report upon the Military Affairs of the United States,* pp. 40, 49, 56, 63–66.

mounted at Fort Sumter had been silenced by the fire of Union batteries located more than four thousand yards distant. On the other hand, guns in casemated works, where they were mounted to fire through an embrasure in the walls, or guns protected by iron turrets or shields, could endure heavy battering, even when the fort was constructed of brick.

As a matter of fact, Gallwey and Alderson were not among the many observers and later students of the Civil War who maintained that rifled siege artillery made brick and mortar fortifications obsolete. The rapid fall of Fort Pulaski in 1861 has usually been interpreted as the dawn of a new era in fortifications; reading Union accounts of the siege, these British officers were "immediately

Among the "novel contrivances" observed by Gallwey and Alderson were hand grenades of this type weighing from one to six pounds. (From sketch included in the Gallwey and Alderson Report.)

struck with the wretched inefficiency of the defence made by the Confederates." They went over the fort, "anxious to see the effect of heavy mortar shells on the arches of the casemates, but with all the firing there was no instance of the kind." As a result of the superior accuracy and effect of rifled ordnance, fortification walls had been thickened from five to eight feet and a new embrasure made of iron had been developed. Illustrative of this new look in fortifications were the partially built defenses of New York Harbor, which Gallwey and Alderson had visited and predicted would be "very formidable" when complete. The *Report* contains an elaborate description of the construction of such works, including even the composition of mortar that was being used.[59]

[59] *Ibid.*, pp. 4–7, 12, 20, 23.

The two observers also visited famed Battery Wagner, a Confederate earthwork constructed to keep the Federal artillery beyond range of Fort Sumter. This work had endured a fantastic siege of fifty-eight days, during which an estimated 1,416 tons of metal had been hurled against it.[60] It had been evacuated several months before the two British officers arrived, so they were able to look over the Confederate defenses for themselves. They were most favorably impressed with the bombproof that had sheltered the garrison. "Strongly built of 12-inch timber, and covered with 10 feet of sand," this work gave no appearance of having been penetrated by Union shell fire. "The reason," they concluded, "why such a fort should have held out for so long a time, and against such a predominant siege, is perhaps that the attacking force had no sappers, and that the conduct of the siege approaches were necessarily slow, and the works of indifferent construction."[61]

With regard to coast defense, the Gallwey and Alderson *Report* drew one important conclusion: everything these two officers had seen or read testified in favor of forts against ships. The armament of Forts Sumter and Moultrie was far inferior to that brought against them; still they had not been reduced or even severely damaged by naval gunfire. In order to reduce a well-constructed fort, provided the guns were adequately protected, it was necessary to land a force and establish siege batteries. The Civil War, like the operations in the Baltic and Black Sea in 1854–55, was proof "that ships cannot contend with forts when the conditions are anything like equal."[62]

Although their first concern was for forts and artillery, both observers had instructions to report upon "novel contrivances" and any other subjects of military interest. Military balloons, they discovered, had "gradually fallen into disuse":

We had conversations on this subject with many general officers who served in the 1862 campaign, including General McClellan, General

[60] John Johnson, *The Defense of Charleston Harbor, Including Fort Sumter and the Adjacent Islands, 1863–1865* (Charleston, 1890), p. 273.

[61] *Report upon the Military Affairs of the United States*, pp. 23–24.

[62] *Ibid.*, pp. 12–13, 23. "The reports on armourplated vessels handed in herewith give voluminous evidence of the performance of the monitors, and of the damage sustained by them, and is well worthy of careful study. . . . Our own extensive experience at Shoeburyness . . . furnish ample means for ascertaining the probable effect of the Federal artillery, as in this Report will be found all necessary information, such as nature of ordnance, weight of projectile, charge, initial velocity, etc." (*ibid.*, p. 58).

Barnard, Chief Engineer, and General Barry, Chief of Artillery; and the former was the only officer who thought that it would be advisable that the army train should include a balloon equipment, and his opinion was somewhat qualified.[63]

They did not comment upon each of the eighty-one different kinds of firearms then reported in use in the Union army.

It appeared to be the general opinion that a certain number of the most intelligent men in each regiment should be armed with breech-loaders. But those officers who . . . may be supposed to be able to give the best opinion, are decidedly against arming the ordinary "line of battle men," with anything but a muzzle loader.

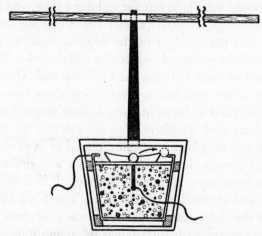

From a Norwegian officer "on a like mission to our own," Gallwey and Alderson obtained this design of a Russian torpedo. Ignited by wires connected to a battery, this floating mine was apt to explode whenever a ship or heavy seas tipped the mine far enough for the copper disk in the center to connect the circuit. (From sketch included in the Gallwey and Alderson Report.)

One Union general even went on record in favor of the smooth-bore musket and ball and buckshot cartridge for the rank and file. They noted that the Union armies on the march were burdened by excess baggage, the lack of which made the Confederates far more mobile. The want of an engineer train, they believed, had been "severely felt."[64]

Because they had been unable to accompany the Army of the

[63] *Ibid.*, p. 31. The unnamed British field officer who visited Butler's command in 1864 likewise wrote that "ballooning as a military resource has been abandoned, and is considered quite useless, except for ascertaining the interior works of a beleaguered city." Quoted in the *Army and Navy Journal*, January 14, 1865.

[64] *Report upon the Military Affairs of the United States*, pp. 28, 58.

Potomac in the field, Gallwey and Alderson had little firsthand knowledge of the trench warfare of 1864 except for what they could observe during the siege of Charleston. They reported that field works had been "extensively utilized," that it had become practice in both armies to throw up a new line of breastworks whenever the troops took up a new position, and that positions fortified with care "have generally enabled the defensive force to withstand the most determined attacks." The abundance of timber and the skill of the American volunteers with pick and ax enabled such works "to be perfected economically and with expedition." In the field works that they inspected, Gallwey and Alderson could see no fundamentally new principle of construction as a result of the introduction of rifled artillery. Even the Washington defenses were built on the same theory as that upon which Wellington's lines of Torres Vedras had been based.[65]

Gallwey and Alderson also commented on the soldiers they saw, and it is evident that they shared the same opinion expressed by most of the earlier British observers: "The soldiers are well behaved, and their bravery is indisputable. Properly disciplined and well commanded, the Federal army would be second to no army in the world, but as present [sic] constituted, with so many great defects, it must as a whole be considered greatly inferior to European armies." From what they could observe, "the artillery were tolerably well drilled, the infantry badly drilled, and the cavalry not drilled at all." The main cause of these shortcomings was inferior discipline resulting from a lack of good regimental and noncommissioned officers. They attacked the replacement system in the Union army, or rather the lack of such a system, and they were critical of the draft, claiming that it was necessary only because "patriotism waned."[66]

In the preface to their *Report*, Gallwey and Alderson recommended "for special investigation and experiment" several subjects, among which were wrought-iron gun carriages and iron embrasures "as constructed in Federal works." They did not recommend the adoption of any new methods of constructing heavy guns, although they did suggest that the Americans' further progress in this field would bear watching.

To what extent did the findings of British observers, official or otherwise, shape military thought in England? In the field of mili-

[65] *Ibid.*, pp. 1–2.   [66] *Ibid.*, pp. 32–33.

tary engineering, it seems obvious that Jervois benefited from his observations; certainly he acknowledged his debt to the Americans in matters pertaining to coast defense. It is worthy of note that copies of Major General Q. A. Gillmore's *Engineer and Artillery Operations against the Defences of Charleston Harbor in 1863* were distributed to all the Royal Engineer libraries.[67] It also appears likely that Sir John Burgoyne, Inspector General of Fortifications, was influenced by the reports of officers he had sent to America. The information provided by Gallwey confirmed some of the views expressed by Sir John before the war: he had predicted, for example, that rifled artillery would give land batteries a marked advantage over ships, and this, according to Gallwey's report, clearly had been the case in the Civil War. It is also probable that the Americans' experience caused Sir John to modify other opinions. In 1855 he had dismissed as "erroneous" the view that the prolonged defense of Sevastopol had been "greatly due to the superiority of earthworks over those of masonry"; early in 1862 he had stated with regard to the defenses of Canada that while permanent works were desirable, they were too expensive and that intrenched positions could be "made very formidable"; finally, in 1870 he went so far as to state that earthworks would provide the best fortifications, all other structures being too costly and requiring too much time to build. By this time he also professed the belief that the increased power of rifled arms would lead to greater dispersion and use of cover than before and that intrenching tools should become standard issue.[68]

Yet it would be a mistake to assume that the Civil War materially influenced the subsequent development of fortifications in Great Britain. After all, Gallwey and Alderson had found nothing specific to recommend except experiments with iron embrasures ("to be fired at by such guns as will be carried by our iron-clad vessels"), and much of what they saw on their trip merely confirmed views that were already popular in their own army. Moreover, rarely if ever does a major power remodel her defenses because of

[67] Extracts from Gillmore's earlier *Official Report . . . of the Siege and Reduction of Fort Pulaski* (New York, 1862) were published in the R.E. *Professional Papers*, XIII, 147–52. These were perhaps the two most influential American military documents on the Civil War as far as most European soldiers were concerned.

[68] Captain George Wrottesley (ed.), *The Military Opinions of Sir John Fox Burgoyne* (London, 1857), pp. 190–91, 397; *Report of the Commissioners Appointed To Consider the Defences of Canada*, Appendix, p. 46; Sir John Burgoyne, "On Hasty Intrenchments in the Field," R.E. *Professional Papers*, XVIII (1870), 93–96.

the so-called lessons of a foreign war, particularly one so remote and unique as the American Civil War. In his important work on fortifications, Sir George Sydenham Clarke concludes:

> In the works constructed within the past thirty years at our home ports and fortresses abroad, no sufficient indication of the results of the experience obtained in the Peninsula, the Crimea, *and the American Civil War* can be traced. . . . It is . . . evident that the rich and varied war experience available was fully appreciated by many minds, and that but for the want of all real organization of scientific thought, the progress of fortification would have been more wisely ordered.[69]

Nor is there much concrete evidence that the several reports on the arms and equipment of the Union army induced the British to make changes in their own matériel. Breech-loading rifled Armstrong cannon had been introduced in the British army before Sumter was fired upon, and during the first year of the Civil War over one thousand Armstrong pieces of various calibers were furnished the Royal Artillery.[70] While it seems likely that the Royal Artillery learned much from the Americans about the performances of the different types of ordnance under fire, it should also be remarked that extensive tests with rifled artillery were being conducted simultaneously in England and that close attention also was paid to developments in artillery in the Danish war of 1864.[71] In 1864 the British army decided to adopt a breech-loading rifle; a special committee appointed to inquire into the subject reported favorably on the performance of breech-loading rifles, citing several instances in the Civil War where the Spencer rifle had been used with conspicuous success.[72] British authorities displayed periodic interest in the military observation balloon; but Beaumont seems to have been the only observer to come back with a favorable report, and little was done in this field for at least a decade. In brief, about all that we can safely conclude from the official reports submitted in 1862 and 1864 is that they contain a wealth of technical information. The Civil War was a proving ground for new arms and equipment, and the experiences it yielded were regarded seriously; but in a decade which saw the Prussian army march to war

[69] *Fortification: Its Past Achievements, Recent Development, and Future Progress* (London, 1890), pp. 81–82. Italics mine.

[70] Fortescue, *History of the British Army*, XIII, 410, 55–52.

[71] *Parliamentary Debates*, CLXXIII, 564; *Report of a Professional Tour of Officers of the Royal Artillery in 1865* (London, 1866), *passim*.

[72] *Army and Navy Journal*, October 1, 1864; Fortescue, *History of the British Army*, XIII, 548.

on three separate occasions, many of the lessons taught in America were outdated before they could be digested.

With regard to Civil War tactics, it is significant that none of the observers really placed his finger on the fundamental reason behind the changes that had taken place. True, the terrain was unusually rugged and heavily wooded, and in the early stages of the conflict both armies suffered grievous shortcomings in discipline, training, administration, and supply: there is no cause to doubt the accuracy of the British observers on these points. It is no less true that many of these faults were eliminated or subdued as the war progressed, as Fletcher and others have indicated. But long after the American volunteers had become hardened veterans, battles still were waged without close direction from the commanding officer on the field; armies remained unwieldy and difficult to maneuver; and there still were remarkably few instances of successful frontal attacks by infantry or mounted assaults by cavalry. The observers who witnessed the fighting before Petersburg and Charleston in 1864 and 1865 could better appreciate the value of intrenchments than those who had accompanied McClellan's army in 1862, but they were no more perceptive in their remarks on cavalry. Harrison and Smyth reacted to this subject in much the same manner as Fletcher and Fremantle. Aside from technical developments relating to artillery and fortification, most British observers tended to dismiss Civil War tactics as aberrations arising from unique conditions, and in so doing they overlooked the basic fact, which now appears obvious—that the new tactics stemmed from an increase in firepower and that infantry now had to extend formations and dig for cover, while cavalry was forced to dismount and rely upon firearms if either were to survive or be effective on a modern battlefield.

Of all British soldiers to visit America during the Civil War, none was to become more famous or influential than Lieutenant Colonel (afterward Field Marshal Sir Garnet) Wolseley, who in later years as commander-in-chief of the British army was instrumental in reawakening English interest in the Civil War. In 1861 Wolseley, then a young veteran of four campaigns, had been ordered to Canada as Assistant Quartermaster General, and, like many of the troops stationed in Canada, he had desired to see something of the war. In September, 1862, he obtained two months' leave and entered Virginia via the "underground route." First he visited Richmond and rode over the Seven Days' battlefields. He then traveled to Lee's headquarters near Winchester, where the Army of Northern Virginia was recuperating after a strenuous campaign in Maryland. Wolseley spent several weeks with Lee and Stonewall Jackson before returning to Canada. Soon afterward he submitted an account of his trip to *Blackwood's Magazine*.

Fletcher, Hartington, and Hewett all had observed the Civil War armies in 1862, and Fremantle made his trip the following spring, so it is not surprising that Wolseley's initial views closely resembled theirs. The Confederate cavalry reminded him of "irregular Indian cavalry." While he admitted the value of mounted infantry in scouting and reconnaissance, Wolseley was convinced that "cavalry that could not fence well would be utterly useless in Virginia." He exceeded Hartington and Hewett (none of the three ever witnessed a major Civil War battle) in his criticism of the volunteer armies, especially those "mobs of Irish and German mercenaries" of the North who had been hired "to fight a cause they know little and care less about."[73] This impression tainted most of Wolseley's later writings, for after thirty years he still looked upon the Civil War armies as "very raw levies . . . who have never gone through any course of military training although they had . . . been present during some . . . fierce but very loose fighting against levies as undisciplined as themselves." Battles fought with such troops and conducted in great part by amateur officers did not, in Wolseley's opinion, convey many useful tactical lessons to the professional and highly trained armies of Europe.[74]

Wolseley's visit with Lee and Jackson kindled an interest that never died. Years later, after he had become one of the foremost soldiers of the empire,[75] he continued to contribute articles on the Civil War to English and American periodicals. In 1887, prompted by the publication of the English edition of A. L. Long's *Memoirs of Robert E. Lee*, Wolseley wrote an eloquent tribute to the late

[73] Wolseley, "A Month's Visit to the Confederate Headquarters," *Blackwood's Edinburgh Magazine*, XCIII (January, 1863), 23, 27. This magazine will be cited hereafter as *Blackwood's*.

[74] Wolseley, "General Sherman," *United Service Magazine*, N.S. III (May–July, 1891), 99–101. Cited hereafter as Wolseley, "Sherman."

[75] In 1870 Wolseley commanded the expedition to quell the uprising in the Red River district of Canada. Three years later he led a successful expedition against the Ashanti in West Africa, and in 1882 he defeated the Egyptians at Tel-el-Kebir. He also played a significant role in the Cardwell Reforms, and in 1895 he succeeded the Duke of Cambridge as commander-in-chief of the British army. His literary life was scarcely less active. See Major General Sir F. Maurice and Sir George Arthur, *The Life of Lord Wolseley* (New York, 1924), *passim*.

Confederate leader.[76] His other Civil War writings include a series of review articles that appeared in the *North American Review* and biographical sketches of Generals Sherman and Nathan Bedford Forrest.

These writings reveal the extent to which Wolseley's opinions had changed since 1862. Then he had merely attempted to describe his visit and to record first impressions; twenty-five years later his approach was essentially that of the professional student of war, for, as Adjutant General in the 1880's, Wolseley was primarily responsible for the condition of Her Majesty's forces. Because England and the United States were both dependent upon sea power and relatively small volunteer armies for defense, obviously they had many problems in common, and Wolseley now looked for lessons in the Civil War that would repay study.

There is no need to itemize the lessons that Wolseley presumably learned from studying the Civil War, for actually the war taught him very little that he did not already know. It would be more accurate to say that he emphasized broad areas which he thought of particular value to the British army and drew upon select incidents to bolster his own ideas. For example, he regarded the "cooperating action of the naval and military services" as one of the "most important lessons taught in the whole history of the American Civil War." This does not mean, however, that Wolseley himself gained any practical knowledge from a study of these operations, for they probably contained little that was new to an intelligent soldier who had fought on three continents and knew well the naval history of his own country. But Wolseley was one of a growing group of British soldiers who feared that since 1871 too much emphasis had been placed upon the study of German military methods, and he used the Civil War to stress timely topics, such as combined operations, coast defense, and amphibious warfare. Writing always with the problems of England uppermost in mind, Wolseley urged a close re-examination of the war in which the North had made decisive use of its sea power:

The originality and force with which all the resources and ingenuity of a great industrial and commercial people were thrown into the struggle, give to these combined naval and military movements a modern form, unique of its kind. . . . Each campaign is full of useful suggestions for us, upon the employment of similar means, should we, as seems

[76] Wolseley, "General Lee," *MacMillan's Magazine*, LV (March, 1887), 321-31.

more than likely, be forced to throw our whole weight into some . . . distant struggle for Imperial existence.[77]

A similar case in point is Wolseley's attitude toward one of the basic problems of a democracy at war—the delicate balance between civil and military authority. He took obvious delight in citing instances where political decisions in Richmond and Washington had seemingly jeopardized the actions of the field commanders;[78] yet it would be absurd to assume that the Civil War was responsible for Wolseley's prejudice on this subject. He had, after all, commanded the unsuccessful expedition to relieve "Chinese" Gordon at Khartoum in 1884, an experience that had caused him to despair the policy of "cant and cowardice" of the Gladstone administration (in which Lord Hartington was Secretary of State for War); and since he had spent his military life in an army ruled by civilian war ministers, Wolseley must have been provoked by similar instances of "meddling" or indecision. Besides, he had a personal ax to grind, for one of the recommendations of the Hartington Commission in 1889—the same year that Wolseley's articles appeared in the *North American Review*—was to limit the powers of the commander-in-chief, beginning with the successor to the Duke of Cambridge—Wolseley himself![79]

Even in purely military matters Wolseley saw nothing really new in the Civil War campaigns. On the contrary, what apparently impressed him most was "the regularity with which the old rules and principles assert their supremacy."[80] He noted that the Civil War armies had made frequent use of field intrenchments, but he held that such tactics were injurious to army morale and had "a very dangerous tendency to unfit soldiers for all rapid offensive action."[81] Possibly Wolseley arrived at this conclusion from his own study of the Civil War, but more likely than not he was influenced by certain of the Continental military writers who were beginning to preach the so-called doctrine of the offensive.[82]

In these later writings Wolseley took an entirely different view

[77] Wolseley, "An English View of the Civil War," *North American Review*, CXLVIII (May, 1889), 556–57; CXLIX (November, 1889), 567.

[78] See *ibid.*, pp. 36–39, 292, 446–47, 540–43, 726.

[79] Dunlop, *Development of the British Army*, pp. 21–22; Maurice and Arthur, *Wolseley*, pp. 204, 290–92.

[80] "English View of the Civil War," CXLVIII, 541.

[81] *Ibid.*, CXLIX, 283–84, 718. [82] See below, pp. 165–66.

of the Civil War cavalry from that which he had held in 1862. As an on-the-spot observer he had found little good to say about dismounted tactics except that they were suited to the forests of North America, but in the 1880's he was an enthusiastic exponent of mounted infantry. He did not completely abandon the *arme blanche*, for in his well-known *Soldier's Pocket-Book* he still extolled the mounted charge—but with reservations. However, Wolseley now recognized the growing importance of mounted infantry. The chief danger as he saw it was that cavalry would try to accomplish too much, becoming a "military Jack-of-all arms," and that any attempt to train cavalry to fight both on horse and on foot would produce a man who "would have the efficiency of neither" cavalry or infantry. He proposed instead the creation of a strong and independent mounted infantry force from the Yeomanry, the Volunteer cavalry. Such a force could "turn to the history of the Confederate war for instructions as to the best mode in which the dragoon can be used in the field." In reversing his earlier position on the Civil War cavalry, Wolseley undoubtedly was influenced by the writings of Sir Henry Havelock and Colonel George T. Denison, two early advocates of mounted infantry. By this time, too, he believed that if England were invaded, enemy cavalry would be ineffective because between the south coast and London "there is no country where cavalry, as cavalry, could maneuver," and "such cavalry as did land could easily be defeated by mounted infantry."[83] Wolseley exerted his influence to establish in 1888 two schools for mounted infantry,[84] although it should be emphasized that his views were far less extreme than those of the later writers who ridiculed faith in "the speed of the horse, the magnetism of the charge, and the terror of cold steel."[85]

Wolseley never lost his enthusiasm for the Civil War or his attachment for the friends he had made in 1862. To the closing days of his life he maintained that Lee was "the ablest soldier of my day," a "highly cultivated military genius,"[86] and when Stonewall

[83] General Viscount Wolseley, *The Soldier's Pocket-Book for Field Service* (5th ed.; London, 1886), pp. 374–78; Wolseley, "General Forrest," *United Service Magazine*, N.S., V (April–May, 1892), 5; "Sherman," pp. 99–100. The views of Havelock and Denison are discussed below, chap. v.

[84] These schools were at Aldershot and the Curragh. *Cavalry Journal*, II (July, 1907), 347–51.

[85] Erskine Childers, *War and the Arme Blanche* (London, 1910), p. 3.

[86] Wolseley to Thomas Nelson Page, March 27, 1909; Wolseley to General Garnett, April 10, 1910. Copies of both letters are in the Robert E. Lee Papers,

Jackson's widow published her biography of her famous husband, Wolseley enthusiastically undertook to help dispose of one hundred copies of the book in England. According to Colonel G. F. R. Henderson:

Lord Wolseley wanted to take the whole lot himself and to hand me over a check, but he is as extravagant in the way of kindness as in his admiration of the Confederates, so I absolutely refused to let him do it. He is not well off for his position [commander-in-chief of the British army], and I guess that Lady Wolseley would have "combed somebody's hair" if the transaction had been concluded.[87]

Although he displayed a sound knowledge of the Civil War campaigns and could often see much in them that was pertinent and timely, Wolseley ought not to be regarded as a profound student of the war. He did not examine it closely or critically, he contributed no original research, and he formulated no new theory on the basis of his observations. His most comprehensive analysis, "An English View of the Civil War," was based almost entirely on the articles contained in *Battles and Leaders of the Civil War*, while most of his other writings were inspired by his naked admiration for Forrest, Sherman, and, above all, Lee.

Wolseley is significant to this study not because of what he wrote about the Civil War but because of his influence in the British army. He was among the first to reintroduce the study of the Civil War to English soldiers and to encourage young officers to undertake serious studies of the American campaigns. Unlike most English soldiers of his day, Wolseley was not held spellbound by the dazzling successes of the Prussian armies over France in 1870. He could appreciate the need for studying other wars as well.

_____

Washington and Lee University, Lexington, Virginia. It was remarks such as these that prompted Sherman to declare that the British "were still judging military matters by antiquated standards" (Lloyd Lewis, *Sherman, Fighting Prophet* [New York, 1932], pp. 643-44).

[87] G. F. R. Henderson to Major Jed Hotchkiss, April 7, 1897. Hotchkiss Papers, Library of Congress.

3

The German Observers

The Civil War aroused less official attention in Prussia and Austria than in either England or France. The overwhelming majority of the population of the German states sympathized with the Union, but most Austrian and Prussian soldiers were too concerned with events nearer home to become interested in the American conflict. Austria had just emerged from an unsuccessful war with France (1859) and faced continuous unrest in Hungary, while Prussia had embarked upon a series of far-reaching military reforms designed to increase the army and strengthen the reserve system.[1] In September, 1862, when the Confederates were invading Maryland and Kentucky, Bismarck was brought to power in order to force army reforms on a hostile Parliament; in the spring of 1864, as Grant and Sherman were preparing their respective drives against Richmond and Atlanta, Prussian and Austrian troops stormed the Danish lines at Düppel (April 18); and in June, 1866, not much more than a year after Lee's surrender at Appomattox, Prussian armies invaded Austria.

The emergence of Prussia as a great military power was not accomplished without considerable intellectual activity within the Prussian army. The Prussian General Staff, under its famed chief, Count Helmuth von Moltke, had made elaborate studies of the latest campaigns in Europe, particularly the war between Austria and France in 1859,[2] and studied neighboring armies with such thoroughness that a French general complained that the Prussians "know more about us than we know ourselves."[3] But the Civil War was totally ignored in these preparations: Prussia's national interests

[1] The best account of the Prussian army reforms in the 1860's is found in Curt Jany, *Geschichte der Königlich preussischen Armee* (Berlin, 1933), IV, 214–32.

[2] The Historical Section of the Prussian General Staff completed an elaborate history of this war in 1862, a work compiled under the close supervision of Moltke himself (F. E. Whitton, *Moltke* [New York, 1921], pp. 73–74).

[3] [General Trochu], *L'armée française en 1867* (Paris, 1870), pp. 14–15. The development of Prussian military thought is traced in Colonel Eugène Carrias, *La pensée militaire allemande* (Paris, 1949), pp. 231–327.

were not involved, and events in Europe offered growing opportunities to study modern warfare.

Despite the large number of Germans who actively participated in the Civil War (an estimated 200,000 native Germans served in the Union army alone),[4] surprisingly few eyewitness accounts were made available in Germany, and often they were little more than popular versions of the writer's trials and triumphs in America. One such book, purporting to be the factual history of a German volunteer in the Confederate army, was actually a work of fiction written by one of the most prolific military writers of the day[5]—which suggests that there must have been a demand for this type of literature. In contrast to the British military observers, most German observers —if they can be properly called such—were either emigrants or soldiers of fortune. The Austrians evidently received technical information from such informal sources,[6] and even the official Prussian observer took an active part in a campaign.

One of the best accounts written by a German soldier in the Civil War is Otto Heusinger's *Amerikanische Kriegsbilder*. Heusinger, who later was commissioned in the Royal Brunswick Infantry, served throughout the war with the 41st New York, a regiment composed largely of German immigrants. He fought in the Shenandoah Valley in 1862, was wounded at Chancellorsville the following spring, witnessed the siege of Charleston, and participated in the final campaigns of the war in Virginia. Believing that the Civil War had been ignored in Germany because of the near-concurrent wars for unification, Heusinger wrote to give his countrymen a picture of the events he had witnessed. Only an occasional comment reveals his professional evaluation of his experiences.

From these casual comments, however, it is apparent that

---

[4] William Kaufmann, *Die Deutschen im amerikanischen Bürgerkrieg* (Munich and Berlin, 1911), pp. 121–25. The German states furnished more soldiers than any other foreign nation. So many people in Berlin clamored to join the Union army that the United States Minister there felt obliged to post a sign declaring: "This is a Legation . . . and not a recruiting-office" (Donaldson Jordan and Edwin J. Pratt, *Europe and the American Civil War* [Boston, 1931], pp. 195–97).

[5] The book in question is Julius von Wickede, *Ein deutscher Landsknecht der neuesten Zeit* . . . (Jena and Leipzig, 1864). See Appendix A.

[6] See above, p. 8 n. Another example of this type of observer was Karl Erdt, described as a "late Captain of U.S. Volunteers." Erdt contributed technical articles to both Austrian and Prussian military journals. See Karl Erdt, "Das Gefecht von Charleston am 7. April 1863," *Oesterreichische militärische Zeitschrift*, IV Jg. (1863), II, 321–40; "Die reguläre Armee der Vereinigten Staaten," *Allgemeine Militär-Zeitung*, Nos. 1–8 (1863); "Die Staatsmilizen," *ibid.*, Nos. 27–36 (1863); "Die Armee der Freiwilligen," *ibid.*, Nos. 28–41 (1865).

Heusinger was both perceptive and well informed. His descriptions are unusually detailed and vivid, and he shows a sound understanding of the tactical conditions. Above all, he respected the firepower of Civil War weapons. The bloody and futile Union assaults at Fredericksburg and Fort Gilmore convinced him of the accuracy and terrible destructive power of modern artillery against infantry, particularly whenever canister was used. He also appreciated the value of field fortifications, and he commented on the durability of the Confederate works protecting Charleston.[7] But his most interesting remarks concern the cavalry. In the Shenandoah Valley in 1864 he had obtained a quite different impression of the Union cavalry than had most observers. By this time the Union cavalry was well led and had acquired valuable experience, with the result that it accomplished—in Heusinger's opinion—"excellent service." "Equipped as lightly as possible" and armed with new, rapid-loading rifles, it could fight as both infantry and cavalry. This new type of cavalry

. . . had the great advantage, expecially in this war, of being able to be sent quickly to a fixed point without tiring a man through great exertion, and the usefulness of this arm was proved first-rate, especially in the case of Sheridan's march toward Richmond, where he destroyed railroads, bridges and canals in the enemy's rear and threw the inhabitants of the city into considerable consternation.

Heusinger credited the cavalry for the Union victory at Five Forks, and he praised Sheridan for his foresight in realizing and developing the potential in mounted infantry.[8] Perhaps he oversimplified the problem, and, as a Union soldier, he may have given Sheridan more credit than was due; in the West, Confederate cavalry under John H. Morgan, Joseph Wheeler, and Nathan Bedford Forrest had performed similar and even greater feats. Nevertheless, Heusinger was one of the first European soldiers to understand and appreciate the characteristics of Civil War tactics— the effectiveness of modern artillery fire, a growing dependence upon intrenchments, and the revolution in cavalry tactics. Like Fletcher, he too detected a marked improvement in discipline as the war progressed.[9]

[7] *Amerikanische Kriegsbilder, Auszeichnungen aus den Jahren 1861–1865* (Leipzig, 1869), pp. 59, 101, 167, 173.

[8] *Ibid.*, pp.. 206–9.

[9] *Ibid.*, p. 148. It is noteworthy that Heusinger thought less of the Civil War generals than many of his contemporaries—perhaps because he had served under some of

Heusinger's views were not shared by a fellow German who had spent two years in the Union cavalry. This anonymous soldier, who had fought in numerous small engagements and had been present at the battle of the Wilderness, did not consider the Union mounted arm cavalry at all. It would ride at the enemy in loose formation, fire a few shots with the revolver (a weapon "which left almost nothing to be desired"), and disappear, provided the Confederates had not done so first. He regarded the Confederates as superior to the Union cavalry in training, discipline, and leadership, and he credited much of their success to frequent use of shock tactics. He thus described a small combat in which a portion of his regiment had taken part:

A detachment 70 strong met with an enemy cavalry detachment of 40 near Fairfax Station. The Union captain, a former hatmaker's journeyman, drew up his men in a single rank and directed them to fire a volley. The Confederates, however, would not enter into any *Feuergefecht*, but instead attacked, saber in hand, at full gallop and in closed ranks. The bullets went way over their heads and in the next moment they had ridden over our company; disbanded in wild flight, our men scampered away, hard pursued by the Southerners. Most of them were either struck down or captured, and only about a dozen saved themselves.[10]

This picture of the Union cavalry, so different from that given by Heusinger, is perhaps explained by the fact that the skirmish described above was not a typical cavalry combat. The behavior of the Union troops on this occasion was so deplorable that a special investigation was undertaken to examine the "disgraceful mismanagement" of the battle.[11] Moreover, the regiment to which this anonymous writer belonged did not participate in any of Sheridan's impressive victories in the Shenandoah Valley in the late summer and fall of 1864; it remained east of the Blue Ridge Mountains and played only a supporting role in that campaign. Nor was the writer

---

them. Sherman and Lee were the only two he regarded as well-rounded generals; the others, Grant, Sheridan, and Jackson included, he considered capable enough, but on a far lower plane (*ibid.*, p. 166).

[10] "Erlebnisse eines deutchen Officiers, in nordamerikanischen Kriege," *Daheimb*, I, No. 36 (June, 1865), 530; No. 37 (July, 1865), 546.

[11] *The War of the Rebellion: A Compilation of the Official Records of the Union and Confederate Armies* (Washington, 1893), Ser. I, XLIII, Pt. I, 742–43, 762. Cited hereafter as *Official Records*. The engagement in question was undoubtedly that of August 9, 1864, when sixty of the 16th New York Cavalry—of which the above writer was a member—were attacked and routed at Fairfax Station by forty of Colonel John S. Mosby's guerrillas.

with Sheridan's cavalry at Five Forks and in the decisive Appomattox campaign. He had been discharged in January, 1865, and had already returned to Germany, glad to have survived his "unfortunate" experiences.[12]

Not all the German officers looked upon their Civil War experiences with such distaste. Several of them acquired glowing reputations in America, and none made better capital of his experiences than Heros von Borcke, a romantic young giant who left Prussia because of financial difficulties and offered his huge Damascus sword to the Confederacy. Commissioned a captain of cavalry, Von Borcke served as a member of Stuart's staff[13] from May, 1862, until incapacitated by wounds the following June. After his return to Europe he wrote of his experiences in a series of articles for *Blackwood's Magazine* (September, 1865–June, 1866) which subsequently were published in book form in England and later in Germany. Although his narrative was non-technical, Von Borcke understood many of the basic tactical changes that had occurred, and amid all the bluster and romantic trappings of his writings are passages which reveal this clearly.

Von Borcke saw enough of the war to respect the increase in firepower that had forced a change in tactics. During the Seven Days' campaign, he "looked with astonishment at the effect of the heavy artillery fire," which at Malvern Hill (July 1, 1862) was "more disastrous than had been before produced by artillery."[14] He took pains to examine many corpses and found so few stabbing wounds that he concluded that "bayonet fights rarely if ever occur, and exist only in the imagination." Medical records lend weight to

[12] "Erlebnisse eines deutschen Officiers," *Daheimb*, I, No. 35, 513; No. 38, 562.

[13] Von Borcke later referred to himself as the "former Chief of Staff" of Stuart's cavalry. Actually he was nothing of the sort. According to another member of Stuart's staff, Von Borcke "got General Stuart to place the body of couriers detailed at headquarters . . . under his command and to give him the title of Chief of Staff in consequence. We could not conceive why he was so tenacious of this trifling matter until his book appeared after the war in which he calls himself Chief of Staff of the Cavalry of the Army of Northern Virginia. This position . . . in European armies is second in importance to that only of the General himself [often, in fact, it was more important]. In our army there was no corresponding position, the Chief of Staff in this case being only the officer who managed the domestic affairs of the military family at headquarters. The General himself controlled directly all the movements of troops" (Lieut. Col. W. W. Blackford, *War Years with Jeb Stuart* [New York, 1945], pp. 159-60). For information on the career of Von Borcke, see Major Edgar Erskine Hume, *Colonel Heros von Borcke: A Famous Prussian Volunteer in the Confederate Army* ("Southern Sketches," No. 2, [Charlottesville, 1935]).

[14] *Memoirs of the Confederate War for Independence* (New York, 1938), I, 71, 74.

his testimony.[15] He also remarked upon the disappointing effects of volley firing by infantry, the value of the signal corps ("an institution peculiar to the American armies"), and the adaptive fighting qualities of the Americans—especially the Confederates. Above all, Von Borcke appreciated the unique problem of supplying an army "in a war of such magnitude, carried on over so vast and thinly populated a territory."[16]

Since Von Borcke, prior to coming to America, had served as second lieutenant in the Second Brandenburg Regiment of Dragoons, his attention naturally centered on the mounted arm. Despite his obvious preference for the saber as a weapon for cavalry, he understood some of the conditions that had made shock tactics impracticable in Virginia. His first major battle convinced him that the lance, "formidable enough in the hand of one accustomed to wield it, is a downright absurdity and encumbrance to the inexperienced." He was aware that the nature of the terrain in Virginia discouraged the operations of cavalry in the regular sense and that "the great improvement in firearms . . . had necessitated a very material change in cavalry tactics." A "genuine cavalry fight, with sabres crossing and single combat" was an event that would "very rarely occur in modern warfare."[17]

Yet Von Borcke was not won over to the new tactics, and in his later years he was inclined to minimize the effectiveness of dismounted fighting. He remained a dashing cavalier and reveled in the mounted charge. Perhaps his experiences with the Prussian dragoons in 1866 persuaded him that the Civil War had been something of an aberration, or possibly, as he aged, the Civil War battles appeared more glamorous. In any case, though he always maintained that a combination of shock and fire tactics for modern cavalry was necessary, he never lost faith in the *arme blanche*, even under modern battle conditions. "How would it have been possible," he inquired

---

[15] *Ibid.*, I, 63–64. In the Civil War "bayonets were so little used that many men threw them away" (E. M. Lloyd, *A Review of the History of Infantry* [London, 1908], p. 248). According to one Union surgeon, "that the armies rarely crossed bayonets was evident from the small number of bayonet wounds, except accidental ones, which were presented to surgeons after a battle. I think half a dozen would include all the wounds of this nature that I ever dressed. Cavalrymen would occasionally get close enough to slash each other with their sabres, but these wounds were few and far between" (Major Albert Gaillard Hart, "The Surgeon and the Hospital in the Civil War," *M.H.S.P.*, XIII [Boston, 1913], 265).

[16] *Memoirs of the Confederate War*, I, 13, 19–20, 160 n., 243–44; II, 7.

[17] *Ibid.*, I, 55, 114; II, 107. For Von Borcke's description of a typical Civil War cavalry skirmish, see *ibid.*, I, 111.

of Lieutenant General Keith Fraser, Inspector General of Cavalry in the British army

. . . to execute that famous ride through McClellan's whole army in the days from June 12 to 15, 1862, with Mounted Infantry? . . . We were obliged to fight all our way through, charging continually and dispersing again and again, sabres in hand, the hostile cavalry. . . . Any development for dismounted fighting would have been out of the question. . . . [Stuart] was a Cavalryman from head to heel, and he wished nothing more than to form his troopers into dashing Cavalry soldiers. . . . Stuart delighted in the charge with sabres drawn.[18]

Von Borcke even went so far as to state:

The Mounted Infantryman will regard his horse as good enough to suit his easy locomotion and very useful to carry him out of a dangerous position. . . . If I was ordered to hold a very important position at all hazards with M[ounted] I[nfantry], I would in the first place have the horses shot to deprive the man of the *arrière pensée* that they were near for their salvation.[19]

Irrespective of the merits of Von Borcke's theories on cavalry, he was probably correct in his contention that Stuart preferred shock tactics whenever possible, for according to a recent biographer Stuart "fought dismounted when he had to—notably and stubbornly in rearguard actions, or when he had to fight for ground. But his feeling was for the white weapon [i.e., the sword, *l'arme blanche*]"[20]

In 1893 Von Borcke collaborated with his close friend and former comrade-at-arms in Virginia, Justus Scheibert, in writing a historical study of the cavalry battle of Brandy Station (June 9, 1863). Both had participated in this fight, and while the views expressed on the subject of cavalry resemble Scheibert's more closely than Von Borcke's, they were certainly approved by the latter. The

[18] Quoted in Charles Sydney Goldman, "Cavalry: Its True Functions in Modern War," *Cavalry Journal*, I (January, 1906), 76–77. Excerpts from several of Von Borcke's letters to General Fraser are published in this article.

[19] Von Borcke to Lieutenant General Fraser, quoted in Captain W. H. James, *The Rôle of Cavalry as Affected by Modern Arms of Precision* (Aldershot, 1894), pp. 7–8.

[20] John W. Thompson, Jr., *Jeb Stuart* (New York, 1930), p. 80. From the accounts of two of Stuart's staff officers, the cavalry of the Army of Northern Virginia fought both on horse and on foot and often blended fire and shock tactics with good effect. Their descriptions of the fighting reveal that whatever Stuart's preferred mode of fighting may have been, the main emphasis was upon firepower; more than once his dismounted cavalry was mistaken for Confederate infantry. See H. B. McClellan, *The Life and Campaigns of Major-General J. E. B. Stuart, Commander of the Cavalry of the Army of Northern Virginia* (Boston, 1885), pp. 48, 49, 56, 78, 120, 124, 156, 173–74, 198, 203, 207–10, 267, 299, 339–40, 363; Blackford, *War Years with Jeb Stuart*, pp. 29–31, 72, 74, 95, 103, 134, 144, 149, 171, 175, 178, 218, 221.

theme of this book is that, beginning in 1863, the Union cavalry had grown and improved to the extent that Stuart's men no longer were able to dominate the field. Thus Sheridan's cavalry, described here as being predominantly mounted infantry, "were victorious principally because they found no enemy before them." Von Borcke and Scheibert implied—and the writings of other foreign observers also suggest—that the Union cavalry had grown dependent upon dismounted tactics not so much to meet the challenge of modern firepower as because it seemed the best way to fight the Confederates.[21]

Von Borcke is best remembered for his *Memoirs*, originally written in England and published later in Germany under the title *Zwei Jahre im Sattel und am Feinde*. The translator, a well-known German cavalry officer, Lieutenant Colonel von Kaehler, recommended the book to his fellow officers as a *Lesebuch für den Reiteroffizier* with the suggestion that it was not to be regarded as a "textbook of military science" or even as a "work of military history," but as a faithful portrayal of the ideal cavalry spirit. "Swords clash and bugles blow on every page."[22] And it was the flavor of the book rather than any specific military comments that so appealed to the German appetite. In a day when the *arme blanche* was exposed to increasing fire in theory as well as in battle, Von Borcke's *Memoirs* were interpreted as evidence that cavalry had not experienced any fundamental change since the days of Frederick the Great. This is why Prince Kraft zu Hohenlohe-Ingelfingen, the great strategist and military theorist, described it as a book that "could make any Cavalry soldier's heart beat fast," and why Prince Frederick Karl and General Karl von Schmidt, the two foremost organizers of modern German cavalry, were both avowed admirers of Jeb Stuart.[23] Even in modern times, Von Borcke's *Memoirs* is one

21 Heros Von Borcke and Justus Scheibert, *Die grosse Reiterschlacht bei Brandy Station* (Berlin, 1893), pp. 63–64. Their estimation of the comparative qualities of the Union and Confederate cavalry in 1863 was probably correct: they claimed that the Union cavalry was vastly improved and was now superior to the Confederates in numbers, armament, and perhaps even in discipline. On the other hand, the Confederate cavalry was composed of better men and horses, had superior leaders, and enjoyed higher morale because of its past victories. It also functioned better as a unit (*ibid.*, pp. 64, 124–25).

22 See Von Kaehler's foreword to the first German edition of *Zwei Jahre im Sattel und am Feinde* (Berlin, 1877); Douglas Southall Freeman, *The South to Posterity: An Introduction to the Writing of Confederate History* (New York, 1951), p. 22.

23 Von Kaehler, *loc. cit.*, p. vi. Prince Kraft is quoted in James, *The Rôle of Cavalry*, p. 7. For the views of Prince Frederick Karl and Von Schmidt, see

of the best-known German books on the Civil War. In the closing campaigns of World War II, an American soldier picked up a copy of *Zwei Jahre im Sattel* which a young German officer had once borrowed from the Würtemberg Military Library and had never returned. The name of this offender was Erwin Rommel, whose brilliant campaigns in North Africa mark him a worthy spiritual descendant of the famed Confederate cavalry leader.[24]

In February, 1863, a young Prussian officer of engineers was summoned to Berlin by Prince von Radziwill, chief of the Corps of Engineers, and informed that he was being sent to America as a military observer. The Prussian General Staff desired specific data regarding "the effect of rifled artillery against earth, masonry, and iron." After conferring with Von Prittwitz, Deputy Inspector General of Fortifications, and Von Roon, the War Minister, Captain Justus Scheibert departed on his mission.[25]

Scheibert was well suited for this task. Possessing the desired social attributes,[26] he was observant, intelligent, and known to be interested in his profession. He was also a capable writer. Early in his career he had attracted the attention of Colonel von Voigts-Rhetz, who later attained a position of considerable influence in the Prussian army, by his habit of spending his annual leave studying army maneuvers and by the pertinent observations of these maneuvers which he recorded in his diary.[27] Others, including several on the General Staff, were impressed by the articles he had contributed to the *Illustrierten Zeitung* on the campaign of 1859 in Italy, articles published anonymously but recognized as coming from Scheibert's pen. He was probably best known, however, for the pamphlet he

---

Von Borcke and Scheibert, *Die grosse Reiterschlacht bei Brandy Station*, p. 62; and Franz Von Schmidt, *Avantgarde: Weg und Welt eines preussischen Reitergenerals* (Berlin, 1941), p. 336.

[24] This copy was sent to the noted Civil War authority, Dr. Douglas Southall Freeman, who once showed the volume to the writer. See also Monroe F. Cockrell, *After Sundown: A Venture into the Shadows of Yesterday* ([Chicago], 1955), Part II, entitled "Did Erwin Johannes Eugen Rommel Visit These Places in the United States???" Mr. Cockrell demonstrates convincingly that, contrary to rumor, he did not, and his conclusions are confirmed by Rommel's widow.

[25] Scheibert, *Mit Schwert und Feder*, pp. 35–36.

[26] A clue to Scheibert's personality is found in Blackford, *War Years with Jeb Stuart*, pp. 203, 206–9. Scheibert's autobiography suggests that he was sociable and met people well. See *Mit Schwert und Feder*, pp. 24–25.

[27] *Ibid.*, pp. 15–16. Generalmajor Konstantin Bernhard von Voigts-Rhetz was named director of the General War Department in the War Ministry in 1859. He later became a prominent staff officer in the campaigns of 1866 and 1870–71 (*Allgemeine deutsche Biographie* [Leipzig, 1896], XL, 216–20).

wrote in 1861 on the influence of rifled artillery on fortress warfare. This was a timely and important subject, and Scheibert soon acquired a reputation as an authority on modern fortifications.[28] Whatever else may have influenced the Prussian authorities in their decision to send Scheibert to America as a military observer, his reputation in this field undoubtedly made him appear a logical choice for the assignment.

Scheibert reached New York the first week of March, 1863. Originally he was to accompany the Union army, but because he wished to examine the effects of modern artillery fire on the defenses at Charleston and was at heart a strong Southern sympathizer, he persuaded his superiors to allow him to visit the Confederate army in an "unofficial capacity." (For diplomatic reasons, the Prussian government chose not to *order* him South.)[29]

After a brief stay in New York, where, like Wolseley, he saw enough of the Union army to form a lasting prejudice against it, Scheibert sailed to Nassau and caught a blockade runner bound for Charleston. He was charmed by this city of the Old South, but since there were no active military operations in progress there at the time, he proceeded to Richmond, where he met with several high-ranking officials of the Confederacy and was guided over the outlying fortifications and battlegrounds. Scheibert hoped eventually to reach the Confederate forces in the West, but first he planned a brief visit to the Army of Northern Virginia, then intrenched on the heights above Fredericksburg.

Arriving in Fredericksburg in April, Scheibert spent a busy week with Lee's army before he met Von Borcke, who persuaded him to join Stuart's cavalry in camp at Culpeper. He remained with Stuart until May, when, mindful of his primary purpose in visiting the Confederacy, he set out to observe the *Festungskrieg* at Vicksburg. Sudden illness and word that Vicksburg had been completely cut off by Grant's forces caused Scheibert to abandon this enterprise and return to the Army of Northern Virginia. He accompanied Lee's staff on the Gettysburg campaign and became acquainted with Fremantle and Fitzgerald Ross, an Austrian soldier of fortune. Following the retreat from Pennsylvania, he and Ross returned to Charleston, which was then besieged by Union naval

[28] Scheibert, *Einfluss der neuesten Taktik und der gezogenen Waffen auf den Festungskrieg: Mit benutzen der von Sebastopol gemachten Erfahrungen* (Berlin, 1861), *passim; Mit Schwert und Feder,* pp. 22–30.

[29] *Ibid.,* pp. 35–36.

and land forces. As soon as he had seen "what was valuable for the Prussian Army," Scheibert journeyed north to Wilmington, and after a tour of the works there he departed for Bermuda and Europe.

An eyewitness of fourteen battles and engagements, Scheibert by this time knew the Confederate army well. He had served as a sort of handyman (*Rittmeister* was the title he preferred) on Stuart's staff, preparing maps, translating letters captured from German-born soldiers, carrying messages, and occasionally even helping in the construction of bridges and breastworks. He had come under fire for the first time in his life at Chancellorsville, had participated in the cavalry battle at Brandy Station, and had viewed Gettysburg from a tall oak overlooking Lee's field headquarters. He was familiar with the rank and file and had observed and conversed with Lee, Stuart, and Stonewall Jackson during anxious moments in battle. He had many personal friends among the junior officers, from whom he had gained much knowledge about campaigns and incidents at which he had not been present. At Charleston he had been given access to confidential information. Like most foreign officers who came to know the Army of Northern Virginia, Scheibert departed for Europe a full-fledged Confederate.[30]

Upon his return to Prussia, Scheibert submitted a detailed report of his findings, discussed his views with various military leaders (among them Prince Frederick Karl and Field Marshal von Wrangel), and lectured before military organizations about his experiences. He was an active participant in the campaigns of 1864, 1866, and 1870, where he was wounded at the battle of Wörth. In 1868 he wrote a popular account of his trip entitled *Sieben Monate in den rebellen Staaten*.[31] Six years later, while stationed at Minden, he prepared a more detailed and technical book on his observations. By this time he was well known for his Civil War experiences (according to Scheibert, none other than Bismarck had requested his services as guide through the captured Danish works at Düppel because of his reputation acquired in America[32]) and could evaluate them in the light of more recent campaigns.

[30] *Ibid.*, pp. 45–168 *passim.*

[31] Scheibert, *Sieben Monate in den rebellen Staaten während des nordamerikanischen Krieges* (Stettin, 1868); the bulk of this work is contained in *Mit Schwert und Feder*. It is significant to note that in 1868 Scheibert did not mention specifically what he had been sent to America to observe.

[32] *Mit Schwert und Feder*, p. 228.

Der Bürgerkrieg in den nordamerikanischen Staaten[33] is a critical analysis of the military aspects of the Civil War. Commencing with a précis of the military operations, Scheibert wrote in considerable detail of the organization, equipment, and tactics of the three arms and also of the engineer, navy, and sanitary services. He devoted a special section to the strategy of the war and even included biographical sketches of the foremost generals on both sides. Because of the controversial nature of the subject, his most interesting observations are those concerning the development of Civil War tactics.

The tactics of infantry posed special problems. Scheibert's own experience with infantry in America had been limited (most of the time he had been with the cavalry or else observing siege operations at Charleston), and he found the printed sources confusing and often contradictory. He noted the French influence in Hardee's *Rifle and Light Infantry Tactics* and Casey's *Infantry Tactics*, which served as the official manuals for the Confederate and Union armies, respectively, and he could see for himself that the Confederates had "acquired great skill" in mastering their formations and could form in line of battle "in an incredibly short time." But he also observed that in combat both armies failed to adhere to the peacetime regulations (which frequently is the case) and that from the chaos and confusion of initial campaigns there emerged a new system of infantry tactics "which merits examination in its different phases."[34]

The first phase, according to Scheibert, was characterized by isolated and disjointed combats, with neither army being sufficiently trained or organized to sustain a major offensive drive. Like Fletcher, Scheibert detected a tendency, especially on the part of the Union troops, to waste ammunition in useless skirmishing at excessive distances. He claimed that the Confederates, with inferior weapons, preferred fighting at close quarters. This period, culminating in the first battle of Bull Run, was one of improvised tactics, inadequate discipline, and uneven leadership. It was the undignified

33 Scheibert, *Der Bürgerkrieg in den nordamerikanischen Staaten: Militairisch beleuchtet für den deutschen Offizier* (Berlin, 1874). Hereafter cited as *Der Bürgerkrieg*. Although Scheibert mentioned an English translation (*Mit Schwert und Feder*, p. 300) and the late Douglas Southall Freeman stated that this volume was "available" in English translation (*Lee's Lieutenants* [New York, 1944], III, 824), no American or English edition of *Der Bürgerkrieg* could be located, nor is it listed in any of the standard bibliographical works.

34 *Mit Schwert und Feder*, p. 67; *Der Bürgerkrieg*, pp. 22-29.

performance of both armies at Bull Run which, in Scheibert's opinion, had caused many European soldiers to lose interest in the American campaigns.[35]

The second phase (1862–63) saw the gradual emergence of linear tactics. By this time both armies had improved substantially in organization, training, and discipline. They had ceased to mass troops on the battlefield because of the growing effectiveness of artillery fire and now deployed in two and sometimes three lines, with skirmishers a hundred paces or so in advance. Usually these lines merged into one confused mass as the battle progressed. Fremantle had noted that the Civil War armies tended to outreach the immediate control of the field commander, and Scheibert observed this same tendency. He once discussed the problem with Lee and was told:

> You must be acquainted with our situation and perceive that my supervision during the battle would do more harm than good. It would be unfortunate if I could not rely upon my division and brigade commanders. I think and work with all my powers to bring my troops to the right place at the right time; then I have done my duty. Once I have thrown the troops into battle, I place the fate of my army into God's hands.

Scheibert described this second phase as a period when the Confederates generally took the strategical initiative and acted on the tactical offensive in most battles.[36]

The third, and to Scheibert the most interesting, phase in the evolution of Civil War infantry tactics was that of the tactical defensive (1863–65). This was the period of the spade and ax, when field fortifications ruled the battlefield. Intrenchments, it is true, had been used before in the war—Scheibert himself had seen them on his tour of the battlefields near Richmond and in the fighting at Chancellorsville—but never to such an extent. Scheibert attributed this development to several factors: it was partly the result of the lack of tactical unity and centralized command that had characterized previous battles, but it was due even more to the fact that after Gettysburg Lee faced overwhelming numbers and had no choice but to resort to the tactical defensive: "In this, the least known period of the Civil War, General Lee . . . first developed his talents

[35] *Ibid.*, pp. 3, 29–31, 34–35.

[36] *Ibid.*, pp. 35–40. See also Scheibert, "General Robert E. Lee, Ober-Commandeur der ehemaligen südstaatlichen Armee in Nord-Amerika," *Jahrbücher für die deutsche Armee und Marine*, XVI (September, 1875), 208–9. This important military journal is hereafter cited as *Jahrbücher*.

as general and tactician, talents which now, having evolved from three years of rich experience and study and supported by experienced troops, produced brilliant results." Scheibert did not advocate the extensive use of intrenchments. He preferred, whenever possible, an offensive in the open field. But in 1864 Lee's forces had not been strong enough to undertake a major offensive against Grant, and Scheibert was forced to admit that in this campaign "the superiority of . . . [defensive] tactics over all other means of fighting was demonstrated to the point that all attempts made to employ different tactics failed completely."[37]

With regard to the tactics of the Civil War cavalry, Scheibert was in basic agreement with Von Borcke. He, too, claimed that the Union cavalry was actually mounted infantry which fought for the most part dismounted, whereas the Confederates had extolled the mounted charge whenever practicable. Both rated the Confederate cavalry superior to the Union cavalry in quality, spirit, and leadership, attributing the success of the Union cavalry in 1864–65 to its overwhelming superiority in numbers. Scheibert steadfastly maintained that shock tactics remained the "fundamental principle of cavalry combat." He recognized the need for occasional dismounted fighting in dense woods and rough terrain, but warned that too great a reliance upon firearms would lower the over-all efficiency of the army and damage the so-called cavalry spirit. And he doubted whether mounted infantry, as opposed to cavalry proper, could operate as effectively in the open fields of Europe as it had in Virginia.[38]

Nevertheless, Scheibert professed wonder "at the great role which cavalry had played in the Civil War, particularly when the terrain was extremely unfavorable for great developments." Recent campaigns in the Crimea—where the famous and futile "charge of the Light Brigade" had occurred—and in Italy had convinced many that the heyday of cavalry had passed and that henceforth infantry would be the most effective arm. The Civil War encouraged Scheibert to think otherwise. The Confederates had combined shock tactics and dismounted fighting to a remarkable degree and had

---

[37] *Ibid.*, pp. 105–6, 306–7; *Der Bürgerkrieg*, pp. 44, 49. It is generally agreed that Lee was at his best during the 1864 campaign against Grant. See Major General Sir Frederick Maurice, *Robert E. Lee the Soldier* (Boston, 1925), pp. 217 ff.; Douglas Southall Freeman, *Robert E. Lee* (New York, 1936), III, 447.

[38] *Der Bürgerkrieg*, pp. 55, 58–59; "General J. E. B. Stuart," *Jahrbücher*, XXV (December, 1877), 289, 297–98. Cited hereafter as Scheibert, "Stuart."

been able to use cavalry as a virtually independent arm. Stuart's men well illustrated the indispensable value of modern cavalry in reconnaissance and in screening the army's movements, while at the same time they had lost none of the "true cavalry spirit." Scheibert did question the value of the strategic cavalry raid, however. He believed that the results of the raids of Stuart, Nathan Bedford Forrest, and John H. Morgan had been exaggerated. Even when executed against untrained troops and armies dependent upon supply depots, in a country with few railroads and an inadequate telegraph system, and where thick forests could mask the movements of entire armies—even under these ideal conditions the Civil War cavalry raids had brought only limited success. In Europe, where such favorable conditions did not exist, cavalry raids were bound to be still less effective.[39]

Scheibert's most fruitful remarks were those concerning Civil War artillery and fortifications, for this is what he had been sent specifically to observe. His comments are all the more interesting because artillery in 1863 was in a period of transition. Rifled artillery was used in both armies, but it had not replaced entirely the old smoothbore, and each type had many vocal advocates. According to Scheibert, Union artillerists preferred the rifled gun, even though they employed the smoothbore "admirably." Lee, on the other hand, is quoted by Scheibert as saying that under certain conditions, particularly where the terrain is heavily wooded,

. . . nothing surpasses . . . the impression of a battery of 12 pound smoothbores which approaches to within 400–600 paces of the enemy and exercises its influence not only with shell and grape shot, but also with the moral effect of its thundering proximity. In such moments rifled artillery, the advantages of which in open country I fully appreciate, cannot replace the smoothbore.

Lee therefore decided to maintain an approximately equal number of both.[40]

39 *Ibid.*, p. 265; *Mit Schwert und Feder*, p. 74; *Der Bürgerkrieg*, pp. 55, 71–72, 75. "General J. E. B. Stuart's letzter groszer Raid," *Jahrbücher*, XXXIII (October, 1879), 164.

40 *Der Bürgerkrieg*, p. 78. Scheibert's observations on the relative value of the rifled gun and the smoothbore seem to be correct. Major General Henry J. Hunt, Chief of Artillery, Army of the Potomac, has written that while many of the younger officers showed a preference for the rifled gun, "General McClellan wisely took the opinion of the older artillery officers, and directed that one-third of the batteries should be of light 12-pounders [smoothbore]. These grew in favor and at the end of the war constituted half the field artillery" ("Artillery," *M.H.S.P.*, XIII, 115). At the time Scheibert was with the Army of Northern Virginia, its artillery comprised

Scheibert detected little fundamental difference in the Union and Confederate field artillery, except that the latter was used more to fire upon the enemy's troops than to silence his guns.[41] In both armies the trend was toward greater centralization, but rarely was artillery used in great masses. Chancellorsville and Gettysburg were the exceptions, and in the case of the latter the artillery barrage preceding Pickett's charge was, in Scheibert's opinion, "a grandiose military spectacle but entirely without consequence on the issue of the battle." He rated the Union artillery especially high and commented on the accuracy of its indirect fire. To this he could testify from personal experience.[42]

Scheibert was particularly impressed by the new rifled siege artillery. The range and accuracy of the Union siege guns convinced him that the day of brick and mortar fortifications had passed. Henceforth earth-constructed forts, particularly those equipped with bomb shelters of the type used by the Confederates at Battery Wagner, would provide the best defense against modern artillery. Scheibert deemed it significant that at Charleston the attacking force, "despite the use of the very latest technical means"—iron-plated ships and rifled siege guns—did not "succeed in taking the fortifications by means of a siege." (Charleston did not actually fall until threatened in the rear by Sherman's army in 1865.) Scheibert further concluded that ironclads had played "only a secondary role" against land defenses and that the torpedo, or submarine mine, was a greater threat to the enemy's morale than to his ships.[43]

In 1889 Lord Wolseley asserted that the "cooperating action of the naval and military services" constituted one of the "most important lessons" of the Civil War.[44] Scheibert, too, was interested in this problem and in fact anticipated Wolseley by two years with his study of this particular aspect of the war. In *Das Zusammen-*

---

103 three-inch rifles, 107 twelve-pounder Napoleons, 30 twelve-pounder howitzers, and 4 six-inch Whitworth rifled guns (Jennings Cropper Wise, *The Long Arm of Lee or the History of the Artillery of the Army of Northern Virginia* [Lynchburg, Va., 1915], II, 571).

[41] According to Wise, the Confederates used their artillery primarily as an anti-personnel weapon in many battles, among them Antietam, Fredericksburg, and the Wilderness (*ibid.*, I, 324, 372; II, 832–33).

[42] *Der Bürgerkrieg*, pp. 80–82.

[43] *Ibid.*, pp. 92–105; *Sieben Monate in den rebellen Staaten*, pp. 109–12; *Mit Schwert und Feder*, pp. 158–61.

[44] Field Marshal Viscount Wolseley, "An English View of the Civil War," *North American Review*, CXLVIII (1889), 597.

wirken der Armee and Marine, published in 1887, Scheibert analyzed the operations of the Union army and navy along the Mississippi. The 1880's were years of increasing agitation within Germany for a more aggressive colonial policy: the Colonial Society, formed in 1882, and the *Kolonialzeitung,* founded two years later, were effective organs for what has been described as a "great outburst of imperialism." Sooner or later, Scheibert reasoned, local wars on distant continents would become unavoidable; there might even be occasion for combined naval and military operations along some of the rivers flowing into the North Sea and the Baltic.[45]

Scheibert's study of the Mississippi River campaigns confirmed an observation he had made earlier at Charleston: naval power alone could not overcome land fortifications. This was evident at Island Number 10 and "in all battles . . . from Fort Henry to the Grand Gulf." A fleet, "despite its mobility and clear superiority in both the calibre and quality . . . of its guns, was not equal to land batteries if unsupported . . . by land forces." Decisive results were possible only through combined naval and military operations. In addition to furnishing valuable tactical support, the Union navy had also enabled the army to solve formidable problems in logistics, for the gunboats had been indispensable in transporting troops and supplies, thus giving the army far greater mobility than otherwise would have been possible. In the light of Germany's new interest in naval and colonial affairs, Scheibert considered the military lessons of this campaign still valid.[46]

Scheibert believed that there was another area in which the military lessons of the Civil War could also be instructive. The introduction of long-range guns and the experiences of the war of 1870–71 had resulted in much confusion of ideas about the future of fortification. Scheibert participated in this *Festungskrieg* controversy, in which he opposed the theories of the Belgian General Henri Brialmont and his enthusiastic followers. Brialmont, creator of the Belgian fortresses made famous by the German invasion in 1914, advocated an elaborate network of barrier forts, fortified cities, and intrenched camps. He regarded the modern fort as a land battleship; sprinkled with many domelike gun turrets called cupolas,

---

45 Scheibert, *Das Zusammenwirken der Armee und Marine: Eine Studie illustriert durch den Kampf um den Mississippi, 1861–65* (Rathenew, [1887]), pp. 2, 62. For a survey of the colonial movement in Germany see William L. Langer, *European Alliances and Alignments, 1871–1890* (2d ed.; New York, 1950), pp. 88 ff.

46 *Das Zusammenwirken der Armee und Marine,* pp. 3–4, 8, 17, 23, 30, 64.

these detached strongholds were designed to guard strategic points even to the point of resisting a determined siege.[47]

Scheibert, on the other hand, contended that such a dependence upon fortifications would result in a defensive attitude and deprive a commander of the troops and freedom of action needed to win victory in the field. The fortress, he argued, had outlived its usefulness as a supply depot. Detached forts could usually be bypassed as easily as most natural obstacles and at best would delay only a detachment of sufficient strength to contain the garrison. It was one thing for a small nation like Belgium to cover her boundaries with permanent works of the type suggested by Brialmont (although, as Scheibert pointed out, the Danish fortifications had failed to contain the Austro-Prussian forces in 1864), and quite another for Germany, with potential enemies on two lengthy fronts, to rely upon a system of fortification for protection against invasion. Scheibert also opposed the idea of intrenched camps, claiming that they would make it easy for a field army to seek refuge behind walls; the experiences of the French at Metz and Sedan in 1870 convinced him that this was a real danger.

In place of Brialmont's elaborate fortification system, Scheibert urged that the field army be considered the first line of defense, to be supported by isolated or improvised works whenever needed. Here Scheibert's views can be traced directly to his experiences during the Civil War. From Lee he had learned the value of field fortifications as a temporary defensive measure, particularly at Falling Waters, where the strength of the Confederate lines on the retreat from Gettysburg had evidently made a lasting impression upon him.[48] At the same time, Scheibert remained convinced that only offensive action won wars. Lee, despite inferior numbers, had

[47] According to an English contemporary, Brialmont "practically contents himself with sprinkling cupolas over his plans, and retains all the objectionable features of the stereotyped fort . . . tricks of drawing office fortification in its most aggravated form" (Sir George Sydenham Clarke, *Fortification: Its Past Achievements, Recent Development, and Future Progress* [London, 1890], pp. 91–92). Brialmont's theories are also summarized in Lieutenant Colonel Louis Charles Jackson, "Fortification and Siegecraft," *Encyclopaedia Britannica* (11th ed.; Cambridge, 1910), X, 679–725.

[48] Brialmont, too, was aware of the value of field fortifications. In his treatise *Hasty Entrenchments* (London, 1872) he gave lip service to this lesson of the Civil War, stating that "never have hasty entrenchments been used with greater success, or more generally, than in the last war in America" (p. 127). Yet it is important to note that Brialmont throughout his book devoted more attention to the wars of Frederick the Great, Condé, and Turenne than to the American campaigns, and in a key chapter entitled "Instances of Fortified Fields of Battle" there is no mention of a single Civil War battle! His examples were taken from the wars of Napoleon and earlier.

been a threat only so long as his army remained mobile; once confined to the trenches at Richmond and Petersburg, the end had been merely a question of time. And in the West, where the Confederates had suffered a series of reverses because of what Scheibert described as a defensive attitude, an entire field army was lost at Vicksburg because it became tied to its fortifications. On the other hand, Sherman's campaigns demonstrated the value of maneuver. The Confederates had been forced to evacuate their defenses both at Savannah and at Charleston to avoid being isolated by Sherman's northward march through the Carolinas. In each case, fortifications had been rendered useless by the mobility of Sherman's army, which is doubtless one reason why Scheibert preferred field fortifications— but only when necessary—to Brialmont's girdle of fortresses and intrenched camps.[49]

Scheibert resigned from the army in 1876 and took up writing as a career. He felt cramped and frustrated in the Engineer Corps, where the prospects for promotion were discouraging and his theories on fortification were unpopular.[50] He soon made a name for himself as military correspondent for the politically conservative *Kreuzzeitung* and as a writer on a wide range of military subjects. In the twilight of Scheibert's career, Count von Waldersee, then chief of the General Staff, brought him out of quasi-retirement to

[49] Scheibert's most important technical work, *Die Befestigungskunst und die Lehre von Kampfe* (3 vols.; Berlin, 1880–86), cannot be located in this country. The views therein are summarized in General Pierron, *Stratégie et grande tactique d'après l'expérience des dernières guerres* (Paris, 1892), III, 425–26, and in two articles by Scheibert: "Strategische Streifflichter auf die Festunsfragen," *Beiheft zum Militär-Wochenblatt* (1891), pp. 49–66; "Allerei Gedanken und Bedenken über den Festungsbau und Festungskrief," *ibid.* (1902), pp. 215–36.

[50] Although in the minority, Scheibert was not alone in his views on fortification. Generals Von Scherff and Von Sauer (who was later converted to Brialmont's theories) both raised similar arguments against the Brialmont school (*Mit Schwert und Feder*, pp. 315–16). Colmar von der Goltz, with whom Scheibert had once collaborated on a technical study of the *Festungskrieg* (*ibid.*, p. 300) espoused the theories of Von Sauer and Major Max Schumann, both of whom advocated a more limited and flexible system of fortification than that proposed by Brialmont (Freiherr von der Goltz and Wolfgang Foerster [eds.], *Generalfeldmarschall Colmar Freiherr von der Goltz Denkwürdigkeiten* [Berlin, 1929], p. 195). Cited hereafter as Von der Goltz, *Denkwürdigkeiten*. See also Pierron, *Stratégie et grande tactique*, III, 421–36. Like Scheibert, Von der Goltz believed that the value of the fortress as a base had diminished appreciably, that fortresses tended to "anchor" large numbers of men in garrisons, and that "an extension of fortificatory works is due to a feeling of weakness. A nation in which a spirit of offensive action dwells will be moderate in their use. He who seeks his safety behind walls and ditches, lacks a sense of strength. More and more will he confine himself to passive resistance, the end of which . . . is sure defeat, be it ever so much delayed" (Von der Goltz, *The Nation in Arms* [London, 1887], pp. 339–49 *passim*).

write on behalf of that organization. As one of the so-called Press Hussars, Scheibert used his pen vigorously in a vain effort to prevent the reduction of the standard term of military service in the German army from three years to two.[51]

After his retirement from the army Scheibert became a prolific writer on Civil War subjects, one reason being, as he candidly admitted, "to pay the rent." With few exceptions, his later writings on the Civil War are thin stuff. They lack substance and tend to be sentimental. Indeed, many of the articles that appear under his name were not written by him at all but were merely translated from American publications. Scheibert actually published dozens of articles and reports written by Civil War soldiers; often they were not even pure translations but were "mixed up by remarks" based on Scheibert's own experiences.[52]

As a historian, Scheibert was partial to the South and often inaccurate. Except for his study of the campaigns in the Mississippi Valley, he manifested little interest in the war in the West; and, like most European soldiers, he attached undue significance to the Virginia campaigns. He seems to have had adequate knowledge of the printed sources, even the *Official Records*, and his studies of Sherman's March to the Sea[53] and the Mississippi Valley campaigns

---

[51] *Mit Schwert und Feder*, pp. 312–17, 332–36; Walter Goerlitz, *History of the German General Staff, 1657–1945* (New York, 1953), pp. 109–14; Heinrich Otto Meisner, *Denkwürdigkeiten des General Feldmarschalls Alfred Grafen von Waldersee* (Stuttgart and Berlin, 1925), I, 374; II, 191–92, 272.

[52] "You will receive," Scheibert wrote a noted Civil War collector, "with the present mail . . . 'Stonewall Jackson's Virginienthal Feldzug,' [published in *Jahrbücher*, XXI (1879), 204–16, 313–28]. I regret very much that you will not find any news in this little study, because it is a mere translation from Col. [William] Allen's lecture in the [Southern] Hist[orical] Society [Papers], only mixed up by remarks which I have given from my personal observations, and some hints about the real unparalleled campaign of Old Stonewall. . . . You would oblige me very much by giving me some hints about new or important publications about the War." Scheibert to John Page Nicholson, January 25, 1880. Microfilm copy of a letter bound in the Scheibert article listed above, John Page Nicholson Collection, the Huntington Library, San Marino, California. See *Catalogue of Brevet Lieutenant-Colonel John Page Nicholson . . . Relating to the War of the Rebellion, 1861–1866* (Philadelphia, 1914), p. 761. In another letter Scheibert listed no fewer than sixteen articles he had lifted from the *Southern Historical Society Papers* alone! Scheibert to J. William Jones, October 13, 1881, *Southern Historical Society Papers*, IX (1881), 570–72.

[53] Scheibert, "Sherman's Marsch durch Georgien: Ein Beitrag zur Geschichte des Sezessionskrieges," *Jahrbücher*, LVIII (1886), 13–35, 173–90. Cited hereafter as "Sherman's Marsch durch Georgien." In this article, one of the best Scheibert wrote after he left the army, he severely criticized Sherman's generalship, particularly on the celebrated March to the Sea. Curiously enough, in 1874 he had indorsed without qualification the remarks of another German student of the war, F. von Meerheimb, who praised Sherman in a lecture before a military audience in Berlin.

together with the book he and Heros von Borcke wrote on the battle of Brandy Station show that he was capable of writing good history. Unfortunately, his unstable financial condition and indestructible loyalty to the Confederacy[54] affected both the quantity and quality of his work.

Scheibert was more thorough as a military observer. One of the first European soldiers to understand the special characteristics of the Civil War armies, he was not deceived by appearances: ragged men could fight. A long war was "a good school to learn how to overcome friction." Believing, as most Europeans did, that the Southerner was intrinsically the better soldier (purer motives, good Anglo-Saxon stock, accustomed to outdoor life and managerial experience on the plantations, etc.), he could see the Northern armies improving steadily in both quality and leadership, mobilizing their vastly superior resources until even Lee's genius was unable to save the South from defeat.[55] Scheibert was particularly impressed by the accomplishments of the Union *Eisenbahn-Abteilung,* an American innovation which had kept the railroads working so well that Prussia in 1866 created a similar Field Railway Section.[56]

Scheibert was not wholly accurate in his analysis of Civil War tactics. His division of infantry tactics into three disinct phases, for example, is basically sound, but oversimplified and distorted. Lee did in fact make greater use of intrenchments after Gettysburg, and partly—as Scheibert suggested—to compensate for his numerical inferiority. But the Confederates had constructed extensive earthworks near Bull Run in 1861 and at Richmond in the year following; Lee fortifications at Fredericksburg in 1862 "marked a definite stage in the evolution of the field defenses," while in the campaign for Vicksburg, where Lee was not even present, "the value of intrenchments was demonstrated to a striking degree."[57]

See F. von Meerheimb, *Sherman's Feldzug in Georgien* (Berlin, 1869), *passim.* Scheibert's remarks on Von Meerheimb's views are found in *Der Bürgerkrieg,* pp. 175-78.

[54] Scheibert once wrote that he and Von Borcke "have brought it about that in the German-Prussian Army nothing concerning the Civil War . . . is so in fashion as accounts of the deeds of Southrons [*sic*]. Sherman and Grant, the pets of ten years ago, are forgotten, and Lee, Jackson and Stuart are now the favorite heroes of our officers." (Scheibert to J. William Jones, October 13, 1881, *Southern Historical Society Papers,* IX, 571.)

[55] *Der Bürgerkrieg,* pp. 16, 22-23, 162-63; "General Lee," p. 99.

[56] "Sherman's Marsch durch Georgien," p. 179. See below, pp. 122-23.

[57] Freeman, *R. E. Lee,* II, 480; III, 204; Arthur L. Wagner, "Hasty Intrenchments in the War of Secession," *M.H.S.P.,* XIII, 139.

Scheibert's arbitrary classification of Confederate cavalry into four neat categories—regular, partisan, scouts, and couriers—and his assertion that the Confederates habitually preferred shock tactics while the Union cavalry generally chose to fight dismounted likewise are subject to question. Stuart himself may have preferred the saber—it would have suited his flamboyant personality—but he did not hesitate to use firearms whenever the occasion demanded. Indeed, one explanation advanced by an officer on Stuart's staff for the comparative decline of the Confederate cavalry after 1863 was a serious shortage of "proper arms," which placed "the Southern cavalry at a disadvantage which can hardly be overestimated. . . . Breechloading carbines were procured only in limited quantities, never more than enough to arm one, or at most two squadrons in a regiment. The deficiency was made up, generally, by Enfield rifles." As this writer pointedly remarked, "the difference between a Spencer carbine and an Enfield rifle is by no means a mere matter of sentiment."[58]

Scheibert repeatedly underestimated the extent to which firepower dominated the battlefields of 1861–65. In fact, he took the position that the breechloader had created a new problem because it encouraged troops to fire ammunition needlessly. Lee had once remarked something to this effect to Scheibert,[59] who apparently failed to consider that the Confederates were plagued by a chronic supply problem and that this condition would not necessarily be such a vital consideration in another war. Scheibert appreciated the fact that intrenchments strengthened the defense, but he attributed the development of trench warfare after Gettysburg more to Lee's inferiority in numbers than to the superiority of modern weapons. He made the same error with respect to cavalry tactics. In stating that dismounted tactics were especially popular with the Union cavalry, it evidently did not strike Scheibert as inconsistent that "inferior" cavalry should resort to allegedly inferior tactics in order to compensate for their inferiority!

This tendency to minimize the effect of firepower on Civil War tactics is explained, in part at least, by the nature of Scheibert's mission to the Confederacy and the time and extent of his visit. He had been sent specifically to observe the effect of modern artillery fire upon fortifications. He returned to Europe while the war was still in what he later designated as the second phase, the period of linear tactics. Scheibert witnessed the battle of Chancellorsville,

[58] McClellan, *Stuart*, pp. 260–61.   [59] *Der Bürgerkrieg*, p. 27.

where miles of breastworks had been erected by both armies, but he was not present to observe the trench warfare of 1864. Similarly, when Scheibert had visited Lee's army, Stuart's cavalry was at its peak. By mere chance he was at Brandy Station, the only major cavalry battle during the entire war in which shock tactics were employed successfully on a large scale. Had he remained long enough to see the gradual decline in the Confederate cavalry after 1863, or had he been able to meet Forrest or witness Sheridan's cavalry in action in 1864, very probably he would have had a better understanding of the transformation that had taken place in cavalry tactics.

These limitations, however, do not detract from the over-all validity of Scheibert's observations. He probably saw more actual combat than the official observers of any of the other European armies; certainly he was the most competent foreign authority on the Army of Northern Virginia, and he was the only foreign observer to make a special study of the tactics of all three arms. Scheibert recognized the problems of recruitment, training, transportation, and supply peculiar to America, and he appreciated the influence that they had exerted upon strategy and tactics. Above all, he was one of the first to interpret the Civil War as a product of the industrial age.

Probably the most significant fact about Scheibert as a military observer is that he really saw very little to recommend for adoption by the German army. Indeed, he stressed the similarities between the Civil War armies and his own. Lee's infantry in 1863 and the Prussian infantry in 1870, according to Scheibert, had many characteristics in common. Both had abandoned the column in favor of the line as the standard combat formation; both had made extensive use of skirmishers. In each case this dispersion of force and the frequent dissemination of the advance echelons had placed a greater burden on the junior officers, resulting in slacker control from the field commander during battle (Scheibert cited Wörth and Spicheren as typical examples). Both armies had also shown a tendency to commit reserve units prematurely. The chief difference, Scheibert decided, was that the Prussian army benefited from superior peacetime training and indoctrination and thus was better able to cope with this new situation. As for the cavalry, Scheibert considered the German cavalry superior to the cavalry of the Civil War in most respects. The one exception was the courier service of the

Confederate cavalry, which Scheibert recommended for adoption by the German army in order to obtain greater cohesion in combat. He also professed to see a basic similarity in the tactics of field artillery in 1863 and 1870.[60]

Why, then, apart from economic considerations, did Scheibert continue to write about the Civil War when he found little that the Germans could learn from the tactics of the American campaigns? In explaining the continued appearance of articles on the Civil War, Scheibert himself revealed why he thought the conflict worth studying:

It may appear odd that the *Jahrbücher* should from time to time return to the war on the other side of the Ocean. But that war is interesting not only because of the significant accomplishments of cavalry, the first use of armored ships, the heavy rifled artillery, the greater application of technical science in war, the colossal development of sanitary methods; it will also remain for centuries an inexhaustible mine for the soldiers who see in the din of war more than mathematical combinations of battalions and squadrons.[61]

Or, as he expressed it elsewhere, "the so-called Rebel army is an inexhaustible store of military and psychological treasures."[62]

Scheibert's observations on the defense of Charleston were confirmed by Lieutenant Colonel von Scheliha, a Prussian who as chief engineer of the Department of the Gulf had "erected a new and extensive line of forts" near Mobile "which proved models of strength and judicious arrangement."[63] After the war Von Scheliha returned to Berlin and wrote a technical treatise on coast defense. Although much of this book was based upon personal experience, it included many actions at which Von Scheliha had not been present and was written "to develop and establish theory from fact." In addition to Confederate accounts it included lengthy extracts from the official reports of officers in the United States Navy. Curiously enough, Von Scheliha's book was published only in England, even though the subject was one of some concern to the Prussian government.[64]

[60] *Ibid.*, pp. 40–44, 71–74, 80, 92–105; "General Lee," pp. 208–9.

[61] "Die letzen Tage der Rebellion: Aus dem Tagebuche eines Kanoniers," *Jahrbücher*, LI (April, 1884), 60.

[62] "Aus dem Soldatenleben der ehemaligen conföderirten Armee," *Jahrbücher*, XXIX (November, 1878), 202.

[63] Ella Lonn, *Foreigners in the Confederacy* (Chapel Hill, 1940), p. 243.

[64] See Brigadier General Albert von Stosch, "Unsere Küsten in einem Kriege mit Frankreich," *Die Grenzboten*, XXVI (1867), II, 246–48.

According to Von Scheliha, the science of coast defense was static at the beginning of the Civil War; it "seemed to have come to a stand-still, and received a new impulse only after the brilliant success of the Federal fleet under . . . [Admiral David Glasgow] Farragut had proved the absolute necessity for the military engineer to cast aside many time-honoured ideas, and to raise himself to the point already reached by the naval architect and artillerist." The South's response to this situation had produced "new combinations and improved methods, which in some cases proved to be of the highest value."[65]

Von Scheliha observed from reports of the operations at Forts Sumter and Pulaski and from his own experience at Mobile "the incapacity of masonry to resist the fire of modern artillery." He became convinced that earthworks, properly constructed, offered "better protection" than permanent fortifications. As evidence he cited the results of the Union bombardment of Battery Wagner in Charleston Harbor, where during a period of forty-two hours 2,864 shells had been fired against this battery: "the bomb-proof had been hit over 1,200 times, the parapet and traverses over 1,400 times, and yet but three guns had been totally dismounted and the bomb-proof remained intact." At Wilmington, Fort Fisher had survived a bombardment of even greater intensity and had likewise remained "substantially uninjured as a defensive work." The meaning was clear: sand and earth were not only the "cheapest" but the "best material" for the construction of shore batteries. The reduction of such works, when left to the navy alone, required much time and enormous quantities of ammunition, and while well-protected guns could often be silenced, they were rarely dismounted or permanently disabled by artillery fire.[66]

But if warships alone could not destroy well-built shore defenses, such works rarely could prevent a steam fleet from forcing a passage "free of obstructions." Hence it was necessary to supplement shore batteries with underwater obstructions such as sunken ships or mines: "Too much importance cannot be attached to this most potent element in coast defence." Von Scheliha devoted three lengthy chapters to a technical discussion of the various types of

[65] Viktor Ernst Karl Rudolf von Scheliha, *A Treatise on Coast-Defence Based on the Experience Gained by Officers of the Corps of Engineers of the Army of the Confederate States, and Comp. from Official Reports of Officers of the Navy of the United States* (London, 1868), p. vii.

[66] *Ibid.*, pp. 32–45. Von Scheliha did not favor guns mounted *en barbette.*

obstructions, paying particular attention to the potentialities of a new weapon, the submarine mine or torpedo. He indorsed whole-heartedly the opinion of Union Rear Admiral David D. Porter, who in his *Report* (February 1, 1865) had stated that "Obstructions and Torpedoes form a better defense than our present Forts."[67]

The experience of the Civil War also convinced Von Scheliha that a successful coast defense depended not only upon strong local fortifications but on co-operating action of land and naval forces as well. Passive defense was not enough, for, as Scheibert also commented, the war had demonstrated that even though defenses could be erected that were practically invulnerable to an attack from the sea, an enemy army by threatening the rear could compel the evacuation of a seaport. Therefore Von Scheliha advocated floating batteries and the construction of railroad lines to points along the coast selected for defense, in order that sufficient reinforcements could be rushed to a threatened area—something the Confederates had rarely been able to do. He felt that the Confederates had erred in trying to defend too much with too little, rather than adopting a more elastic defense and concentrating only on the more important ports and river entrances.[68]

Von Scheliha arrived at nearly the same general conclusions as Scheibert except for his estimate of the torpedo, which he rated more highly. Both realized that earthworks formed the best protection against modern artillery fire and that naval action alone could not reduce coastal fortifications. Von Scheliha's formula for a successful coast defense was based on two vital ingredients: a series of strategically important and well-constructed local defenses complete with shore batteries and channel obstructions and an efficient communication system to insure prompt relief in the event of an enemy landing in force.

Von Scheliha's work is probably the most authoritative study on the Civil War of its kind. Not only was he able to draw from his own vast experience; he made skilled use of published documents as well. His deductions from the siege of Charleston, for example, were substantiated in the "official" Confederate history of *The Defense of Charleston Harbor*, which appeared in 1890. The author of this book testified to the effectiveness of earthen fortifications and

[67] *Ibid.*, pp. 48–77, 177–218 *passim*.
[68] *Ibid.*, pp. 3–6. Confederate General P. G. T. Beauregard, commander at Charleston in 1863, made the same criticism (T. Harry Williams, *P. G. T. Beauregard: Napoleon in Gray* [Baton Rouge, 1954], p. 175).

torpedo defenses ("The iron-clad squadrons of Rear-Admirals DuPont and Dahlgren were as effectually stopped for more than two years by fear of these as by anything else"), and confirmed Scheibert's and Von Scheliha's observations in stressing the need for a co-operating land army both in the attack and in the defense of a fortified harbor.[69]

[69] John Johnston, *The Defense of Charleston Harbor, Including Fort Sumter and the Adjacent Islands, 1863–1865* (Charleston, 1890), pp. 261–76.

4

The French Observers

In contrast to what was happening in England and Prussia, no military reforms of consequence were pending in France at the time of the Civil War. Not that none was needed—the unheeded warnings of General Trochu[1] and the subsequent collapse of France in 1870 were later to reveal grave weaknesses in army organization and training. But in 1861 the French army was still basking in the glow of the Napoleonic tradition. More recently it had waged successful campaigns in Indochina and Algeria, and it had performed creditably in the Crimea and in Italy, campaigns that had earned the respect of Europe. Other armies, including both Union and Confederate, borrowed from French regulations, copied French military institutions, and even imitated French uniforms. "Everything took on a slightly French look."[2] For obvious reasons, then, the French military leaders were inclined to be complacent:

The very ease of the success won with deplorable conditions of preparation, organization and command had the most fatal effects upon the spirit of the army. It favored the natural tendency of the French to neglect effort, to believe that dash and bustle were all that were necessary to solve military problems. The Imperial Government, absorbed by domestic political considerations, was persuaded that it could have an army fit for war without spending in advance the necessary sums for its maintenance and preparation. Thus the victories of Magenta and Solferino marked the route to Sedan.[3]

The Civil War was only a few months old when several prominent French civilians, some of them with previous military experi-

[1] Général Trochu, *L'armée française en 1867* (Paris, 1870), *passim.*

[2] Cyril Falls, *A Hundred Years of War* (London, 1954), pp. 31, 38. "The American Civil War, to give an obvious example, was fought both by the North and South, in what were, in effect, French uniforms, even to the peculiar form of the *képi.*" (The képi was the military cap most common among Civil War soldiers; it had a round, flat top that sloped toward the front, and a visor.) James Laver, *British Military Uniforms* (London, 1948), p. 20.

[3] Marshal Franchet d'Esperey, "Du Directoire à 1914," *Histoire militaire et navale de la nation française* (Vol. VIII in Gabriel Hanataux (ed.), *Histoire de la nation française* [Paris, 1927]), p. 382. Cited hereafter as D'Esperey, "Du Directoire à 1914."

ence, arrived in the United States. The first of these was Prince Napoleon, a nephew of Napoleon Bonaparte and cousin of Napoleon III, the French emperor.[4] Prince Napoleon landed in New York in July, 1861, and, accompanied by two officers on his staff, paid a brief visit to both the Union and Confederate armies. He witnessed no fighting, and because he saw the Civil War armies in embryonic stage his views deserve only passing mention. The militia he described as "detestable troops," but the volunteers he inspected in the camps around Washington struck him as being somewhat better: they marched "well enough," their discipline was at least adequate, and they were "so-so" in their drill. He held a similar opinion of the Confederate soldiers, although those he viewed in the encampments at Bull Run impressed him as being better raw material than what he had seen in the North. Nothing the Prince wrote, however, suggests more than a casual interest in military matters.[5]

This was true also of his military aide, Lieutenant Colonel Ferri Pisani. This officer was distressed by the lack of military protocol and the weak chain of command in the Union army. He showed disgust at the theatrical displays of many of the officers he met, and he considered the American soldiers inferior to those of the standing armies in Europe. Did such volunteers compare favorably with the professional armies? "No, a thousand times no."[6] Ferri Pisani's piquant remarks reached many readers, for his book was among the first to appear in Europe with information about the troubles across the Atlantic.

A more detailed and sympathetic picture of these events was given by the Prince de Joinville,[7] a former rear admiral in the French navy and a well-known and influential writer on naval matters. The Prince de Joinville had sailed for America in August, 1861,

[4] Prince Joseph Charles Paul Napoleon was the son of Jerome Bonaparte, youngest brother of Napoleon I. Napoleon III was the son of Louis, another of Napoleon Bonaparte's brothers.

[5] Prince Napoleon, "Voyage du Prince Napoléon aux États-Unis, 1861," *La revue de Paris,* V (September–October, 1933), 241–72, 549–87. Prince Napoleon landed in New York toward the end of July, spent the first week of August in and about Washington, and then departed for Canada and the West. He returned to France in September, convinced that the North would win the war (*ibid.,* p. 242).

[6] *Lettres sur les États-Unis d'Amérique* (Paris, 1862), pp. 170–72.

[7] François Ferdinand d'Orléans, Prince de Joinville, was the third son of Louis Philippe, King of France from 1830 until his abdication in 1848. For his early career see Lady Mary Loyd (trans.), *Memoirs of the Prince de Joinville* (New York, 1895), *passim.*

accompanied by a son whom he hoped to enrol in the Naval Academy and two nephews, the Comte de Paris and the Duc de Chartres.[8] He remained with his nephews, who had enlisted in the Union army and had been appointed to McClellan's staff, and together they participated in the Peninsular campaign. In July, 1862, when diplomatic relations between Washington and Paris became "very strained" because of French activities in Mexico,[9] the Orléans princes took leave of the Army of the Potomac and returned to Europe. In October the Prince de Joinville's account of the Peninsular campaign was published in the *Revue des deux mondes*.[10]

As an unofficial member of McClellan's headquarters, the Prince de Joinville was able to observe flaws in the organization of the Union army. It suffered from poor staff work,[11] an inadequate replacement system, and an unwieldy supply service. "If their primi-

---

[8] These Bourbon princes were the sons of Ferdinand, Duc d'Orléans, the eldest son of Louis Philippe. After the death of his father in 1842, the Comte de Paris, as eldest son, became heir apparent to the French throne. They had been in exile since 1848. The Marquis de Flers, *Le Comte de Paris* (London, 1889), pp. 45–81.

[9] On January 9, 1862, a "small French Army Corps" disembarked at Veracruz. Moving inland in April, this force was defeated before La Peuble, and substantial reinforcements were rushed from France. This was in direct defiance of the Monroe Doctrine and raised anew the question of French diplomatic recognition of the Confederacy. When news of the failure of McClellan's army before Richmond reached France, "the stage seemed . . . cleared for action. Even the French Minister in Washington believed that the moment had come when European mediation was possible," and it was not until the spring of 1864 that Napoleon III "definitely abandoned the South." Donaldson Jordan and Edwin J. Pratt, *Europe and the American Civil War* (Boston, 1931), pp. 209–15.

[10] A. Trognon [the Prince de Joinville], "Guerre d'Amérique: campagne du Potomac, Mars–Juillet 1862," *Revue des deux mondes*, V (October, 1862), 798–867. The Prince de Joinville used a pseudonym because the government would allow nothing to be published in France under the rightful name of one of the Orléans princes (De Flers, *Le Comte de Paris*, p. 96). Even though such an article might not be altogether free from political implications, Prince Napoleon believed that if what the Orléans princes wrote under pseudonyms "is good, well composed . . . and in favor of the good cause of the North, the *Revue des deux mondes* should be permitted to publish it" (Jordan and Pratt, *Europe and the American Civil War*, p. 230). In Europe this article, which was published in book form the following year, has often been attributed to the Comte de Paris; the American edition, in which the Prince de Joinville is identified as the author, is entitled *The Army of the Potomac: Its Organization, Its Commander, and Its Campaign* (New York, 1862). All citations to this work refer to the American edition.

[11] "In the United States there is no such thing as a corps of the General staff . . . whose duty it is to regulate, centralize and direct the movements of the army. . . . The functions of the adjutant-general are limited to the transmission of the orders of the general. He [the adjutant general] has nothing to do with seeing that they are executed. The general has no one to bear his orders but aides-de-camp, who have the best intentions in the world, and are excellent at repeating mechanically a verbal order, but to whom nobody pays much attention if they undertake to exercise any initiative whatever" (*ibid.*, p. 52).

tive organization had been better, the survivors of this rude campaign . . . might be regarded as the equals of the best soldiers in the world." When well led, the American soldier was brave, a willing worker ("nothing was so remarkable as to see a detail fall to work at making an abatis in the woods"), and admirably suited for campaigning.[12] The real fault with the Union army, the Prince decided, was the volunteer system itself. Writing in a day when French military leaders "unanimously averred" that it took years for a soldier to acquire "the requisite knowledge, discipline and spirit," the Prince de Joinville concluded:

> In Europe . . . we have learned to recognize the comparative value of the regular soldier, and of this costly and capricious amateur soldier, who is called a volunteer. . . . An army of sixty thousand regulars would have done more than double or triple the number of volunteers; but in America they do not know this, and besides, they do not wish to know it. It would involve a renunciation of the general and deeply rooted creed, that every American, when he wishes to do a thing, may find within himself, without any apprenticeship, the power to do it.[13]

The Prince de Joinville made few tactical deductions. He described a cavalry action as "one of those fights with the cold steel which have become so rare in these days," and which, in this instance at least, was "all so much valor thrown away." He did not comment on the tactics of infantry beyond stating that the Union soldiers preferred to fight a defensive battle; this, however, the Prince attributed more to "the national character" than to an appreciable increase in firepower. As for the artillery, the rifled gun, according to the Prince, was "the rage of the hour, and fit only to be fired . . . at long range in an open country." For thickly wooded terrain he still preferred the familiar smoothbores, the "real fighting guns," firing either round projectile or "a good dose of grape."[14]

Despite occasional factual errors and a few shaky generalizations (readers will be interested to know that delay is "a characteristic trait of the American people"), the Prince de Joinville was a discerning observer. His detailed knowledge of military matters and the fact that he was able to view a major Civil War campaign from

[12] *Ibid.*, pp. 80, 96; see also pp. 28, 64, 79.

[13] *Ibid.*, pp. 12–13. The official French view toward military organization and recruitment is summarized in Richard D. Challener, *The French Theory of the Nation in Arms, 1866–1939* (New York, 1955), pp. 14–15.

[14] *The Army of the Potomac*, pp. 50, 71–72, 74.

Running the blockade. The "special artist" of the *Illustrated London News* bound for Wilmington on a blockade runner. (From the *Illustrated London News*, July 16, 1864.)

Count Zeppelin (*seated in center*), later a pioneer in developing the airship, and a Lieutenant Rosencranz (*far right*), a Swedish officer on McClellan's staff, in the Peninsula, 1862. Others are Major Ludlow (*seated on left*), Lieutenant Colonel Dickinson (*with straw hat*), and Captain Ulric Dahlgren (*standing*). (From F. T. Miller [ed.], *Photographic History of the Civil War* [New York: Review of Reviews Co., 1912], Vol. I.)

Unidentified British officers with General W. F. Barry during the Peninsular campaign. (From Miller, *Photographic History of the Civil War,* Vol. I.)

The famous bombproof at Battery Wagner. (From *Official Photographs Taken on the Battlefields during the Civil War* by Matthew B. Brady and Alexander Gardner [privately printed].)

Sketch of portion of Battery Wagner the morning after the assault of July 18, 1863. By the "special artist" of the *Illustrated London News*. (From *Illustrated London News*, September 26, 1863.)

Assault on Battery Wagner, July 18, 1863. By the "special artist" of the *Illustrated London News*. (From *Illustrated London News*, September 26, 1863.)

Confederates laying mines by moonlight in the Harbor Channel, Charleston. By the "special artist" of the *Illustrated London News*. (From *Illustrated London News*, May 16, 1863.)

Typical Civil War battlefields before 1863. Second Bull Run (*above*) and Antietam (*below*) were fought before the armies became accustomed to intrenching. (From Miller, *Photographic History of the Civil War*, Vol. II.)

Typical Civil War battlefields, 1864. Grant's position on the North Anna (*above*) and Sherman's defense before Atlanta (*below*) illustrate the extent to which pick and ax were used after 1863 to improve an already formidable position. (From Miller, *Photographic History of the Civil War*, Vols. I, V.)

The power of rifled artillery. Fort Pulaski after two days' bombardment, April, 1862. (From Miller, *Photographic History of the Civil War*, Vol. I.)

The power of rifled artillery. Fort Sumter in September, 1863. (From Miller, *Photographic History of the Civil War*, Vol. I.)

The Comte de Paris (*left*) and the Duc de Chartres (*center*) with their party during a lull in the Peninsular campaign. (From Miller, *Photographic History of the Civil War*, Vol. I.)

Two popular guns. *Above*, twelve-pounder smoothbore Napoleon in the Washington defenses. *Below*, a twelve-pounder breech-loading Whitworth rifle in Confederate service. (From Miller, *Photographic History of the Civil War*, Vol. V.)

A controversial arm. These Confederate cavalry were armed with carbines and doubtless fought most of the time dismounted. (From Miller, *Photographic History of the Civil War*, Vol. IV.)

Rehearsal for battle. Union infantry drilling at Chattanooga, with skirmishers advanced and the main line preparing to "charge." (From Miller, *Photographic History of the Civil War*, Vol. II.)

Another task for the construction corps. Damaged bridge across Bull Run. (From Miller, *Photographic History of the Civil War*, Vol. II.)

Bridge repaired by the construction corps. (From Miller, *Photographic History of the Civil War*, Vol. II.)

Field telegraph in operation in 1864. (From Miller, *Photographic History of the Civil War*, Vol. VIII.)

Professor Lowe's famous balloon before Richmond in 1862. (From Miller, *Photographic History of the Civil War*, Vol. VIII.)

the command level enhanced the importance of his observations, which were written in a style that was, according to the translator, "equally free from the carelessness of the amateur, and the pedantry of the professional soldier."[15]

The same could also be said of the Prince de Joinville's nephew, the Comte de Paris, who with his brother had enlisted in the Union army, receiving the honorary rank of captain, and had accompanied McClellan during the Peninsular campaign as a bona fide member of the staff.[16] Upon his return to England in the summer of 1862, until June, 1871, when the French National Assembly repealed the law that had sent his family into exile, the Comte de Paris spent much of his time engaged in literary pursuits. During this period he began work on his massive *History of the Civil War in America*, the first volume of which appeared in 1874.[17] From this date until his death twenty years later, the Comte de Paris devoted what time he could salvage from his political activities and illness to what he regarded as his "great work." Although he had served with the Union army for only one campaign, he set out to describe in detail every battle of the war. He looked upon his work as "essentially a military history," written in the hope that his countrymen "would not reject without examination precious examples and dearly bought experience under the pretext that what has succeeded in America cannot be applied to Europe."[18]

Like Fletcher, who had also accompanied the Army of the Potomac in 1862, the Comte de Paris was skeptical of the worth of the American volunteer at this stage in the war. "Good soldiers they were not—indeed, they were scarcely soldiers." But he, too, could detect a steady improvement in the armies as the war progressed, al-

---

[15] *Ibid.*, pp. 3, 23.

[16] According to Miss Lonn, the princes "laid down the condition that they were to receive no pay but should, on the other hand, be free to resign whenever they desired" (Ella Lonn, *Foreigners in the Union Army and Navy* [Baton Rouge, 1951], p. 278). The Comte de Paris always insisted that he and the Duc de Chartres were both "regularly mustered into the U.S. Volunteer Service." The Comte de Paris to John Page Nicholson, August 24, 1887. Microfilm copy of a letter contained in a bound volume entitled "A Collection of Autograph Letters from Philippe Comte de Paris to John P. Nicholson, relating to the Civil War." (Cf. *Catalogue of Library of John Page Nicholson*, p. 230.) Cited hereafter as Nicholson Papers.

[17] *Histoire de la guerre civile en Amérique* (8 vols.; Paris, 1874-83); American edition, L. F. Tasistro (trans.), *History of the Civil War in America* (Philadelphia, 1875-88). All citations refer to the American edition.

[18] Comte de Paris to John Page Nicholson, April 12, 1893, Nicholson Papers; *History of the Civil War*, I, 2.

though he thought that the Americans had required "a long time to learn that, upon ground where the fighting had to be done at short distances, it was almost always less dangerous to rush upon the enemy than to be decimated by his fire while standing still." After several campaigns, however, the Civil War soldiers, though they "still bear the name of volunteers," had in fact become real veterans. With obvious reference to those republican reformers in France who advocated conscription and a reduction in the length of service, the Comte de Paris pointedly remarked that it was not to the Civil War "that the partisans of levies *en masse* and improvised armies must look for confirmation of their theories."[19]

The Comte de Paris' comments on Civil War tactics do not differ greatly from those of other observers. Infantry seldom used the bayonet; "everything was in favor of the party acting on the defensive." Like Scheibert, he credited Lee with inaugurating the system of improvised field works that played such a conspicuous part after 1864.[20] He likewise noticed that Civil War generals had often lost control over their armies in battle, which he blamed on poor staff work and the unusually rugged terrain, "a circumstance which could never be lost sight of in the study of this war." He was more critical than Scheibert of Lee's system of command, claiming that at Gettysburg "the extreme independence" that Lee encouraged among his subordinates "rendered the best conceived plans . . . fruitless."[21]

The Comte de Paris believed that the tactics of Civil War cavalry in a sense grew out of the earlier campaigns against the Indians in the West, since most of the prewar cavalry had actually been dragoons or mounted rifles and had been so designated. By 1861, long-range weapons had rendered all distinction between dragoons and regular cavalry "useless in a contest in which the dragoon should be the true type of all cavalrymen." The Comte de Paris agreed with most critics that unfavorable terrain, inadequate training, and—in the case of the Union cavalry—poor horsemanship also had dis-

19 *Ibid.*, I, 176, 191, 256; see also p. 366; II, 34. Manifestly the French legislators and military leaders did not look to the Civil War "for confirmation" of their theories. Their eyes were glued to the Rhine, and not the far side of the Atlantic, as they set about to repair the damage of the Franco-Prussian War. France abandoned the long-term professional army in favor of the German short-service model, which was based on a rigorous system of conscription. The first conscription law was enacted in 1872 (Challener, *The French Theory of the Nation in Arms*, pp. 32-48).

20 *History of the Civil War*, I, 192; III, 812.

21 *Ibid.*, I, 191, 556; III, 587.

couraged the use of shock tactics.[22] Evidently the Comte de Paris preferred a combination of fire and shock tactics, for his pages abound with favorable descriptions of cavalry "fighting alternately on foot and on horseback."[23] He was also of the opinion that the cavalry raid, so called, had played a "novel" but "important" part during the war.[24]

With regard to sieges and coast defense, the Comte de Paris repeated the conclusions of Scheibert and Von Scheliha. He believed that the Civil War offered proof that uncovered batteries could not withstand heavy bombardment, that works of masonry were largely rendered obsolete by the new rifled siege artillery, and—here he disagreed with Scheibert—that underwater mines or torpedoes were effective in harbor defense.[25] Recalling the experience of the French in 1870, when a relieving French army, the Army of the Loire, and desperate sorties by the besieged garrison of Paris had failed to break the Prussian stranglehold on the capital city, the Comte de Paris paid particular attention to the operations around Vicksburg. Because the Union army had been forced to invest a fortified city and at the same time ward off the parries of a relief force under Johnston, he wondered "if the German officers, who have shown so much discernment in selecting in the American war all that was applicable to the European continent, have not derived some useful information from the siege of Vicksburg for the campaign of 1870."[26] If the Prussians actually benefited from studying this particular campaign, there is no written record of it. Scheibert, it will be recalled, had been unable to reach Vicksburg during the siege, and no other Prussian military writer of consequence had paid particular attention to the Vicksburg campaign before 1870.

Because he had been in America for but a short time and had witnessed only one major campaign, the Comte de Paris had to depend upon printed sources and the testimony of friends for his *History*. His is essentially a secondary work, an expert synthesis of the interpretations of contemporary observers. In scope it resembles Fletcher's *History of the American War*, except that it is more detailed and was never finished. The Comte de Paris was meticulous in his research. In addition to studying the standard works on the war, he

22 *History of the Civil War*, I, 24-25, 71, 194.

23 *Ibid.*, II, 448, 480; III, 15-16, 243; IV, 130, 203.

24 *Ibid.*, II, 83, 480.

25 *Ibid.*, I, 447, 460; II, 232; IV, 361, 383.   26 *Ibid.*, III, 364.

used many of the lesser-known pamphlets and even some manuscript material. Through the good offices of President Grant he was furnished copies of original Confederate reports several years before they were published in the *Official Records,* and his American friends sent him numerous documents and personal recollections relating to the various campaigns.[27] Although former Confederates found the work prejudiced in favor of the North, the Comte de Paris' *History of the Civil War,* considering the handicaps of the author and the conditions under which he wrote, is a reasonably reliable study and compares favorably with histories of similar scope written in the United States. Better than any other European military writer before him, the Comte de Paris had digested the information brought back by the military observers and soldiers of fortune. In 1886 he was again exiled for political reasons, and work on his *History* lagged appreciably thereafter. He died in 1894, having barely carried his narrative through the year 1863. Before his death, however, he did manage a brief visit to the United States, an event he regarded as "a pilgrimage of a former member of the Army of the Potomac."[28]

The Orléanist princes, of course, had not observed the Civil War in any official capacity, and no French soldiers were sent to America as official military observers during the first years of the war. Indeed, on September 28, 1861, the French Minister of War decreed by order of the emperor that henceforth no leave would be granted to any army officer intending to visit America. The French government, anxious to avoid unnecessary diplomatic entanglement, did not absolutely prohibit departures, but no officer could leave and still retain his rank.[29] This was too great a risk for any officer with a career to protect; hence there were no French counterparts to Fletcher, Fremantle, or Von Borcke.

Because French soldiers were thus discouraged from traveling to America during the early part of the war, the published report of the official Swiss military observer, Major Ferdinand Lecomte, received wide attention in France. A staff officer in the Swiss army

[27] The Comte de Paris to John Page Nicholson, June 24, 1878, Nicholson Papers. The Nicholson Papers contain many letters from the Comte de Paris thanking Nicholson for sending him material and mentioning similar favors from other former Union officers.

[28] The Comte de Paris to John Page Nicholson, August 10, 1890, Nicholson Papers.

[29] Lonn, *Foreigners in the Union Army,* p. 280.

and editor of the *Revue militaire suisse*, Lecomte was first prompted "to make a military excursion" to America by reading Ferri Pisani's *Letters on America;* in December, 1861, he was officially authorized to make the trip. He became attached to McClellan's staff as a voluntary aide-de-camp and saw service at Yorktown before returning to Switzerland. No stranger to an assignment of this nature, Lecomte had also been an observer in the war between France and Austria in 1859, and his official *Report*[30] and a three-volume *History*[31] he subsequently wrote contain many cogent technical observations.

Lecomte was the only official foreign observer whose report was published and made generally available while the Civil War was still in progress. (The British official reports were classified "confidential.") Although he saw even less of the Peninsular campaign than the Prince de Joinville and the Comte de Paris, his analysis of the Army of the Potomac in 1862 testifies to his acumen as an observer. He noted, first, that this army suffered "from lack of authority in the generals. . . ." He deplored the influence of politics in the selection of higher officers and governmental interference in what he considered to be strictly military matters. Second, he thought the mode of recruitment defective, particularly the practice in the North of giving bounties to volunteers and by so doing attracting undesirable elements. Personally, Lecomte favored the Swiss system of conscription.[32] Third, he was opposed to the election of officers by the rank and file and to the custom of giving commissions to those who had recruited a company or regiment for Federal service; all too often such officers had "no other title to their commissions than having known how to entice a few recruits to inns or clubs." Fourth, he maintained that the lack of a "really organized staff" further weak-

[30] Ferdinand Lecomte, *Guerre des États-Unis d'Amérique: Rapport au département militaire Suisse* (Paris, 1863). American edition, *The War in the United States: Report to the Swiss Military Department: Preceded by a Discourse to the Federal Military Society Assembled at Berne, Aug. 18, 1862* (New York, 1863). Cited hereafter as Lecomte, *Report*.

[31] *Guerre de la sécession: Esquisse des évenements militaires et politiques des États-Unis de 1861 à 1865* (Paris, 1866–67). Lecomte also edited a volume of translated documents entitled *Campagnes de Virginie et de Maryland en 1862* (Paris, 1863).

[32] *Report*, pp. 91–92. "If the army were recruited by conscription, or if each citizen, subject to service, were held to military duty, as in Switzerland, the various classes of society would be more equally and more directly identified with the war, and would better comprehend the necessity of the sacrifices which it demands" (*ibid.*, p. 93). The Federal government passed a national conscription law in 1863.

ened army leadership.[33] Fifth, the regiments were too numerous and as a result were too weak in effective force. This was partly because of unsound recruiting practices, but even more it was the result of a vicious replacement system whereby newly raised troops were formed into additional regiments rather than sent as replacements to veteran organizations. Lecomte thought it would be better to introduce replacements into the regiments that already had combat experience, even if this meant establishing regimental depots. Furthermore, "there would be fewer places for officers to bestow, fewer favors to be distributed, and less . . . political intrigue."[34] Sixth, the Union army appeared to be burdened with excessive baggage—a characteristic fault, one might add, of most American armies, even in World War II and Korea. Seventh, there seemed to be a lack of adequate pensions, medals, and other recognition "to boost morale of the soldier."[35] And finally, Lecomte observed that the enforcement of discipline was "fundamentally defective." Courts of inquiry and courts-martial were "multiplied to infinity, diverting, at every turn, a good number of soldiers from active service." Lecomte thought that the Union soldiers possessed too strong a spirit of individual independence, "laudable in civil life but . . . fatal to military discipline."[36]

This was certainly a fair appraisal of the Union army in 1862. Like most of the others who had been personally familiar with the Army of the Potomac during the Peninsular campaign, Lecomte later stressed the fact that as the war progressed, many of these weaknesses were remedied. After the war he wrote that the campaigns of 1864 and 1865 had demonstrated "an infinitely superior degree of execution," indicating that the Americans had been able "to profit from the lessons of experience." Even in his *Report* he stated that the American armies "have shown military capacities equal to those of the best troops in the world."[37]

[33] "At the moment when the government made the greatest sacrifices for the army, the artillery, and armament in general, it neglected almost completely the formation of a good general staff" (*Guerre de la sécession*, I, 80).

[34] *Report*, p. 95; *Guerre de la sécession*, I, 143.

[35] *Report*, p. 96. Actually the Congressional Medal of Honor had already been proposed on February 17, 1862. This proposal became law on July 12 of that year, only a few months after Lecomte's departure for Switzerland.

[36] *Ibid.*, pp. 97–98. Lecomte also considered it a source of weakness to the North that Washington was situated on the military frontier and that undue preference was given to its defense.

[37] *Guerre de la sécession*, I, 228; *Report*, pp. 53–54. "The general information of the men in all which concerns encampments and the establishment of routes, bridges

Not all that Lecomte had to say about the Army of the Potomac in 1862 was critical. On the contrary, he recommended that the Swiss authorities consider adopting some features of the organization and equipment of the Union forces. For example, he thought that the Union supply system, based upon the principle "that the soldier ought to be able to subsist on his rations, without being obliged to disburse a fraction besides . . . ought also to be practised" in the Swiss army. He also was impressed by the revolution that had occurred in naval warfare. "If we should ever be under the necessity of arming our frontier lakes," he reported, "we ought not to forget that vessels of wood . . . can no longer hold out against the heavy calibres and iron plates of the American system, which are already imitated by the European powers." He urged the Swiss authorities to "renounce the bivouac" and to furnish the troops instead with a tent, as in America, and he recommended that the Swiss cavalry adopt the McClellan saddle.[38] He commented favorably on the United States army revolver, which he anticipated would "certainly be of great advantage" in Switzerland, and on the practical features of the American military uniform. Most important of all, however, was the fact that his experiences in America confirmed an earlier conviction "that spades, axes, and mattocks are articles of the first necessity, and of daily use in all the corps."[39]

Although he claimed he could detect "nothing in particular to notice" in the strategy of the Civil War, Lecomte did grasp the importance of two developments destined to influence strategy. The Union navy, he felt, had compensated "for the disappointments which the land army had experienced." The blockade of the Southern coast was "effective," and the "frequent transportation of troops . . . with all their supplies and *matériel* of the heaviest calibre, prove that the most difficult and extensive operations can be seriously undertaken by an army, as well as seconded on all the navigable waters." At the time, combined operations in the Crimea had been

---

and abatis, their patience and their *sang froid* under disappointments, their force of will, and their persistence against obstacles, are truly remarkable. On the other hand, the etiquette of discipline, the respect for authority, and the good order of the internal service, fall short of what is desirable" (*ibid.*, pp. 73–74).

[38] So named after Captain (later General) George B. McClellan, who had brought back from Europe in 1856 a saddle "used by the Prussians, framed on a Hungarian tree." A modified version of this saddle remained standard equipment for the United States cavalry until horse cavalry was abolished in 1942 (Herr and Wallace, *The Story of the U.S. Cavalry*, p. 78).

[39] *Report*, pp. 100–104.

looked upon almost as "the eighth wonder of the world," but according to Lecomte "about fifty" such landings had taken place during the Civil War, with superior skill and much less fanfare.[40] He also recognized the strategic importance of railways. In his *Report* he stated that no other army had made "so important and so frequent" use of railroads, and in his later work he cited a recent brochure written by the aged Jomini, the dean of strategists, in which it was stated that railroads would exercise an ever increasing influence on future military operations. Lecomte suggested that the Civil War furnished all the material necessary for this new chapter on strategy.[41]

Observing the troops in the field, Lecomte was concerned more with questions of organization and equipment than with tactics. In his *Report* he scarcely mentioned Civil War cavalry, for example, except to state that it was "excellent as light cavalry and for foraging." Like Fletcher and Wolseley, however, he later changed his mind, afterward asserting that cavalry had derived greater benefit than any other arm from the improved weapons. With increased firepower the Civil War cavalry had become "also at the same time swift and powerful infantry." Lecomte marveled at the results it had attained with the breechloader, and he seems not to have regretted the gradual passing of shock tactics—but then, he was not a cavalryman. He also believed that much could be learned from the American cavalry with respect to skirmishing and outpost duties.[42] For his time Lecomte showed an unusual appreciation for the firepower of Civil War weapons and the resulting use of field fortifications on an ever increasing scale, although apparently he did not count this among the more important lessons of the Civil War.[43]

"In matters of organization, discipline, maneuvers *en masse*, military uniform, and hierarchical spirit" the Civil War, according to Lecomte, "has furnished nothing." Yet Lecomte, like Scheibert, saw much to be learned in the broad field of military technology. Breech-loading and repeating rifles, artillery of "enormous calibre," armored ships, and Gatling guns were correctly interpreted by Lecomte as weapons of the industrial revolution destined to alter

[40] *Ibid.*, p. 88; *Guerre de la sécession*, III, 290.

[41] *Report*, pp. 75–76; *Guerre de la sécession*, III, 290–91.

[42] *Report*, p. 73; *Guerre de la sécession*, III, 12, 259, 291.

[43] *Ibid.*, I, 53, 172; II, 93, 187–88; III, 45, 98, 123. In his summary of the tactical lessons of the Civil War, Lecomte mentioned only the development of mounted infantry and the tactics of the skirmish line and outpost duties. *Ibid.*, III, 291.

the concepts of war, while prodigious feats in military engineering, the "admirable use" of the field telegraph and signal system, improvements in camp equipment and medical services, likewise persuaded him that the Americans had made an immense contribution to the development of "the military art in general."[44]

No matter how informative was Lecomte's *Report*, however, the French military authorities eventually felt the need to send their own trained observers to America. *Le Moniteur* had maintained a regular correspondent in America since early in the war, and articles on the military developments in America appeared occasionally in periodicals such as the *Revue des deux mondes,* but these were written mostly by civilians for the general public. In 1862 the leading French military journal, *Le spectateur militaire,* hired a former French officer then serving in the Union army to write articles that would give French officers "a true picture of military life in the United States,[45] and the following year a personal emissary of Napoleon III observed the various governmental departments and some of the military establishments and arsenals of the Confederacy as well. The published account of this visit, however, is of a general nature and concerns social and political conditions rather than military matters.[46]

In 1864 the French government finally sent an official military mission to America. In May of that year, Colonel François De-Chenal and Captain Pierre Guzman, both of the French Artillery Corps, sailed from Liverpool with instructions to study American military techniques, "especially" those "innovations in artillery." DeChenal was a court favorite who had asked the emperor to be assigned to this mission. Described by a Union staff officer as "a per-

44 *Ibid.,* III, 289–91.

45 Ulric de Fonvielle wrote a series of articles on soldier life in western Virginia, where he was a member of General John C. Fremont's command. He wrote only of events he himself had witnessed, and although he often commented on the conduct of the war, his articles contain little technical military information. Like most European soldiers, De Fonvielle admired the individual soldier of the Civil War and deplored the replacement system. He seems to have distrusted improvised armies, and he attempted to draw no conclusions from the "strange war" he was fighting. De Fonvielle served with Colonel Gustave Paul Cluseret, a military adventurer who in 1871 became commander of the communard military forces during the period of the Paris Commune. Both had served previously under Garibaldi. Ulric de Fonvielle, "Guerre d'Amérique," *Le spectateur militaire,* XXXIX (August, 1862), 207–25; XL (October–December, 1862), 40–52, 161–82, 376–86; XLI (January, 1863), 97–108; XLII (June, 1863), 418–31, *passim.*

46 Charles Frederick Girard, *Les États Confédérés d'Amérique visités en 1863: Mémoirs addressé à S. M. Napoléon III* (Paris, 1864), *passim.*

fect specimen of an old Frenchman, who has spent most of his life in provincial garrisons," DeChenal apparently was interested in "all sorts of things, from antiquities down to rifled projectiles." Curiously enough, despite the nature of his mission and the fact that he had an American wife, DeChenal "utterly refused to learn a word of English."[47]

If his biographer is correct, the working member of the French military mission in 1864 was a Captain Guzman, an ordnance expert and a capable linguist. Because the mission arrived before the consent of the United States government had been secured, Guzman and DeChenal were forced to wait nearly a month for permission to visit the Army of the Potomac. Even the French diplomatic officials were slow to render assistance, evidently fearing that the mission might "pluck some feathers from their wings." Guzman and De-Chenal used this time to inspect arsenals, hospitals, and military installations in New York, Philadelphia, and Washington. On June 19 they were notified that they could visit the field army, and three days later they reached Grant's forces at City Point, where they were invited to accompany the staff of General George G. Meade, commander of the Army of the Potomac. The two French officers spent July, August, and September at Meade's headquarters. During the final three months of the year they made numerous trips to other military establishments throughout the United States, and in January, 1865, they returned to France.[48]

Before leaving America, Guzman submitted six detailed reports on what he had learned about foundries and the manufacture of ordnance and munitions. Later he submitted a general report embracing the following subjects:

1. Summary of the causes of the Civil War
2. The division of the states
3. The character of the Union army
4. The meaning (*esprit*) of the military operations
5. The material resources of the country
6. The report of Sherman's chief of engineers
7. An analysis of the major campaign maneuvers of 1864
8. The mess and clothing of the troops

[47] Colonel Theodore Lyman, *Meade's Headquarters, 1863–1865* (Boston, 1922), pp. 178–79. See also Philippe Régis Denis, Comte de Trobriand, *Four Years with the Army of the Potomac* (Boston, 1889), p. 595.

[48] Lt. Col. François Dumas, *Le commandant Guzman* (Paris, 1887), pp. 34–41. According to this account, Guzman was designated as DeChenal's assistant quite by accident. He was, however, a most fortunate choice.

According to his biographer, this report was a basis for what appears to have been an intelligence estimate of the capabilities of the United States forces in 1866,[49] and it is supposed to have "created a sensation" when it was placed before the influential Artillery Committee. Like Scheibert's, Guzman's military reputation was made in America. Whenever documents pertaining to the Civil War were received in Paris, it was Guzman who was sent for to recommend those of special significance to the French army. And when Lieutenant General John Schofield, a former army commander under Sherman, visited France after the war, it was Guzman who was designated the official host, partly, it appears, in order to find out details of the logistics of Sherman's operations. The Minister of War wanted to know "what means were employed to mobilize the only American army that had really been capable of movement," what rolling stock, for example, had been used and what *impedimenta* had been necessary to sustain an army at great distances from its bases. Guzman was sent to the United States on two subsequent missions. In 1867 he accompanied another officer on an eight-month tour in the United States, England, and Belgium, to investigate the possibilities of manufacturing abroad the new Chassepot rifle. Again in 1871 he visited America, this time to supervise the transfer of twenty-five batteries of artillery purchased by the French government to replace those lost at Orléans.[50]

Guzman's reports were not circulated under his own name, but probably he was responsible for much of the material included in DeChenal's *The American Army in the War of Secession*, which was first published in France in 1872.[51] As official head of the military mission in 1864, DeChenal had been compelled to devote much of his time to the necessary work of public relations, leaving to his subordinate the task of compiling the official reports.[52] In his preface DeChenal indicated that his book contained the second part of his official report, that dealing with the organization and administration of the Union army. It also included new material gleaned from the

49 See below, pp. 144–46.

50 Dumas, *Guzman*, pp. 50–52, 55, 59, 100 ff.

51 General DeChenal, *L'armée américaine pendant la guerre de secession* (Paris, 1872); the American edition was published at Fort Leavenworth in 1894. All citations refer to the American edition.

52 The preliminary drafts of these reports were found among Guzman's papers, and were written in his hand (Dumas, *Guzman*, p. 48).

reports and documents furnished DeChenal by General Meade as well as from secondary sources.[53]

DeChenal's reactions to the Civil War—perhaps because his book does not represent his views alone—were decidedly mixed. He claimed that the Americans as a rule made good soldiers: "At the core, and in all that is essential, the discipline of the American is as good as, if not better than, that of European armies; but it has not the external marks, and an observer who merely passes through . . . may thus be deceived." But DeChenal did not believe that patriotism, devotion, and discipline could "entirely atone" for a lack of military knowledge, which the Civil War soldier had to acquire in battle, "sometimes at great cost." The armies he had observed did not appear as skilled in those "great movements of parade" as a regular army in Europe; they revealed a "certain unwieldiness" that he thought would handicap such an army fighting under European conditions. ("But one would seek in vain in America for plains like that of the camp at Châlons, where so many armies have clashed.") Like most of the foreign observers, DeChenal also criticized the Union army for its replacement system and lack of a general staff.[54]

What the Americans lacked in formal drill and organization, however, DeChenal believed they made up for in other ways. The army engineers, for example, had accomplished wonders, and the forts protecting New York Harbor were models of military construction. DeChenal also praised the work of the railroad construction corps, the signal corps, and the services of supply and transportation. "It would be difficult," he wrote, "for a commissariat service to work more smoothly," especially since the American army was unable to live upon the country and had to carry all its supplies.[55] DeChenal was so impressed by "the admirable sanitary condition" of the Union army that one naturally wonders how the French soldier was able to survive normal camp life in the mid-nineteenth century. He even brought back to France detailed instructions for digging a camp latrine, which he claimed had kept the

---

[53] "Will you see in France our mutual friend Deschanel [sic]—he talked of writing for the benefit of the French public and I sent him all the reports, documents, and books I could collect about the war." General George G. Meade to General Régis de Trobriand, August 28, 1867. Marie Caroline Post, *The Life and Memoirs of Comte Régis de Trobriand* (New York, 1910), p. 347.

[54] *The American Army*, pp. 17, 224, 228, 231.

[55] *Ibid.*, pp. 43–48, 200. DeChenal's book demonstrates the official French interest in the logistics of Sherman's marches. *Ibid.*, pp. 180–81.

Army of the Potomac "free from the horrible odors which are found in rear of every line of quarters in the camp at Châlons."[56]

DeChenal's book contains a wealth of statistical information about the organization, equipment, and regulations of the Union army. He reported that the infantry knapsack, though "very awkward looking . . . does not seem to fatigue its wearer and holds more than ours"; that the Springfield rifle was "an excellent arm, leaving nothing to be desired"; that the "weight and great liability to get out of order" made the Spencer carbine "unsuitable for cavalry" (a debatable statement); and that the Schenkl projectile was "the best" of the American artillery projectiles, "its fire being accurate" but displaying a tendency to "subject the piece to great wear." Even the nosebag for horses received notice.[57] Not content merely to describe the West Point curriculum, DeChenal even included the dimensions of the main buildings at the Military Academy. His book is burdened with statistical tables and charts indicating monthly pay rates, subsistence allowances, ordnance stores, clothing allotments, and bits of miscellaneous information. He reported, for example, "It has been found that the average length of service of a cavalry carbine is five years; of pistols, sabres and cavalry equipments, four years; of infantry equipments, six years; of the infantry musket, seven years."[58]

DeChenal treated the subject of tactics only casually; yet even his occasional remarks were cogent and to the point. Recalling the superiority of the Confederate horse in the first years of the war, he reported that by the time the French military mission joined the Army of the Potomac in 1864, the Union cavalry enjoyed "the advantage in all encounters." Stuart was dead, and it was during this period that Sheridan won his great victories in the Shenandoah Valley. DeChenal observed: "There have been very few cavalry battles during the war. In most cases, the cavalry dismount and fight on foot like infantry. The American cavalry throw up intrenchments like the infantry and with equal skill. One of the finest earthworks that we have seen, was constructed by a regiment of cavalry."[59]

Like so many European soldiers, he questioned the value of raids, believing that the damage resulting from them was usually more apparent than real and that the raids incurred an enormous waste in horseflesh. DeChenal (or was it Guzman?) examined "one by

56 *Ibid.*, p. 171.   58 *Ibid.*, p. 152.

57 *Ibid.*, pp. 23–36, *passim.*   59 *Ibid.*, p. 28.

one" some six thousand unserviceable mounts that had been sent back to City Point after one of Sheridan's long raids. Discovering that the horses "were all thin, mostly broken-down in front . . . with some broken knees," but that there was not a single instance of saddle rub, he took a McClellan saddle back to France and recommended it to the Minister of War for use in the French cavalry.[60]

From his comments on infantry tactics it is evident that DeChenal appreciated the effect of modern firepower. The American soldiers, he reported, "understand the great necessity for cover. . . . They throw up intrenchments without waiting for the order."

Hardly has the army halted . . . before it is intrenched without waiting for the engineer officer; and when the latter arrives he finds few things that need rectifying; the lines are defiladed, the traverses are well placed, abatis is prepared, the vedettes are placed in small trenches which furnish them perfect cover; the army is secure against surprise. . . . If the position has to be held, all these rough works are perfected and lines and redoubts are built which are quite as artistic as the best of military constructions. All arms are equally skillful and the cavalry rivals the sappers of the engineers.

DeChenal seems to have grasped the significance of Civil War intrenchments better than most contemporary European soldiers. At least he recognized that frontal attacks had become prohibitive and that only turning or outflanking movements were practicable. He considered Sherman's Atlanta campaign "a masterpiece of this kind of maneuver," presenting "a series of marches and countermarches which can not be studied too much by any soldier who is interested in his profession."[61]

DeChenal's book is not free of errors and inconsistencies. No historian of the Civil War would accept his categorical statement that "the habit of obedience to the law and of considering it a sufficient guaranty against the caprices of power has prevented among the [Union] generals any idea of insubordination," or that "aptitude was the sovereign rule in the selection of officers"; and there are many who would question his statement that alcoholic beverages and venereal disease were virtually unknown among Sherman's troops on their march through Georgia.[62] Nevertheless, despite his habit of overworking superlatives, DeChenal's book made it abundantly clear that the Union army in 1865 was a good army, well

60 *Ibid.*, pp. 29–31, 234–35.

61 *Ibid.*, pp. 27, 231–33. 62 *Ibid.*, pp. 85, 229–30.

equipped and schooled by four years of hard campaigning. If Napoleon III and his advisers ever seriously considered persevering in the Mexican venture against the active opposition of the United States, and if they were familiar with the reports of Guzman and De-Chenal, surely these reports must have exercised a sobering influence upon French policy.

There was other evidence, too, of the military capabilities of the Union army. Auguste Laugel, a director of an important French railroad, visited Grant's army in the trenches before Petersburg and came away convinced that four years of war had forged the "raw soldiers" of 1861 into an effective military organization. Laugel concluded that there was "nothing that might not have been undertaken with the troops under Grant's orders that were camped before Richmond and Petersburg."[63] Another distinguished Frenchman, Ernest Duvergier de Haurranne, was equally surprised to find that the discipline and organization of the Union army before Petersburg were superior to anything the Europeans had expected of a volunteer army. He came to regard the Army of the Potomac as the equal of a long-service, professional army, commanded by officers who were surely better "than those of our garrison veterans who became generals without ever having been under fire." De Haurranne returned to France convinced that he had witnessed a new kind of warfare, a war where armies had transformed "an entire region into a citadel."[64] Still another French visitor, the Marquis Adolphe de Chambrun,[65] wrote letters in praise of the Union forces in 1865. Repeating the opinions of "several foreign observers who constitute themselves experts in military matters," the Marquis de Chambrun described Sherman's Georgia campaign as a "work of genius." His army was "first class," made up of men who were used to "all kinds of work and are exceedingly good at enduring fatigue." Sherman himself possessed "an extraordinary combination of sol-

[63] Auguste Laugel, *The United States during the War* (New York, 1866), pp. 204, 230.

[64] Ernest Duvergier de Haurranne, "Huit mois en Amérique à la fin de la guerre, lettres et notes de voyage, 1864–65: X, une visite à l'armée du Potomac," *Revue des deux mondes*, LXI (March–April, 1866), 590, 604, 609.

[65] The Marquis de Chambrun, a lawyer and journalist, came to America in January, 1865, with the blessing of the French Minister of Foreign Affairs, Édouard Drouyn de Lhuys, who "was naturally eager to obtain the report of an impartial observer on the progress of the war between North and South and also learn the real truth concerning what was happening in Mexico" (General Aldebert de Chambrun [trans.], *Impressions of Lincoln and the Civil War: A Foreigner's Account* [New York, 1952], p. vii).

dierly gifts." The Marquis was tremendously impressed by the American war effort, by "their immense resources, their military strength, their six hundred-and-fifty war vessels created during four years." The numbers of the Union forces actually engaged during the last month of the war were "terrifying." "It is certainly prodigious that any people, after four years of war, should still possess such resources."[66]

One other French writer deserves mention. Régis de Trobriand, the son of a former French general and a well-known literary figure, had emigrated to America in 1847. In 1861 he was elected colonel of the 55th New York Volunteers, and by the time the war ended he had reached the rank of brevet major general. His memoirs, written soon after the war to acquaint the French people with what had occurred in America, confirm the testimony of other foreign observers. The Army of the Potomac had improved with age, until by 1863 it could be considered on "the level of the regular armies of the old world." As a soldier the American "was not inferior to any other," although he suffered from a cruel replacement system. According to De Trobriand, if recruits

had even been sent to us by squads or companies to fill up our depleted ranks, we would have quickly made them serviceable soldiers. Intermingled with tried men, placed under the orders of experienced officers, they would have soon conformed to discipline and been efficient in drill. They would have quickly learned their trade, and marched under fire with the confidence which the example and support old soldiers give to newcomers.

He concluded that infantry "can be quickly prepared for the field" but that cavalry "cannot be improvised. Our experiences . . . proved that."[67]

The writings of nearly all the French observers, official or otherwise, lead to one inescapable conclusion: the Civil War armies, amateurish as they might have been in 1861, by 1865 had become strong and efficient fighting forces. No one could read the accounts of the Prince de Joinville, the Comte de Paris, Lecomte, Guzman, and DeChenal, and indeed of Scheibert and many of the English observers as well, without gaining the impression that despite—or perhaps even because of—its deviations from accustomed modes of warfare, the Civil War was an event of military significance. The only

[66] *Ibid.*, pp. 6, 7, 31, 62.

[67] De Trobriand, *Four Years with the Army of the Potomac*, pp. 82, 331, 338, 414-15.

question was, would the European armies interpret the information furnished from these varied sources to mean that the war of 1861–65 represented an important step in the evolution of warfare, or would they come to regard the American campaigns as essentially an interesting—but uninstructive—aberration?

5

The View from England
1861-86

Professional interest in the Civil War was in no way limited to those who had journeyed across the Atlantic. There were many soldiers in Europe, including some of high rank, who were familiar with the major campaigns. The military journals often contained news from America; in Prussia, France, and England a number of military writers focused their attention upon the war, and many others who made no special study of the military operations as they unfolded allotted them proportionate space in general works or treatises on tactics and strategy.

In examining the reaction to the Civil War among soldiers in England, one is struck by the prominence of those who wrote about the war, foremost among whom was Captain Charles Cornwallis Chesney, professor of military history at the newly established Staff College and one of the most competent military writers of his day. Chesney became best known for his *Waterloo Lectures*, published in 1874, but he first made his reputation as a military critic through his writings and lectures on the Civil War.[1] He used the campaigns in Virginia and Maryland to illustrate lectures at the Staff College, lectures which he subsequently enlarged into a two-volume history. Described by a contemporary critic as "by far the clearest and most scientific view of the operations yet published in England," Chesney's *Campaigns in Virginia*[2] was the first detailed study of a Civil War campaign to reach the British public. It enabled Englishmen for the first time to see the war as one of their leading military critics

[1] Stanley Lane-Poole, "Charles Cornwallis Chesney," *Dictionary of National Biography* (London, 1908), IV, 195; Whitworth Porter, *History of the Corps of Royal Engineers* (London, 1908), II, 499.

[2] [Colonel E. B. Hamley], "Books on the American War," *Blackwood's*, XCIV (December, 1863), 349. *Campaigns in Virginia, Maryland, etc.* (2d ed.; London, 1865). Originally appearing in 1864, this work was revised and published "in more complete form" the following year. *Ibid.*, I, vii.

described it. No longer were the names of remote places and obscure generals without meaning. Chesney had captured the essence of the eastern campaigns, and his books enabled an interested audience to understand the crucial events that had occurred there. His writings also served as a springboard for later studies of the Civil War.

The first commandant of the Staff College, Colonel (later Sir) Patrick MacDougall, was another who was well acquainted with the Civil War. The son-in-law of Sir William Francis Napier, the famous historian of the Peninsular War, MacDougall drew heavily from the experiences of Wellington's army for most of his theoretical writings,[3] but in a new work written while the Civil War was in progress, he did not hesitate to utilize whatever information he could gather about the events across the Atlantic. He cited the campaigns to illustrate specific points, and while he appears to have done little original research, he at least was familiar with much of the literature that had been written about the Civil War. His was the first English military text to incorporate some of the military lessons of the American conflict.[4]

Of all British officers who studied and wrote about the Civil War during the 1860's, none was to become more influential than Colonel (later General Sir Edward Bruce) Hamley. In 1859 Hamley, having served with distinction at various military posts throughout the empire and in the Crimea, had been named professor of military history at the Staff College, where his lectures laid the foundation for his monumental work which appeared in 1866, *The Operations of War*. In this single volume Hamley accomplished "more than any other Englishman to make known to English officers the value of a methodical treatment of the study of campaigns." Exploring the whole progressive science of modern war, "Hamley was the first to show ... that success in war lay in the discovery of basic principles and their application to existing circum-

3 MacDougall's best-known work probably is *The Theory of War: Illustrated by Numerous Examples from Military History* (London, 1856). This book was translated into French and German and was used widely as a military text in England. The paper which MacDougall wrote in 1857 entitled "The Senior Department of the Royal Military College" probably led to his selection as commandant of the Staff College when it was founded in the following year. He relinquished the post in 1861. Robert Hamilton Vetch, "Sir Patrick Leonard MacDougall," *D.N.B.*, XXII, Supplement I, 993–94; Major A. R. Godwin-Austen, *The Staff and the Staff College* (London, 1927), p. 127.

4 *Modern Warfare As Influenced by Modern Artillery* (London, 1864), *passim*.

stances."[5] Written with trained literary skill (for Hamley had contributed various essays and literary pieces to *Blackwood's*), this book was remarkably free from the usual professional pedantry. Probably no officer was more influential in the British army in the 1860's than Hamley; certainly no military treatise was more widely read by following generations than *The Operations of War*.[6]

Hamley's initial reactions to the Civil War were typical of many European soldiers. He felt the common contempt of the professional strategist for the clumsy efforts of the improvised Civil War armies. The first battle of Bull Run, seen through the candid eyes of William Howard Russell,[7] had discredited the war in the minds of many. To Hamley this battle was "certainly the greatest joke in the world"; he only hoped that the proceedings in America would meet the derision he felt they deserved. He also made the common error of underestimating the war potential of the North. By 1862, however, when the first observers reached the scene, Hamley began to see the war in a different light, and he watched the later campaigns with a growing interest. According to his biographer, "Long before the termination of the war, he had come to the conclusion that the Northern American, like the Gascon, could plan and fight as well as swagger. . . ." Hamley delivered a series of lectures at the Staff College on the Civil War, and he contributed several articles about the subject to the magazine of his good friend John Blackwood.[8]

Hamley shared the sympathetic feelings most British officers expressed for the South; so much so, in fact, that on one occasion Blackwood suggested that he give more credit to the North "for the energy which turns out such enormous armies operating over so vast a field." Hamley was especially harsh in his criticism of Sher-

[5] Colonel F. Maurice, *War: Reproduced with Amendments from the Article in the Last Edition of the Encyclopaedia Britannica, to Which Is Added an Essay on Military Literature and a List of Books with Brief Comments* (London, 1891), p. 9. Godwin-Austen, *The Staff and the Staff College*, p. 134.

[6] Hamley worked hard in other ways to promote professional knowledge among British officers. In 1865 he was appointed to the Council of Military Education, which was intrusted with the military instruction of the army. In 1870 he was named commandant of the Staff College. For many years he also acted as judge for the Wellington Prize Essay contest, held annually to determine the best essay written on a military subject. Alexander Innes Shand, *The Life of General Sir Edward Bruce Hamley* (Edinburgh and London, 1895), I, 119, 179, 198, 210.

[7] William Howard Russell, *My Diary North and South* (London, 1863), II, 202–50.

[8] Shand, *Life of Hamley*, I, 135–37. Mrs. Gerald Porter, *John Blackwood* (Vol. III of *William Blackwood and His Sons, Their Magazine and Friends* [London, 1898]), p. 268. Unfortunately, these articles appeared anonymously, and only one, "Books on the American War" (December, 1863), has been positively identified as coming from Hamley's pen.

man for his "barbarous" campaign in Georgia, and when the latter read Hamley's treatment of this campaign in *The Operations of War*, he sent Hamley copies of relevant orders to enable him to correct several errors of fact. Hamley thought this "a very handsome way of meeting objections," and his revised account of the Atlanta campaign in subsequent editions earned praise from Sherman.[9]

Significantly, both Chesney and Hamley looked upon the Civil War essentially as one in a series of wars, to be neither ignored for its irregularities nor heralded as the dawn of a new day in warfare. Obviously this war had different characteristics from those which had preceded it in Europe; yet Chesney attempted to show that the Civil War had but demonstrated the validity of universal military principles and that therefore it ought not to be regarded, as it was by many, as "a sort of chaos of butchery, a series of indecisive battles of which nothing could ever come." In discussing general problems of tactics, logistics, and strategy, Hamley frequently pointed to examples from the Civil War, but it is obvious that he, too, did not regard the lessons of that war as in any way unique. Equally important for his purposes were the Napoleonic Wars and the campaign between Austria and France in Italy in 1859.[10]

Quite naturally, the views of Chesney, MacDougall, Hamley, and others in England who wrote about the Civil War often resembled opinions expressed by observers who had witnessed some part of the campaigns. Thus Chesney described the Union army of 1861 as "an armed and dangerous mob," which, by 1863, had so improved that it could counterbalance the superior leadership of the Confederates and the individual excellence of the Southern soldier. Good discipline and sound organization were the keys to a successful volunteer army, he concluded, and the Civil War gave heartening assurance to Chesney that the volunteer system was not in itself a vice. If the British army could avoid the administrative abuses that had impaired the effectiveness of the Civil War armies, the English Volunteer need never be inferior to any soldier on the Continent.[11] Mac-

[9] *Ibid.*, pp. 269–71; Shand, *Life of Hamley*, I, 186–91.

[10] Chesney, "Sherman's Campaign in Georgia," *Journal of the R.U.S.I.*, IX (1866), 204. Cited hereafter as Chesney, "Sherman's Campaigns." Edward Bruce Hamley, *The Operations of War Explained and Illustrated* (London, 1866), *passim*.

[11] *Campaigns in Virginia*, I, 14–15; II, 112, 203–4. Like most of the observers, Chesney believed that the Southerner, because of his life out of doors and early familiarity with rifle and horse, was naturally much better suited to soldiering than the city-bred recruit from the North.

Dougall too was influenced by what the observers had written. He was impressed, for example, by the Prince de Joinville's statement that the Union army in 1862 lacked anything remotely resembling a general staff. This in itself was ample proof of McClellan's "unfitness to lead an army to victory," and it was inconceivable to MacDougall that a general with a reputation as an organizer par excellence "should have entirely neglected the one measure which alone could have a practical value to the discipline and bravery of his troops. . . ."[12]

Like most foreign observers, MacDougall and Chesney also disapproved the role of American cavalry. MacDougall criticized dismounted tactics, claiming that this turned the cavalryman into "a hybrid and inferior soldier." For close fighting he would replace the carbine with a good revolver. Chesney at first shared the prevalent prejudice against dismounted tactics. The Americans, he wrote, did not understand the correct use of cavalry. They relied too much upon infantry and artillery; they were reluctant to attack infantry in the traditional manner; and they were too willing to fight on foot, a development "most detrimental to their usefulness, and likely to be confirmed into an evil tradition" Chesney blamed this reliance upon firepower on the nature of the country and defective discipline. He also questioned the value of the much-publicized cavalry raids which, save in isolated instances, had caused substantial waste of horseflesh for what appeared to be meager results.[13] Later he was to revise his estimation of Civil War cavalry, embracing this time the views of a group of "Young Turks" who wanted to sweep away much of the time-honored tradition of the mounted arm.

Because those who followed the progress of the Civil War from England were influenced by the views expressed by the various observers, one might reasonably expect to find in their writing some digestion of the technical data reported by the several official missions sent to the United States from the Royal Artillery and the Corps of Royal Engineers. This does not appear to have been the case. Gillmore's *Engineer and Artillery Operations against the Defences of Charleston Harbor* is mentioned frequently, but in none of the books and articles on the American Civil War that appeared in England in the 1860's and 1870's is there any reference to official reports of British observers. Probably there were many who did not

[12] *Modern Warfare As Influenced by Modern Artillery* (London, 1864), p. 272.

[13] *Ibid.*, pp. 15, 135; Chesney, *Campaigns in Virginia*, II, 105-8, 226-27.

know of the existence of such reports, although Sir Thomas Fraser looking back over a long and successful military career, later recalled that as a young officer of the Royal Engineers he was informed of the engineering methods developed during the Civil War.

As the technical reports reached us I took in hand a number of their new methods; and, under service conditions, tested and adopted some of them, particularly for military bridging. . . . These experiments took several years, but they supplied the means for exact calculations, and were done once and for all. In due time they were embodied in the textbooks of "Military Engineering."[14]

It is odd that in his treatise on the attack of fortifications, written in 1877, Sir Thomas himself ignored the official reports. Gillmore is cited, to be sure; even Livy and Thucydides have their place in the bibliography; but of the Royal Engineers who had been sent to America to observe the effects of rifled artillery upon permanent fortifications there was not a word.[15] The main reason for this neglect probably was that the documents were designated "confidential," and as such they must have been rigidly restricted. It is also likely that more recent tests at Woolwich and the experiences of the Danish War of 1864 and the Franco-Prussian War of 1870 robbed the reports of much of their importance.

Few Englishmen thought that the American campaigns offered new lessons in strategy. Chesney maintained that the guiding principles of strategy during the Civil War were, or ought to have been, the same "which animated Caesar, Hannibal, and Napoleon. . . . At no time, save in exceptional cases, could generals deviate from those principles without meeting evil consequences." Sherman, "a man of original genius," was the possible exception, and even he had been forced to adhere closely to certain axioms of strategy.[16] For his part, Hamley could see nothing even in Sherman's March to the Sea that would "modify existing theories."[17]

Railroads, however, had injected a new element into strategy, and this subject was explored by Captain H. W. Tyler in a lecture be-

[14] Major General Sir Thomas Fraser, *Recollections with Reflections . . . a Memoir of a Scottish Soldier in Ireland from the Seventeenth Century* (Edinburgh and London, 1914), pp. 119–20.

[15] *The Attack of Fortresses in the Future* (London, 1877), *passim*.

[16] "Sherman's Campaigns," pp. 205–6; "Sherman and Johnston in the Atlanta Campaign," *Fortnightly Review*, XCIII (December, 1875), 619.

[17] *The Operations of War Explained and Illustrated* (new ed.; Edinburgh and London, 1909), pp. 19–20.

fore the Royal United Service Institution. Tyler recognized, as indeed had many of his fellow officers, that the railroad had become of paramount importance in war. Because at times during the Civil War trains furnished the only practical means of moving and supplying armies, railroad lines had become primary objects of attack. Special expeditions had been undertaken to tear up rails; great battles had been waged for the possession of junctions. Tyler concluded that the Civil War taught a number of useful lessons about the military use of railroads. It demonstrated, first of all, that trains could be used with great advantage in moving and supplying troops. It also revealed that railroads were more vulnerable than regular roads; they were more quickly and easily destroyed, but if the necessary materials were at hand, they were also more readily repaired.

The American campaigns indicated that a single line of rails, provided with a proper number of sidings, could supply an army in the field, although Tyler recommended that any new railroads constructed for strategic purposes should be laid with double lines of rails. Tyler deduced that it was not safe for a commander to rely upon railroads as the sole line of communication in hostile territory. Finally, he concluded that railroads lent themselves more to defensive than to offensive operations.[18] Had Tyler waited but six months to give his lecture, he would have been able to find in Sherman's Atlanta campaign some clues to the problem of maintaining an army in enemy country on a single railroad. And could he have foreseen the movements of the Prussian armies in 1866 and again in 1870, he would have been forced to revise his conclusion that railroads were of primary advantage in defensive operations.

Most English soldiers of Hamley's generation who wrote about the Civil War occupied themselves largely with tactical problems. MacDougall, to cite one example, was concerned particularly with the effect of improved artillery upon tactics. He interpreted the Civil War to mean that increased firepower would force infantry to adopt less rigid and more extended battle formations:

The experience of the present contest in America would seem to point to the conclusion that a position in an open country, which has been prepared for defence, cannot be carried by direct attack by troops moving in close order, exposed to the present field artillery. In nearly all the great battles of the Civil War, the assailants, except where a surprise

[18] "Railways Strategically Considered," *Journal of the R.U.S.I.,* VIII (1864), 342.

was effected as at Corinth [Shiloh], or when operating in a wooded country as at Chancellorsville, have been defeated by artillery fire.[19]

MacDougall predicted that the destructive power of modern artillery would limit infantry in future battles to holding strong points and prepared defensive positions. Because it had been demonstrated that "comparatively inferior troops" were capable of holding a strong defensive position (most British observers to the Civil War had noted that even hastily raised volunteers could fight respectably when behind cover), MacDougall believed that the general effect of increased firepower would be "to diminish the difference in value between volunteers and troops of the line." The great battles of the future would be decided principally by artillery. Cavalry would play "but a secondary part . . . for its only power lies in the offensive, and it cannot act at all unless in motion."[20]

Discussion of tactical matters usually centered on two main topics of current interest: the use of intrenchments and the role of cavalry. With regard to the former, Chesney seems to have been the first in England to demonstrate that intrenchments had "formed a very important part" of Sherman's Atlanta campaign. No one who heard his lecture on this campaign could have missed the tenor of his remarks. Certainly the Duke of Cambridge, commander-in-chief of the British army, had been an attentive listener, for as he commented afterward:

I would only remark that two things struck me very much in what has fallen from the lecturer. One is, that in this war, and, I think, in all future wars, the spade must form a great element in campaigns. It is quite clear, from what has been stated, that there was no movement made without instant entrenchments, both on the part of the attacking force and of that of the defensive; and that even the movements in advance were instantly confirmed . . . by the position being entrenched in a manner which would preclude the danger of attack. Now that I think is a very great and new element in the features of war, and probably the necessity for it has been greatly increased by the improvements in arms, both artillery and musketry.[21]

In a lecture before the same body five years later, Colonel Gerald Graham echoed the remarks of Chesney and the Duke of Cambridge: "This great American contest proved the advantage of cover in all field operations, and the later Bohemian campaigns of

[19] *Modern Warfare As Influenced by Modern Artillery*, p. 424.

[20] *Ibid.*, pp. 14–15, 135, 272.

[21] Quoted in the *Journal of the R.U.S.I.*, IX (1866), 220.

1866, by displaying the startling effect of the breech-loading rifle, made it obvious that, in future warfare, troops will have to be kept under cover as much as possible, whether acting on the offensive or defensive."[22] While British soldiers duly noted the Americans' use of intrenchments, particularly in the latter stages of the war, most of them attached no particular significance to this fact. Those that did anticipate a greater dependence upon intrenchments in future wars could read the same lesson from the war of 1870, where, according to one British observer, "an immense development of intrenching" had followed the initial decisive field operations. Here again the Civil War appeared to be but one step in a general trend in warfare.[23]

Not so with the cavalry. As early as 1865 the advantages of cavalry armed with breech-loading carbines had been noted,[24] and the following year the Duke of Cambridge, discussing Chesney's speech before the Royal United Service Institution, expressed his opinion that

if there was one feature in the explanations of the lecturer which struck me more forcibly than another, it was that he clearly brought before my mind the absolute necessity of a large, handy body of cavalry, with this difference perhaps, that whereas it was considered in former years that cavalry should be of a very heavy calibre, they ought now to be made as light as possible. . . . Probably the day of heavy cavalry has somewhat passed by.[25]

By heavy cavalry the Duke undoubtedly meant cavalry armed with lance and saber and trained exclusively for shock tactics. It is significant that in his lecture on Sherman's Atlanta campaign Chesney appeared to be less critical of the use of cavalry than in his account of the earlier campaigns in Virginia. His views on the subject were shortly to change still more.

22 "Shelter Trenches, or Temporary Cover for Troops in Position," *ibid.*, XIV (1871), 448–78. Graham mentioned a "Shelter Trench Exercise" which had recently been introduced into the proposed new field exercises and which soon was to be submitted to the Duke of Cambridge.

23 "This drove home the lesson, as I understood it, of the great war of the sixties in the United States . . ." (Fraser, *Recollections*, p. 120). See Fraser, "Notes on the Combined Use of Intrenchments, Defended Posts, and Redoubts, for Strengthening Positions, War of 1870–71," R.E. *Professional Papers*, XXI (1873), 17–25; Robert Home, *A Précis of Modern Tactics: Compiled from the Works of Recent Continental Writers at the Topographical and Statistical Department of the War Office* ([London], 1873), p. 137.

24 "The Last Campaign in America," *United Service Journal*, CIX (September–December, 1865), 370.

25 Quoted in the *Journal of the R.U.S.I.*, IX, 220.

The most radical proposals came from a young hero of the Indian Mutiny, Major (later Sir) Henry Havelock. The son of a prominent English general, Havelock's career had been brief but brilliant. He had distinguished himself at the defense of Lucknow, and in the relief of Cawnpore he had been awarded the Victoria Cross. Although he was alleged to have seen some part of the operations in America,[26] it is extremely unlikely that he did so, for neither his own writings nor the sketch in the *Dictionary of National Biography* mentions such a visit: in 1863–64 Havelock was busy fighting Maoris in New Zealand. In March, 1867, he succeeded Wolseley as Assistant Quartermaster General in Canada, in which capacity he served for two years. It was during this period that he wrote his controversial *Three Main Military Questions of the Day*.[27]

One of the questions raised by Havelock concerned the cavalry. Like most of his contemporaries, he was interested in finding a way for cavalry to meet the challenge of the breechloader. He had been an early advocate of mounted infantry, having experimented with such a body in India as early as 1858.[28] In Canada he had had occasion to learn something about the mounted infantry techniques developed during the Civil War. The experiences of the Americans had convinced him that here was struck "the first blow given to the supremacy of what we may call a purely 'sabre cavalry.'"[29]

According to Havelock, the American cavalry at the commencement of war in 1861 had been simply a poor model of its European counterpart. The first battle of Bull Run made it evident that this type of cavalry no longer was adequate against improved firearms and that henceforth, in order for cavalry to be of much value, a new organization based on firepower would have to be developed. Havelock credited the Confederate cavalry leader, Brigadier General John H. Morgan, with devising the so-called mounted rifle plan of fighting, a development which gained ground rapidly in both

[26] Colonel G. F. R. Henderson (Captain Neill Malcolm [ed.]), *The Science of War: A Collection of Essays and Lectures 1891–1903* (London, 1906), p. 236.

[27] R. H. Vetch, "Havelock-Allen," *D.N.B.*, XXII, 826. Havelock's father was Major General Sir Henry Havelock, whose premature death in 1857 was caused by his exertions in the Indian Mutiny.

[28] Havelock had actually formed a tiny body of mounted infantry in India in the autumn of 1858 and had early demonstrated (to himself, at least) the value of such a force. The advantage of mounted infantry in India was that it could substitute firepower for shock action in dealing with elusive native bands. See J. W. Fortescue, *A History of the British Army* (London, 1899–1930), XIII, 397.

[29] *Three Main Military Questions of the Day* (London, 1867), pp. 34, 44.

armies and which, "improved upon by experience, and lavishly supplied by the almost boundless resources of the North . . . became, more than any one thing else, the weapon that gave the Confederacy its death blow."[30]

The essence of this new doctrine was that cavalry had become mobile firepower, dependent upon the horse primarily as a means of locomotion. Civil War cavalry had fought most of the time on foot, using magazine rifles, shelter afforded by the terrain, and hastily constructed breastworks to enable it to contend—often successfully —with larger bodies of infantry. Mounted supports and reserves behind the lines were moved to threatened positions on short notice, where they could either charge if the opportunity presented itself or else dismount in an attempt to catch the enemy in a destructive cross-fire. In Havelock's estimation, troops "thus armed, trained, and instructed were equal to any contingency, and could act upon any sort of ground."[31]

As the classic example of this new mode of fighting, Havelock pointed to Sheridan's action at Five Forks in April, 1865, and the ensuing pursuit of Lee's army to Appomattox. The defensive power of dismounted cavalry was evident in the fighting preceding the battle proper, when Sheridan's troopers, intrenched and well armed, had inflicted heavy casualties on the Confederate infantry assaulting them. The following day they had displayed their effectiveness in offensive action by skilfully co-operating with the Union infantry to defeat the Confederates at Five Forks. This action proved to be the lever that finally pried Lee out of his trenches, so Havelock concluded that it was the Union cavalry that had been the chief factor in bringing the remnants of Lee's army to bay near Appomattox. British cavalry, lacking the arms, training, and equipment of Sheridan's mounted infantry, would have been totally unprepared "to play this part of independent . . . action at a distance from the other two arms." Indeed, Havelock doubted seriously whether any European cavalry armed with lance and saber and fighting by shock tactics alone could have thus prevented Lee from making good his escape.[32]

Here was a revolutionary doctrine. Unlike most foreign observers, Havelock denied that the Civil War cavalry had been incapable of charging in the most "dashing European manner." They simply had better sense, realizing "the reckless ineffectual folly of a

[30] *Ibid.*, pp. 110–11.   [31] *Ibid.*, pp. 47–48.   [32] *Ibid.*, pp. 78, 99.

mounted charge." The Union cavalry was ten times as effective "by making a liberal use, dismounted, of their repeating fire." Thus Havelock boldly refuted the arguments of Fletcher, Fremantle, Hewett, and the other British observers, whom he accused of judging Civil War cavalry by what he termed obsolete European standards.[33] He appealed to his readers to shake themselves loose from unsound Continental doctrines, to reshape British cavalry from "the jangling, brilliant, costly, but almost helpless unreality it is" into a force cut after Sheridan's pattern. With his own experiments in 1858 in mind, he suggested that such cavalry would be particularly effective in India, where the country was no better suited than the wilds of Virginia and Tennessee for the employment of traditional cavalry tactics. "If Mounted Riflemen could achieve such great things against the steadfast stubborn veterans of Lee," he reasoned, "there is practically no limit to what they could do for us in India against our contemptible, half-disciplined, ill-armed, disunited Asiatic enemies." Havelock thus became the first English soldier to indorse wholeheartedly the tactics of Civil War cavalry, which offered "the one special lesson which with its proffered reward of immediate economy in time, men, and money, the Great American war holds out to us English. If we neglect its teaching . . . then indeed it may be said of us that contemporary military history is enacted before our eyes—in vain."[34]

In 1868, just one year after the appearance of Havelock's polemic, similar views were advocated by Lieutenant Colonel George T. Denison, a Canadian cavalry officer. Denison had served under Wolseley during the Fenian disturbances in 1866, where he had greatly impressed Wolseley with his skill in leading cavalry. Denison was also a good friend of Havelock, whom he credited with giving him the advice and encouragement needed to write his own work entitled *Modern Cavalry*.[35] Denison's theories, particularly those concerning dismounted action of cavalry, were derived al-

---

[33] *Ibid.*, pp. 47–49.

[34] *Ibid.*, pp. 112–14. Havelock subsequently accompanied the Prussian armies as an observer during the war of 1870, where he became acquainted with General Sheridan, representing America in a similar capacity. See Philip Henry Sheridan, *Personal Memoirs of Philip Henry Sheridan* (New York, 1902), II, 418–25.

[35] Wolseley later described Denison as "one of the ablest, and professionally one of the best read officers I ever knew," better fitted for high military command than 95 per cent of the officers in the British army (*The Story of a Soldier's Life* [New York, 1904], II, 148–49); Lieutenant Colonel George T. Denison, *Soldiering in Canada* (Toronto, 1900), pp. 142–53.

most entirely from his study of the Civil War. Much of his information came from conversations with ex-Confederates who, like the former Lieutenant General Jubal A. Early, had refused to accept the verdict of the war and were sulking in Canada. He also corresponded with former Confederate cavalry officers, and he was well versed in the published source materials.[36]

In the main Denison accepted Havelock's thesis that mounted infantry or light cavalry—he used these terms interchangeably—could accomplish more than regular cavalry under modern battle conditions. He did not go as far as Havelock in advocating complete abandonment of the old-style cavalry, but then Havelock had been concerned primarily with what would prove beneficial in India. Denison believed that at least one-fourth of all cavalry should still consist of "real cavalry, armed as such, and taught that nothing can withstand a well-executed charge." But even here, he would modify the *arme blanche*:

If there is one principle which the works on cavalry lay down more positively than another, it is that cavalry using the sabre will always overcome cavalry using any description of fire-arms. This was undoubtedly correct formerly, when the old flint-lock horse-pistol was the weapon used. ... But now, with revolvers, the whole features of the case are changed. These arms will carry from 200 to 300 yards, and comparatively good shooting can be made with them up to 75 or 100 yards, while in a melée they are most deadly weapons. ... A number of instances occurred in the war in America showing the value of this arm as compared with the sword.

From conversations with former Confederate officers and from the books he read and the letters he received about their campaigns, Denison concluded that the bulk of the cavalry in a modern army should consist of light dragoons or mounted rifles, armed with the Spencer carbine "and taught the power of accurate firing on foot." Occasions favoring the mounted charge undoubtedly would still arise, but they would not be as numerous as before.[37]

Denison was a more judicious student of war than his friend Havelock, whom he suspected of overstating the case for Union

[36] Among those with whom Denison "was in the habit of frequently discussing military matters" were Jefferson Davis, Generals J. C. Breckinridge, John McCausland, Richard Taylor, John B. Hood, Harry Heth, W. S. Preston, "and many other officers of lower rank." Denison devoted an entire chapter in his autobiography to recollections of former Confederates. *Ibid.*, pp. 58–82.

[37] *Modern Cavalry: Its Organization, Armament, and Employment in War* (London, 1868), pp. 30–31, 73–75.

cavalry in the final campaign of the war. By 1865, he pointed out, the South was "completely exhausted . . . and overpowered by overwhelming numbers." A personal friend of Jubal Early, Sheridan's old opponent in the Shenandoah Valley, he could not share Havelock's admiration for the Union general, even though he was forced to admit that Havelock was correct "to a certain extent" in his analysis.

In 1874 Denison learned that the Grand Duke Nicholas of Russia was offering a prize for the best work on the history of cavalry. After three years' intensive study, during which he consulted an estimated seven hundred books pertaining to cavalry, Denison submitted his entry. His *History of Cavalry* won first prize, possibly because mounted infantry had many adherents in Russia,[38] and at once became regarded as the definitive work on the subject. In this book, fortified by the experiences of the Franco-Prussian War, Denison plugged essentially the same theories that had gone unheeded in his earlier work. He continued to advocate the use of mounted infantry in reconnaissance, outpost duties, and strategic raids, with "cavalry proper" (still in the proportion of one to three) being saved to exploit the dwindling opportunities that modern battle offered. He wrote with the conviction of one who had seen his prophecies confirmed by the experiences of more recent wars. As late as 1913 he could still claim that "thirty-six years of consideration and study" had not "varied my views, or modified them in any way."[39]

Although Havelock was a professional reformer and had the reputation of being eccentric, while Denison was only a militia officer and a militia officer from Canada at that, their writings soon won over many adherents. Probably they were responsible for Fletcher's and Wolseley's partial conversion to mounted infantry. Chesney, too, altered his opinion of Civil War cavalry. If his earlier writings

---

[38] In 1884 a former British military attaché at St. Petersburg wrote that "there has been for some years past an influential section of officers in the Russian army who have constantly advocated the theory that European cavalry of the present day, equipped and drilled after the old-fashioned methods, is unsuited to the requirements of modern warfare, and who have insisted that a cavalry . . . taking as its model and example, both as to armament and method of fighting, the American cavalry of the Civil War, is the kind of cavalry which will make its mark in future warfare." The Czar's cavalry made a practice raid into Russian Poland in the autumn of 1876. Colonel F. Chenevix Trench, *Cavalry in Modern War, Being the Sixth Volume of "Military Handbooks for Officers and Non-commissioned Officers"* (London, 1884), pp. 75–77.

[39] *A History of Cavalry from the Earliest Times with Lessons for the Future* (2d ed.; London, 1913), pp. xv, 415–43.

agreed with what observers on the scene had reported, his later views were undoubtedly shaped by the arguments of Havelock and Denison. By 1874 he was willing to admit that Sheridan's tactics at Five Forks had succeeded perfectly: "No general had mastered like this young American commander, the new art of using . . . mounted riflemen."[40] His brother, Sir George Chesney, was one of the first to advocate converting the Yeomanry, or Volunteer cavalry, into mounted infantry, asserting that "30,000 such horsemen would, if handled boldly, wholly cripple and confound an opposing army of 300,000! Riding to and fro in rear of an army, intercepting its communications, cutting off its supplies, destroying its reserve ammunition and material, such a force would undoubtedly create panic and confusion far and wide."[41]

The official manuals naturally were reluctant to adopt the theories advanced by Havelock and Denison. Clery rejected their ideas outright, asserting that "the force of a cavalry soldier dwells in his horse, and its application in the impetuosity of the charge." Cold steel was "the only weapon" a cavalry soldier should rely on. Home, leaning upon the theories of Continental writers, believed that "the danger to cavalry on the battlefield of smokeless powder and increased accuracy of fire has probably been exaggerated." Home recognized the conflict between lance and carbine; he admitted that modern firepower would limit the role of cavalry in battle; but he still had faith in the massed cavalry charge and shock tactics.[42]

One manual, however, did incorporate the teachings of Havelock and Denison. Colonel F. Chenevix Trench appreciated the "brilliant and, in some cases, extraordinary services" of the Civil War cavalry:

By far the most striking instance in any modern campaign of important results being achieved by the action of dismounted cavalry was the

[40] *Essays in Military Biography* (New York, 1874), p. 76.

[41] Quoted in Henderson, *Science of War*, p. 267. See also Sir George Chesney, "A True Reformer," *Blackwood's*, CXIII (April, 1873), 474. Sir George, a well-known soldier and military writer, was best known as the author of "The Battle of Dorking: Reminiscences of a Volunteer" (*ibid.*, CIX [May, 1871], 539–72), which purported to be the story of a successful German invasion of England; it was written to urge action in improving the efficiency of the Volunteer forces. The Chesney Gold Medal, to be awarded "to the author of the most original literary work treating with naval or military science and literature which has a bearing on the welfare of the British Empire," was instituted in 1899 in memory of Sir George Chesney. The first recipient, curiously enough, was an American, Captain A. T. Mahan (information obtained in correspondence with Captain B. H. Liddell Hart).

[42] Lieutenant Colonel Clery, *Minor Tactics* (5th ed.; London, 1880), p. 122; Home, *Précis of Modern Tactics*, pp. 59–74.

part played by the Federal cavalry during the last closing scenes of the American Civil War. . . . With such . . . feats to rely upon . . . any cavalry officer may feel himself justified in thinking that in the wars of the future, dismounted cavalry, when properly trained, skilfully handled, and boldly led, may oftentimes have a great part to play.

It made little difference whether such troops were called cavalry or mounted infantry; the point was that they fought equally well on foot and on horseback and were capable of producing great results. Against cavalry, Sheridan's men fought sword in hand on horseback; when opposed to infantry, his men dismounted and used the rifle.[43] Chenevix Trench also could see merit in the strategic cavalry raids characteristic of cavalry on both sides during the Civil War.[44]

It is unlikely that the Civil War, though widely studied in England, had any direct bearing upon official doctrine. Chesney and Hamley had studied it precisely because it seemed to reveal the soundness of established principles. Individual writers sensed the significance of intrenchments, but neither this lesson nor that preached by Havelock, Denison, and their disciples received official recognition, at least not until after the turn of the century. The official reports on the Civil War remained more or less a closed book.

We need not look far for the reason behind this neglect—only across the Channel. In 1866 and again in 1870 the Prussian army had startled the world by tumbling, in a series of swift and decisive victories, the two major military powers on the Continent. Austria was crushed in a campaign of only seven weeks' duration in the summer of 1866. France's turn came four years later, when the German armies poured across the frontier, bottled up the two main field armies in Metz and Sedan, and laid siege to the capital. The German Empire was proclaimed amid surroundings furnished by Louis XIV, and the military center of gravity shifted from Paris to Berlin.

These convincing victories caused the British army to sit up and take notice. No longer was it a case of an occasional writer or lecturer referring to selected lessons of a distant war; British officers now intently scrutinized the German campaigns and made a methodical, at times even a dogmatic, study of German military theories and institutions. Students at the Staff College were fed a regular diet of Moltke and his campaigns by instructors like Colonel

---

[43] *Cavalry in Modern War*, pp. 165–66, 179, 188–90, 211–12.

[44] *Ibid.*, pp. 193, 214.

Lonsdale Hale, who reputedly had "so minutely studied" the war of 1870 that "at any moment, he could inform an inquirer of the exact position of all the German and French units down to companies at any given time in any battle." Granted that this may be an extreme example, it nevertheless illustrates the practical value placed upon study of the wars for German unification.[45] To some extent the Cardwell Reforms of 1870–71, brought about because of military weaknesses exposed in the Crimean War and the Indian Mutiny, also came under the German influence. Although basically English in origin and designed to correct evils peculiar to the British army, these reforms incorporated some ideas from the Germans, particularly certain features of the newly adopted short service and enlistment on a territorial basis. Army maneuvers were instituted in 1871, and even the Prussian *Pickelhaube* replaced the French kepi as standard headdress in most British regiments, a "new look" reflecting the change in military thinking.[46]

The Civil War was overlooked in this rush to study everything German. A new military literature appeared, stressing questions of tactical interest and for the most part disregarding campaigns conducted before 1866 on the broad assumption that "you can't draw any deductions from what occurred before the [universal] introduction of the breech-loader."[47] For a generation after 1871 military texts seldom cast more than a fleeting glance at the American campaigns, and the subject was practically ignored in the technical treatises and military journals.[48] There does not appear to have been a single book devoted exclusively to the Civil War written in Eng-

[45] Major General J. F. C. Fuller, *The Army in My Time* (London, 1935), p. 123. See also Godwin-Austen, *The Staff and the Staff College*, p. 198; Major General Sir John Adye, *Soldiers and Others I Have Known* (London, 1925), pp. 136–37.

[46] Sir George Arthur, *From Wellington to Wavell* (London, 1942), p. 72; General Sir Robert Biddulph, *Lord Cardwell at the War Office* (London, 1904), pp. 189, 212–13; James Laver, *British Military Uniforms* (London, 1948), p. 21. Lest American readers think the British naïve in going to such lengths to imitate the Germans, it should be remarked that in 1881 the *Pickelhaube* was officially introduced into the United States Army as well. Richard Knötel, Herbert Knötel, and Herbert Sieg, *Handbuch der Uniformkunde: Die militärische Tracht in ihrer Entwicklung bis zur Gegenwart* (Hamburg, 1937), p. 400.

[47] Lieutenant F. Maurice, *The System of Field Manoeuvres Best Adapted for Enabling Our Troops To Meet a Continental Army* (London, Wellington Prize Essay for 1872), p. 10; *War*, p. 110.

[48] See, for example, Clery, *Minor Tactics, passim*; Home, *A Précis of Modern Tactics, passim*; Fraser, *The Attack of Fortresses in the Future, passim*; Col. C. B. Brackenbury, *Field Works: Their Construction and Tactical Application* (Vol. VII in "Military Handbooks for Officers and Non-commissioned Officers" [London, 1888]), *passim*.

land during the fifteen years that followed the downfall of France
in 1871. Hamley continued to devote proportionate space to the
Civil War in later editions of *The Operations of War;* Chesney's
interest in the war survived the Germanization of British military
thought;[49] and proponents of mounted infantry could still find comfort in the exploits of Sheridan, Forrest, and Stuart, but they were
clearly a minority. For the rest, it would not be entirely amiss to
state that the exploits of those Civil War generals would have
caused greater attention in England in the 1870's had they written
their memoirs in German.

Inevitably a reaction set in. By the mid-1880's there were many
who were beginning to wonder if other wars might not offer more
useful lessons to a colonial power. Germany, these new voices
argued, was after all a land power dependent upon a conscript army
for protection, while Britain's first line of defense was still the Royal
Navy, her small volunteer army bearing the double responsibility
for home defense and policing the empire. Men like Wolseley and
Colonel Frederick Maurice now looked beyond the period of the
German wars, pointing to lessons "which have in no wise been diminished in value by the changes which have come over the face of
war." Maurice, who had ignored the Civil War in previous writings,
decided there was much "to be derived by a careful student from
the American war," and Wolseley, writing always with the problems of England uppermost in his mind, strongly advised his officers
to "copy the Germans as regards work and leave their clothes and
their methods alone."[50] Even from far-off India came a strong appeal to look again at the Civil War, in many respects "a far more

[49] "The military excellence displayed in . . . the American Civil War has been unduly depreciated by comparison with later events on the continent. There is a
disposition to regard the American generals and the troops they led as altogether
inferior to regular soldiers. . . . The conditions of war on a grand scale were illustrated to the full as much in the contest in America as those more recently waged
on the continent. In all that relates to the care of feeding and supplying an army
in the field, the Americans displayed quite as much ability as any continental power,
while if the organization and discipline of their impoverished troops were inferior,
the actual fighting was in fact more stubborn, for no European forces have experienced the amount of resistance in combat which North and South opposed to each
other" (*Essays in Military Biography*, pp. iii–iv).

[50] Maurice, *War*, pp. 12, 107; Maurice and Sir George Arthur, *The Life of Lord
Wolseley* (New York, 1924), p. 222. See also Maurice, "How Far the Lessons of the
Franco-German War Are out of Date," *United Service Magazine*, N.S. X (March,
1895), 555–77; Miller T. Maguire, "Our Art of War As Made in Germany," *ibid.*,
XIII (May–June, 1898), 124–34, 280–91; Spenser Wilkinson, "Introduction," W. Birk-
beck Wood and Major J. E. Edmonds, *A History of the Civil War in the United
States, 1861–65* (New York, 1905), p. xiv.

likely source of information . . . than the histories of struggles between French and Germans." "A True Reformer" complained that
"for 15 years the tactics of timidity have been dinned into our ears,
and month after month our officers have been condemned to pass
examinations in books compiled from others which have long since
found a resting place in the dusty cellars of German publishers."[51]
So when a young officer named Henderson, then practically unknown outside his own regiment, set about to write a history of the
Fredericksburg campaign, the time was ripe for a revived interest
in the Civil War.

[51] "A True Reformer," *Letters on Tactics and Organization* (Calcutta, 1888), pp.
299, 312. "A True Reformer" was Captain F. N. Maude, who later became a well-
known military writer.

6

The View from Germany
1861-1914

Although most Prussian soldiers naturally were preoccupied with
events directly concerning their own army—the reforms of 1860–61
and the war with Denmark in 1864—thoughtful attention was paid
to the Civil War. Books and articles were written to acquaint the
public with the broad outlines of the war; individual battles and
campaigns were analyzed for the benefit of military readers; and
technical treatises elaborated upon American innovations in the
fields of artillery and military engineering. Even when the war of
1866 against Austria and preparations for a probable clash with
France became favorite topics in barrack-room conversation and in
the military journals, the Civil War was not forgotten.

In Prussia, as in England, comparatively little was written about
the Civil War until 1863. This was the year, it will be recalled, when
the Prussian General Staff became sufficiently interested in the war
to send Scheibert to the scene as an official observer. By 1863, military writers in Prussia also began to scrutinize events in America:
Captain Constantin Sander published the first edition of his history
of the Civil War,[1] and the important *Preussische Jahrbücher* carried
a series of anonymous articles about individual campaigns of the
war. If the Civil War did not attract the attention of writers as influential in the Prussian army as Chesney, MacDougall, and Hamley
were in their own, at least it was not totally ignored by men of
prominence. Colonel Albrecht von Stosch, a brilliant General Staff
officer who later distinguished himself in the wars against Austria
and France and who ultimately became Chief of the Admiralty,
wrote a series of articles entitled "The American War from a Military Standpoint" for *Die Grenzboten*.

As history these early studies leave much to be desired (Stosch,

[1] See Constantin Sander, *Der amerikanische Bürgerkrieg von seinem Beginn bis
zum Schluss des Jahres 1862* (Frankfurt-am-Main, 1863).

in fact, even placed the Rocky Mountains in Virginia),[2] but they are significant for the attitudes they reveal. Being for the most part professional soldiers belonging to an army based upon conscription, these writers shared a low opinion of the American militia. To Sander, for example, the Civil War underscored the need for military preparedness; to Stosch, it demonstrated the need for an organization similar to the Prussian General Staff and for an adequate replacement system. In varying degrees these writers understood the special characteristics of the Civil War—the lack of decisive military victories, the influence of untrained volunteer armies upon generalship, the new importance of rivers and railroads, and the special problems in supply, communications, and command caused by the vast and difficult nature of the theater of war. They even showed some awareness of the vital role of sea power, although this subject lay outside the scope of their studies.[3]

Much of the Civil War literature written in Prussia in the 1860's was devoted to the study of technical aspects of the war. Like their counterparts in England, Prussian engineers were anxious to learn more about the influence of rifled artillery upon fortifications; consequently, few operations of the Civil War drew greater notice than those involving coast defense. Scheibert had been sent over specifically to ascertain the effects of rifled artillery on the works protecting Charleston; Von Scheliha wrote a lengthy treatise on the subject; Stosch, in an article discussing problems in coast defense that might arise in a future war with France, perceived that the experiences of the Americans contained "a lesson for us," while still another officer of the Prussian General Staff told a military audience that this subject constituted one of the most important lessons of the Civil War.[4]

In 1865 Constantin Sander brought out a revised and enlarged edition of his history of the Civil War, in which he showed much

2 "Der Krieg in Nordamerika vom militärischen Standpunkt," *Die Grenzboten,* XXIV (1865), Vol. I, p. 64. Cited hereafter as Stosch, "Der Krieg in Nordamerika." Stosch is identified as the author of these articles in Frederic B. M. Hollyday, "Albrecht von Stosch: A Political Study of the Bismarckian Period" (Ph.D. diss., Duke University, 1955), pp. 36 ff.

3 Stosch, "Der Krieg in Nordamerika," XXIII (1864), Vol. IV, pp. 326, 327–33; XXIV, Vol. I, pp. 59–60; Vol. II, pp. 228, 250; Sander, *Der amerikanische Bürgerkrieg,* pp. 56, 121; "Der Feldzug 1863 in Nord-Amerika," *Preussische Jahrbücher,* XII (1863), 488, 490, 500.

4 [Stosch], "Unsere Küsten in einem Kriege mit Frankreich," *Die Grenzboten,* XXVI (1867), Vol. II, p. 248; Colonel F. von Meerheimb, *Sherman's Feldzug in Georgien* (Berlin, 1869), p. 51.

greater concern than before for technical developments. As an officer of the Royal Prussian Artillery, he was especially interested in the effect of rifled artillery on fortifications, and in his description of the operations before Charleston in 1863, he borrowed heavily from a professional paper he had contributed to a publication of the Prussian Artillery and Engineer Corps.[5]

The most systematic study of the influence of modern artillery on coast defense is that by Captain C. Jacobi on the siege of Charleston. Based upon information contained in Gillmore's *Engineer and Artillery Operations against the Defences of Charleston Harbor*, which has been circulated in most of the major armies of Europe,[6] Jacobi's book dealt mainly with technical subjects—the various types of rifled artillery in use at Charleston, materials, effective ranges, and so forth. He wrote primarily for those in the Prussian artillery and engineers, confident that the operations he described would furnish "rich and valuable material for the study of siege operations."[7]

Although Jacobi's book was published before those by Scheibert and Von Scheliha, he arrived at the same general conclusions. He, too, affirmed that a naval attack against land installations would seldom succeed without the aid of co-operating land forces and that earthworks afforded far greater protection against modern artillery than works built of brick and masonry. He predicted that the increased range of siege artillery would make it necessary in the future to erect defensive works much farther away from the city or installations they were intended to protect. The surest way to defend a harbor or river entrance, he concluded, was to block it with obstacles lying within range of shore batteries. Finally, Jacobi regarded bomb shelters of the type constructed by the Confederates at Battery Wagner "indispensable" to modern coastal fortifications. Calling attention to subjects such as the effectiveness of mortar fire

[5] Sander, *Geschichte des vierjährigen Bürgerkrieges in den Vereinigten Staaten von Amerika* (Frankfurt-am-Main, 1865), p. 241. Sander's article, which unfortunately cannot be located, is entitled "Artilleristische Aphorismen aus dem gegenwärtigen amerikanischen Bürgerkriege," *Archivs für die Officiers der Königl: Preussischen Artillerie- und Ingenieur-Corps* (28 Jahrgang).

[6] Mention has already been made of Gillmore's influence in England. His official *Report* was also circulated in Prussia, Austria, and France. In addition to Jacobi's study, it was analyzed by Julius von Wieruth in the Austrian publication *Mittheilungen über Gegenstande der Ingenieur- und Kriegs Wissenschaften* (Vienna, 1865).

[7] *Die gezogenen Geschütze der Amerikaner bei der Belagerung von Charleston von 1863 bis 1865 in ihrer Verwendung, Wirkung, und Haltbarkeit.* (Berlin, 1866), p. 1.

against fortifications, the use of wire ("it is quick to erect and suffers but little from enemy fire") and sandbags, armored vessels versus shore batteries, and the practical difficulties of storming a prepared position, Jacobi was clearly of the opinion that the Prussians could profit from studying the operations of the Americans at Charleston.[8]

The Prussians were also interested in railroads. The Americans had been the first to wage war over great distances largely by means of the railroads, and the creation of a separate corps to operate trains and maintain equipment, the use of armored trains, and the evolution of the hospital car can all be traced directly to the Civil War. The campaign in Italy in 1859 had first indicated the importance of railroads in war, but it was the Civil War that actually demonstrated how they could be used for military purposes.[9]

The Prussians had commenced study of the military possibilities of railroads several years prior to the Civil War. For more than a decade the Great General Staff had worked on schemes to use railroads for transport and concentration, but by 1861 nothing had been done to organize military transport by rail other than the issuing of a series of ordinances dealing with the movement of troops. In 1864, however, "directly influenced by the developments of the Civil War," the Prussians added a Railway Section to the Great General Staff, just in time for it to function in the war with Denmark that same year. In May, 1866, on the eve of the war with Austria, the Prussian War Minister created a Field Railway Section (*Feldeisenbahnabteilung*), which was modeled directly on the Construction Corps of the Union army and designed to perform similar functions. That same year a translation of the report of Brigadier General D. C. McCallum, Military Director and Superintendent of Railroads in the Union army, was published in Prussia, soon to be followed by "a long series" of technical papers, pamphlets, and books on the wartime use of railroads.[10] In this new literature the

[8] *Ibid.*, pp. 17 n., 26, 29, 36, 64–67.

[9] Edwin A. Pratt, *The Rise of Rail-Power in War and Conquest, 1833–1914* (London, 1915), p. 9.

[10] *Ibid.*, pp. 104, 122–27; Major Hille and Major Meurin, *Geschichte der preussischen Eisenbahntruppen*, I: *Von 1859 bis zur Beendigung des deutsch-französischen Krieges* (Berlin, 1910), pp. 4–5; Frederic Canonge, *Histoire militaire contemporaine* (Paris, 1886), I, 358–59. German interest in McCallum continued after the establishment of the *Feldeisenbahnabteilung*. Cf. "General MacCallum und das militär Eisenbahnwesen während des nordamerikanischen Bürgerkrieges," *Militär Wochenblatt* (May 28, 1879), No. 43, pp. 754–64.

Civil War provided many practical illustrations of the functions and maintenance of military railroads. Even the more theoretical works make it clear that the Civil War was commonly regarded in Prussia as a testing ground for the military application of railroads.[11] It is interesting to note that in Austria, too, a study was made of the Union Construction Corps only weeks before the Prussians adroitly applied in the Seven Weeks' War the lessons learned from the operations of railroads during the Civil War.[12]

In the years preceding the war of 1870, Prussian writers manifested little interest in Civil War tactics or strategy. Stosch's views were typically conventional. American cavalry, he wrote, was in reality mounted infantry; even when it fought on horse, it derived most of its punch from firearms rather than "the vehemence and force" of shock tactics. Like most European soldiers, Stosch expressed preference for the Confederate cavalry, and he attributed the rise of mounted infantry more to rough terrain than to the destructive power of modern weapons.[13] He made the same error in explaining the changes that had occurred in infantry tactics, crediting them notably to "inexperienced troops" (after three years of fighting!) and difficult terrain. Stosch disapproved Grant's strategy of attrition in 1864, claiming: "It's the same old story, that inferior commanders prefer the conquest of fortifications to a decisive battle and thereby lose more time, men, and money than in the bloodiest battle."[14]

Colonel F. von Meerheimb, a more thorough student of the Civil War, better understood the tactical and strategical lessons of the war. Almost alone among his fellow officers, Von Meerheimb did not discount the fundamental military lessons of the war because it had been fought by amateurs. As early as 1868 he predicted:

11 See J. E. Lassmann, *Der Eisenbahnkrieg* (Berlin, 1867), pp. 1, 35, 68, 78–79, 87, 89, 92–93, 95. The only title the present writer could find referring specifically to railroads in the Civil War is entitled *Abhandlung über die Thätigkeit der amerikanischen Feldeisenbahnabteilungen der Nordstaaten: Bei den Directionen der Staatseisenbahnen* (Berlin, n.d.). Unfortunately, no copy of this work could be located. See Pratt, *The Rise of Rail-Power*, p. 377.

12 See Captain Wendelin von Boeheim, "Das Eisenbahnbau-Corps der Armee der Vereinigten Staaten: Seine Errichtung, Versuche und seine Leistungen im letzten Kriege," *Streffleur's österreichische militärische Zeitschrift* (1866), II, 1–27. Von Boeheim, an officer in the Pioneer Corps, derived much of his information from a report received by a Captain Boleslawsky, formerly a member of the Austrian army and serving at the time the article was written in Mexico. See above, p. 8 n.

13 "Der Krieg in Nordamerika," XXIV, Vol. I, pp. 229, 251.

14 *Ibid.*, p. 262; XXIII, Vol. IV, pp. 395, 456.

The American war shows in heavy lines the picture of the war of the near future, and the Georgia campaign clearly throws most of the characteristic features into bold relief. The extended use of railroads and telegraph and the indirect strokes against these communication lines of the enemy, the constant employment of field fortifications, the transformation of terrain for tactical purposes and the altered use of cavalry appear to be the essential points wherein the Civil War is distinguished from previous wars in Europe. The combination of modern long-ranged, rapid firing weapons and prepared positions give the defensive such a great superiority that frontal attacks will succeed only on the rarest occasion. Flank movements, involving great marching ability on the part of the troops, consequently will be used more frequently than before.[15]

With the exception of the military use of railways, the Civil War does not appear to have had any direct influence upon official doctrine in Prussia. Prussian leaders knew about the war, to be sure, but there is no reason to believe that any high-ranking official regarded the Civil War as being particularly instructive in a military sense.[16] Possibly the Prussians learned something new in coast defense from the Americans; at least they were aware of what the Americans had accomplished, and several competent studies on the subject were readily available. But there is no specific evidence to indicate any change in policy as a result of American experiences in coast defense. The Prussians had been experimenting with breech-loading rifles since 1841, so it is obvious that the Civil War did not awaken any new interest in this subject. Even so, it does seem odd that no one studied the Civil War battles for clues to probable effects of this new weapon upon tactics, especially since careful attention had been paid to rifled artillery and siege operations. Quite likely the reason for this neglect is that few soldiers in Prussia became professionally interested in the Civil War before 1863, at which time the majority of troops in both armies were still armed with muzzle-loading weapons. By 1864 the Prussians could observe the effect of their own breechloader, the needle gun, in the war with Denmark, and the campaign of 1866 obviated any real need to look to distant wars for information about breech-loading firearms in battle.

[15] *Sherman's Feldzug in Georgien*, p. 51.

[16] See Theodor von Bernhardi, *Aus dem Leben Theodor von Bernhardis* (Leipzig, 1893–1906), V, 114–16, 182–83; VI, 136, 193–94. A prominent military writer who had the ear of many high-ranking officers, Theodor von Bernhardi's memoirs show that he and his circle of friends were well informed about the main events of the Civil War. Bernhardi himself confessed to a *soldaten-sympathie* for the Confederates.

The popularity of mounted infantry in some circles in England did not spread far into Prussia. A German translation of Denison's *Modern Cavalry* was published early in 1870, but his views were neither widely accepted nor officially indorsed. There is no evidence to support Denison's claim that his theories influenced the Prussian cavalry in the war with France.[17] It is of course possible that Karl von Schmidt, the famed Prussian cavalry leader of 1870–71, profited from the example of Civil War cavalry. He might have learned something about American cavalry tactics from correspondence with his nephew in the Union cavalry, although the youth had died before Sheridan's arrival from the West in 1864; it is known that Von Schmidt considered Jeb Stuart "an ideal cavalry leader" and thought his methods of fighting "worthy of exhaustive study." But Von Schmidt's views on dismounted action probably can be traced more to his own experiences during the campaigns of 1870–71, when his command frequently deployed and fought on foot.[18] Another well-known leader of cavalry, Prince Frederick Karl, was also an avowed admirer of Jeb Stuart. The prince was well acquainted with Von Borcke, who had served first on his staff in 1866 and later as his personal adjutant,[19] and doubtless he was familiar with the exploits of the Confederate cavalry. Considering Von Borcke's opinion of dismounted tactics, however, it does not

[17] "My views about throwing cavalry two or three days ahead of the army, which I advocated and which the Germans did not use in 1866, were adopted and used with great effect in 1870" (G. T. Denison, *Soldiering in Canada: Recollections and Experiences* [Toronto, 1900], p. 159). Previous to the appearance of a German edition of *Modern Cavalry*, Denison's views seem to have attracted little attention in either Prussia or Austria. See Constantin Braun, "Bewaffnung der Cavallerie und berittenen Schützen im Letzten amerikanischen Kriege," *Streffleur's österreichische militärische Zeitschrift* (1869), II, 117. In a volume of commentaries that accompanied the German edition of Denison's *History of Cavalry*, Lieutenant Colonel Prix, an officer of the Royal Prussian War Ministry, weighed Denison's proposal to arm cavalry with revolvers but remained throughout a typical advocate of shock action. *Anmerkungen und Zusätze zu Denison's Geschichte der Cavallerie* (Vol. II of Denison, *Geschichte der Cavallerie seit den frühesten Zeiten mit Betrachtungen über ihre Zukunft* (Berlin, 1879), pp. 818–25. According to Hans Delbrück, the great German military historian, this work by Denison "has no scholarly historical value" (*Geschichte der Kriegskunst im Rahmen der politischen Geschichte* [Berlin, 1920], IV, 137 n.).

[18] Von Schmidt, quoted in C. von Bredow, "Über die Leistungen der amerikanischen Cavallerie im Secessionskriege," *Jahrbücher für die deutsche Armee und Marine*, XXIII (April–June, 1877), 347. Cited hereafter as Von Bredow, "Leistungen der amerikanischen Cavallerie." Franz von Schmidt, *Avantgarde: Weg und Welt eines preussischen Reitergenerals* (Berlin, 1941), pp. 254, 271, 289, 343.

[19] Wolfgang Foerster, *Prinz Friedrich Karl von Preussen* (Stuttgart and Leipzig, 1910), II, 24, 502 n.; Major Edgar Erskine Hume, *Heros von Borcke* (Charlottesville, 1924), pp. 15–16.

seem possible that the prince could have learned much of military value from this source.

Nor does the high command seem to have been influenced by the Civil War. Moltke is supposed to have remarked that the affair in America was nothing but a matter of "two armed mobs chasing each other around the country, from which nothing could be learned."[20] Conceivably Moltke did say something of the sort, although some writers think otherwise;[21] in any case, even had Moltke made such a statement in 1862 or 1863, he would have found many competent soldiers in Europe—among them Hamley—to agree with him. Rarely did Moltke mention the Civil War. In his *Selected Works* there is a fleeting reference to the naval operations of Admiral Farragut, and in the debates over the military law of 1874 Moltke reminded supporters of the proposed militia legislation that the Civil War offered convincing arguments against the use of militia,[22] but his views on tactics and strategy were untouched by events across the Atlantic.[23] In the absence of evidence to the contrary, we can only assume that Moltke was far too involved in the momentous events taking place in Europe to cast more than a cursory glance at the war in America. His genius lay primarily in the realm of organization and strategy, and with the exception of the military application of railroads there was little that he could learn from the Civil War in either respect.

Prussia's victories over Austria and France changed both the map

20 Quoted in Major General J. F. C. Fuller, *War and Western Civilization, 1832–1932* (London, 1932), p. 99.

21 "It is not true that Moltke ever referred to those campaigns [in America] as 'the struggle between two armed mobs,' [although] the expression does . . . fairly truthfully indicate the attitude of the average German military mind in the matter" (Captain [F. N.] Maude, *Attack or Defence: Seven Military Essays* [London, 1896], p. 9); Lieutenant Colonel G. F. R. Henderson, *The Science of War*, ed. Captain Neill Malcolm (London, 1906), p. 233. To the present writer's knowledge, no one has ever documented Moltke's alleged statement.

22 Generalfeldmarschall Graf von Moltke, *Ausgewählte Werke*, Vol. I: *Feldherr und Kriegslehrmeister* (Berlin, 1925), pp. 444–46; *Gesammelte Schriften und Denkwürdigkeiten*, Vol. VII: *Reden* (Berlin, 1892), p. 112. During the war with Denmark Moltke picked Scheibert for a special task because of the latter's experience at the siege of Charleston. *Moltke's Militärische Werke*, Vol. I: *Militärischen Korrespondenz: Krieg, 1864* (Berlin, 1892), p. 125.

23 It is interesting to note, however, that although Moltke did not refer to the Civil War, he was aware of at least one of the fundamental tactical lessons it taught. In 1865 he wrote that "the fire of stationary troops was so much more effective than that of troops advancing that it would be well to combine as far as possible a tactical defensive with a strategical offensive" (*Militär Wochenblatt*, July 8, 1865, quoted in Fuller, *War and Western Civilization*, p. 100). After 1870, Moltke's views on cavalry tactics were no less cognizant of modern firepower. See Colonel Eugène Carrias, *La pensée militaire allemande* (Paris, 1948), p. 245.

of Europe and conventional military precepts. Politically, these wars led to the unification of Germany and the foundation of the German Empire under the hegemony of Prussia. The army reforms of 1860–61, the needle gun (which had been adopted in 1841 and enabled infantry to fire rapidly and to reload in a prone position), and meticulous organization and planning paved the way for the military victories. Thoroughly grounded in the theories of Clausewitz, the famous philosopher on war, Moltke had shaped his own doctrines to make efficient use of the products of the Industrial Revolution. His strategy capitalized upon recent improvements in communications—new and improved road networks, railroads, and the military telegraph; his theories were implemented by a corporate brain, the famous Prussian General Staff, while superior peacetime training and indoctrination further lubricated a military machine that, after 1870, was universally regarded as the best in the world.

The successes of the Prussian army inevitably gave rise to a wealth of new military literature—memoirs, official histories, technical studies, and books on tactics and strategy. In Germany two trends became at once apparent. So successful were Moltke's campaigns that after 1870 there were few who dared criticize his strategy, and his ideas received almost universal acceptance.[24] Moreover, the wars for unification stimulated interest in military history in general. In contrast to the reaction in England, German military writers were not entirely blinded by their dazzling successes, and from 1866 until the Russo-Turkish war of 1878, German officers probably were more actively interested in military studies than those of any other army; Moltke himself placed a high value on the study of military history, "especially after 1866, in order to test and enlarge his own experience by the facts."[25] Manifestly, the German campaigns received the greatest attention, for they were the most recent, the best documented, and by far the most convincing, but the Civil War was also studied for lessons that might be applicable.

[24] Ibid., pp. 260–61. For a concise summary of German strategical thought after 1871, see Lieutenant General von Caemmerer, The Development of Strategical Science during the 19th Century (London, 1905), pp. 157–77. The emergence of Moltke and the General Staff as the controlling force in the Prussian army is traced in Walter Goerlitz, History of the German General Staff 1657–1945 (New York, 1953), chap. iv. See also Spenser Wilkinson, The Brain of an Army: A Popular Account of the German General Staff (London, 1897), passim.

[25] Capitaine Breveté Niessel, Tendances actuelles de l'infanterie allemande (Paris, 1905), pp. 1–2; Friedrich von Bernhardi, On War of Today (London, 1912), I, 46.

After 1870, most German writings on the Civil War appeared in the military journals, notably the *Jahrbücher für die deutsche Armee und Marine*. The scope and caliber of these writings varies enormously. Some writers did little more than review or summarize current American literature on the Civil War;[26] others translated excerpts from American publications and pieced them together under enticing titles, a practice which Scheibert was not long in adopting.[27] A few attempted to write serious history. Major F. Mangold, an instructor in the Royal Academy of Artillerists and Engineers, revised Sander's *History of the Civil War* and wrote an authoritative study of the Second Bull Run campaign, a book that was acclaimed by one American reviewer as "a most remarkable production, exhibiting the profoundest research [and] a wonderfully intimate knowledge of the topography."[28] Mangold was anxious to give his brother officers "a reliable and impartial history" of the Civil War, and his book was devoid of the didactic passages so often found in the military literature of this period.[29] Others beside Man-

[26] Typical of this sort of review article is "Die Kriegführung am Mississippi *1862–63*," *Beiheft zum Militär-Wochenblatt* (1876), Part V, pp. 241–68.

[27] Most of the articles signed by Captain A. von Clausewitz belong to this category. See Von Clausewitz, "Aus dem americanischen Secessionskriege, I: Die Schlacht von Fredericksburg am 13 December, 1862," *Allgemeine militär Zeitung* (1868), pp. 72–73. Von Clausewitz also translated a portion of Sherman's *Memoirs* (Vol. II, chap. xv), which he published under the title "Ein Eisenbahnkrieg im amerikanischen Sezessions-Krieg," *Militär Wochenblatt* (1876), No. 32, pp. 571–81. He even wrote to Lee after the war, seeking permission to translate the autobiography of the Confederate general, which he understood was soon to be published in the United States. To bolster his case, he stated that he had already translated selections from E. A. Pollard's *Southern History of the War* (Richmond, various dates), and he claimed that he was motivated by "l'enthusiasm le plus pure" rather than "une spéculation de libraire." Lee, of course, never wrote his memoirs. Von Clausewitz to Robert E. Lee, March 13, 1866. Robert E. Lee Papers, Washington and Lee University. Lee's answer is reprinted in the Rev. J. William Jones, *Life and Letters of Robert Edward Lee, Soldier and Man* (New York, 1906), p. 249.

[28] Constantin Sander, *Geschichte des Bürgerkrieges in den Vereinigten Staaten von Amerika 1861–1865* (2d ed., completed and revised by F. Mangold; Berlin, 1877); F. Mangold, *Der Feldzug in Nord-Virginien im August 1862* (Hanover, 1881). The review quoted above is from the *Army and Navy Journal*, XXVII (November 2, 1889), 178. Mangold was a partisan of Major General Fitz-John Porter, the Union officer who had been relieved from command in 1862 and found guilty of disobeying orders at the battle of Second Bull Run. Porter's case was re-examined in 1879, and at a new hearing he was cleared of all charges. The proceedings of this hearing prompted Mangold to write his monograph. A by-product of his research is "Richmond und Washington: Eine strategische Studie aus dem amerikanischen Bürgerkrieg," *Jahrbücher für die deutsche Armee und Marine*, XLV (October–December, 1882), 27–38.

[29] F. Mangole [*sic*] to Rev. Dr. J. William Jones, August 16, 1878, reprinted in *S.H.S.P.*, VI, 190. This letter reveals Mangold's difficulties in locating Confederate source materials, which he confessed "have been flowing very scantily," and it

gold approached the Civil War from a historical point of view, but most of them based their writings upon too scanty information to be regarded seriously.[30]

Most German officers who wrote of the events of 1861–65 had specific military "lessons" in mind. They were strikingly influenced by Scheibert, whose *Bürgerkrieg in den nordamerikanischen Staaten* appeared in 1874, and for the next decade they wrote articles analyzing the tactics of the American armies—the significance of field fortifications, the use of artillery, innovations in the function of cavalry. They dramatized the weakness of improvised armies of militia and untrained volunteers; they stressed problems in logistics and advances in military technology. Because they were so alike in their evaluation of the military aspects of the Civil War, it is not necessary to study the views of each writer separately. Their collective views, however, reveal some interesting facts.

First, almost without exception those who interpreted the military characteristics of the Civil War accepted Scheibert's analysis.[31] They agreed with his observations on the power of rifled artillery and its limitations in dense woods;[32] they shared his opinion of Civil

---

shows his desire for accuracy: "Nothing more will be printed before the manuscript of the whole is finished, and it seems to me now more than likely that I shall then suppress the first volume and write that over again also."

[30] For examples of the historical treatment of Civil War campaigns, see "Aus dem amerikanischen Secessionskriege: Feldzüge von 1861 und 62 in den westlichen Alleghany Gebirgen," *Jahrbücher für die deutsche Armee und Marine*, XX (July–September, 1876), 48–68, 183–97; "Aus dem amerikanischen Secessionskriege: Feldzüge in Ost und West Tennessee 1863," *ibid.*, XXVI (January–March, 1878), 183–95, 276–97; H. von Clausewitz, "Die Einnahme von New Orleans durch die Flotte der Nordstatten von Amerika am 23 April 1862," *ibid.*, XXVII (April–June, 1878), 21–47.

[31] The conclusions in this and succeeding paragraphs are derived from a study of the following: "Aus dem amerikanischen Secessionskriege: Feldzüge am Mississippi 1862 und 1863," *Jahrbücher für die deutsche Armee und Marine*, XIV (January–March, 1875), 59–82, 166–87, 251–82; "Beitrag zur Charakteristik des nordamerikanischen Secessionskrieges," *ibid.*, XIX (April–June, 1878), 177–88, 247–60; C. Von Bredow, "Über die Leistungen der amerikanischen Cavallerie im Secessionskriege, Historische Studie," *ibid.*, XXIII (April–June, 1877), 200–221, 347–58; M. von Wedell, "Operationen der Potomac-Armee unter General Grant im amerikanischen Secessionskriege 1864 und 1865," *ibid.*, XXIV (July–September, 1877), 79–86, 282–325; E. W., "Über die Verwendung der Feld-Artillerie im nordamerikanischen Secessionskriege," *ibid.*, XXX (January–March, 1879), 55–69, 134–47; and "Charakteristische Momente der Kriegführung im nordamerikanischen Secessionskriege," *ibid.*, XXXVII (October–December, 1880), 32–51, 152–66, 261–74.

[32] This was really an academic question in the mid-1870's because in the recent war against France all the Prussian guns were rifled, and, as the technical treatises clearly demonstrate, they had proved vastly superior to the bronze smoothbores of the French artillery. Prince Kraft zu Hohenlohe-Ingelfingen, *Letters on Artillery* (2d ed.; London, 1890), p. 29.

War cavalry and his conviction that the strategic raid was not applicable in Europe; they indorsed his explanation of the rise of intrenchments, and most of them refused to attach much significance to the "abnormal" *Spatenkrieg* of 1864–65.

It is also apparent that these writers understood many of the distinctive characteristics of the Civil War. They recognized the tremendous problem in logistics. As one writer commented, in Europe armies usually dispersed on the march in order to live and concentrated to fight, while in America, where most of the land was still wilderness, dependence upon rivers and railroads as lines of supply forced the armies to remain more or less concentrated much of the time.[33] These writers were aware of the unique contribution of the Union navy in blockading the Confederate ports and supporting the army along inland waters. They respected the industrial power of the North and the creative achievements in military technology. Military engineers, the *Eisenbahnabteilungen*, the sanitary services —these and kindred organizations received frequent and favorable mention. Because they understood these forces at work, the Germans in the 1870's could appreciate the reasons for some of the changes that had occurred in strategy and to a lesser extent in the tactics of the Civil War. The important fact to note, however, is that these writers were unanimously of the opinion that the Civil War had deviated from European patterns because of unique political and geographical conditions. It was precisely because it was unique that they continued to find it of interest.

We may safely conclude that the Germans did not, in any real sense, learn the basic tactical lessons of the Civil War. They found the war instructive in matters of matériel and technology; it even offered useful examples in coast defense and joint army-navy operations. But insofar as the tactics of the three arms was concerned, the Germans placed their trust in their own experiences. How could they give priority to a war which not only was fought before the general introduction of breech-loading firearms and artillery, but about which much remained to be learned? One student of Civil War artillery complained that available sources "were so varied . . . and so inaccurately reported, that we cannot speak of definite principles." The Americans would mention, for example, "only that the artillery went into position, but not where, how, and why."[34] No

[33] "Charakteristische Momente der Kriegführung im nordamerikanischen Secessionskriege," p. 264.

[34] E. W.,"Über die Verwendung der Feld-Artillerie im nordamerikanischen Secessions-Kriege," pp. 136, 139.

German soldier anticipated the use of intrenchments in Europe to the extent that they had been employed in the American campaigns: "A carry-over of this method of fighting . . . would imply a want of appreciation for the purposes of every battle—the overthrow of the enemy."[35] While intrenchments were known to augment the power of the defensive, they were considered of value primarily to raw troops and militia, not to the well-trained, offensive-minded army that Germany maintained. Besides, who ever won a decisive victory sitting behind trenches? Examples were few and far between, even in the later stages of the Civil War.

In matters regarding the handling of cavalry, the Germans found the experiences of the Americans "stimulating," "interesting," even "of great significance," but they were not won over to the idea of mounted infantry. They studied the dismounted tactics of Civil War cavalry, for this was a subject being thrashed out by those who formulated official doctrine, but the over-all impression was that the *Fuszgefecht* had been used and found successful in America only because special conditions there had precluded the use of regular cavalry. Even Von Schmidt, whose experiences in 1870–71 had convinced him that it was "indispensably necessary" for cavalry to learn to fight on foot, preferred shock tactics: "It cannot too often be repeated that the main thing to do is carry out the mission in hand *at any price;* if possible this should be done mounted and with the *arme blanche;* but should that not be feasible, then we must dismount and force a road with the carbine. . . . The object must be attained under any circumstances."[36]

This does not sound like Havelock or even like Denison; furthermore, it was not the American Civil War but the war against France that caused Von Schmidt to press for adequate firearms for cavalry and increased instruction in dismounted fighting. As a member of the Cavalry Commission, appointed in 1874 to formulate new regulations, he did his utmost to see that appropriate attention was devoted to this neglected phase in the training of cavalry. The "Draught for the Instructions of Dismounted Fighting for Cavalry," issued by the commission in 1874, provoked a storm of protest throughout the army. Where would time be found for additional training? What would happen to the exuberant cavalry spirit? Von Schmidt defended the proposed regulations and managed to salvage

[35] "Charakteristische Momente der Kriegführung im nordamerikanischen Secessionskriege," p. 159.

[36] Karl von Schmidt, *Instructions for the Training, Employment and Leading of Cavalry* (London, 1881), pp. 186, 188.

most of the provisions for the German Cavalry Regulations of 1875, but he was not completely satisfied with the work of the Cavalry Commission. The new regulations still were "entirely insufficient" in the space allotted to dismounted tactics.[37]

One other fact arouses comment. Most German soldiers who studied the Civil War in the 1870's nourished similar prejudices. Long years of peacetime training and preparation had paid off handsomely in 1866 and 1870; hence they tended to scorn non-professional armies and militia organizations. (When a promising young officer of the General Staff suggested in 1877 that the armies Gambetta had improvised in France in the last year of the Franco-Prussian War had introduced a new element, the *levée en masse*, into warfare and that the Germans had better take heed, such an outcry resulted that the officer was quickly transferred to a small garrison in Thuringia.)[38] Time and again they stated that improvised armies composed of militia and untrained volunteers were inadequate for the exigencies of modern warfare. Lacking proper discipline, sufficient good officers, and a general staff to plan and coordinate movements on the battlefield, the Civil War armies by their very nature were responsible for the lack of decisive victories and the "unnatural" duration of the conflict. Similarly, Clausewitz had preached annihilation of the enemy; Sadowa and Sedan had shown that this was possible, and the Civil War had been barren of many decisive military victories. German officers therefore were critical of Civil War strategy, which they interpreted generally as one of attrition and struggle for the mastery of supply lines. Of American strategists they seem to have had the most respect for Lee and Sherman, Lee for his accomplishments in the face of an enemy greatly superior in numbers and Sherman for his logistics.[39] Napoleon and

[37] Franz von Schmidt, *Avantgarde*, pp. 336, 340-43, 371-73; Kaehler, *Die preussische Reiterei von 1806 bis 1876 in ihrer inneren Entwicklung* (Berlin, 1879), pp. 308-412 *passim*. Kaehler, the translator of Von Borcke's *Memoirs of the Confederate War*, does not mention the Civil War.

[38] Friedrich Freiherr von der Goltz and Wolfgang Foerster, *Generalfeldmarschall Colmar Freiherr von der Goltz Denkwürdigkeiten* (Berlin, 1929), pp. 84-88; Carrias, *La pensée militaire allemande*, pp. 296-97. The book that created this excitement was Colmar von der Goltz, *Léon Gambetta und seine Armeen* (Berlin, 1877). The burden of this book was that Germany, faced with the likelihood of a war on two fronts, might have to resort to improvised armies to supplement the regular army against an invasion by superior numbers. The experiences of the French in raising such forces were not to be ignored, therefore, even though Germany had won the war.

[39] The best analysis of Sherman's strategy is found in the writings of Von Meerheimb. See *Sherman's Feldzug in Georgien, passim*, and "Der amerikanische

Moltke, however, still ranked as the foremost framers of modern strategy.

By the mid-1880's most Germans had ceased to write about the Civil War. Scheibert, now dependent upon his pen for a livelihood, continued to grind out articles for the *Jahrbücher für die deutsche Armee und Marine*, but the subject no longer stimulated interest or even controversy. This is scarcely surprising in view of the fact that almost no German soldier thought the American campaigns as instructive in a practical sense as the campaigns of 1866 and 1870–71. Nor had any prominent officer such as Lord Wolseley in England become interested in the Civil War and thus encouraged further study of that conflict. Perhaps interest in the Civil War died also because in the 1880's the Historical Section of the German General Staff had began work on a multivolume history of the wars of Frederick the Great. This project, together with the staff studies of the Franco-Prussian War, consumed much of the energy that might have gone into the study of other campaigns.

German interest in the Civil War was revived slightly at the turn of the century, when several books and articles on the individual battles and campaigns of the war were published.[40] Most of these were historical summaries, and only one, Baron von Freytag-Loringhoven's three-volume critique of the war in the East, is worthy of special mention. A General Staff officer and one of Germany's most prominent military writers, Freytag-Loringhoven originally did research on the Civil War for a series of lectures at the Kriegsakademie which he never gave.[41] In many ways Freytag-

<hr>

Bürgerkrieg," *Deutsche Rundschau*, IX (1876), 233; XI (1877), 243–50. Von Meerheimb did not consider Sherman's tactics of significance, but he thought the latter's use of maneuver to overcome obstacles "admirable." Although he did not organize his observations as Liddell Hart was to do half a century later, he clearly recognized the keystone to Sherman's strategy as being what Liddell Hart was to term "alternative objectives." See below, chap. ix.

40 See "Charleston 1860–1865," *Beiheft zum Militär Wochenblatt* (1893), pp. 268–403; Scheibert and Von Borcke, *Die Grosse Reiterschlacht bei Brandy Station* (Berlin, 1893); M. von Ahlefeld, "Das Generalstabswerk über den nordamerikanischen Burgerkrieg," *Militär Wochenblatt* (August 11, 1900), No. 74, pp. 1779–82; Georg Funke, "Die Operationen der Konföderirten um Richmond im Mai und Juni 1862," *Beiheft zum Militär Wochenblatt* (1901), pp. 277–95; K. von Golsler, "Die Schlacht bei Gettysburg am 2. und 3. Juli 1863," *ibid.* (1913), pp. 197–258.

41 Freiherrn von Freytag-Loringhoven, *Menschen und Dinge wie ich sie in meinem Leben sah* (Berlin, 1923), pp. 109–10. According to Spenser Wilkinson, lectures at the Kriegsakademie at this time consisted during the first year's course "of one or more of the campaigns of the French Revolution and Napoleon," and during the third year the "campaigns of the period since Napoleon, especially those of the time of the Emperor William I" (Wilkinson, *The Brain of an Army*, p. 89).

Loringhoven may be compared to his English contemporary, Lieutenant Colonel G. F. R. Henderson.[42] Both were reliable historians; both taught in advanced military schools, Henderson at the Staff College and Freytag-Loringhoven at the Kriegsakademie; and both were especially interested in the psychology of generalship.[43] Each was a serious student of military history; each sought to relate the Civil War to contemporary military problems; and each produced what was in effect a synthesis of his own army's interpretations of the Civil War.

Like most Germans who wrote about the Civil War, Freytag-Loringhoven understood the conditions that had determined the nature of military operations in America. He, too, appreciated the extraordinary difficulties of supply, the importance of the railroad and telegraph, and the indispensable role of the Union navy.[44] He, too, distrusted improvised armies; to him the Civil War signified the failure of the militia system. Even though the American soldiers of 1865 were comparable in many ways to professional soldiers of Europe, this did not alter the fact that in 1861 the militia and volunteers had not been equal to the emergency. They were, wrote Freytag-Loringhoven, "completely inadequate."[45]

The invention of smokeless powder and improvements in high explosives had increased interest in the subject of fortifications,[46] and Freytag-Loringhoven paid more attention than his predecessors to the improved fortifications of the Civil War. He attributed the development of trench warfare in 1864–65 to reasons other than the increase in firepower, but at the same time he noted that

. . . without thorough artillery preparation, without previous attainment of fire superiority over the defender, the attack against fortified field positions was already impracticable with the effect of weapons at

[42] See below, chap. viii.

[43] See Freytag-Loringhoven, *Die Macht der Persönlichkeit im Kriege* (Berlin, 1905).

[44] Freytag-Loringhoven, *Studien über Kriegführung auf Grundlage des nordamerikanischen Sezessionskrieges in Virginien* (Berlin, 1901–3), I, v, 87; III, 12, 139–40; *Krieg und Politik in der Neuzeit* (Berlin, 1911), p. 211.

[45] *Ibid.*, p. 273; *Studien über Kriegführung*, I, 28–32, 51, 59, 90; II, 21–23; III, 106. For similar evaluations of improvised armies see Funke, "Die Operationen der Konföderirten um Richmond," pp. 279–80; Von Golsler, "Die Schlacht bei Gettysburg," pp. 254–55.

[46] "The training of officers and men for the *Festungskrieg* met with increased attention in the last decade before the [First] World War." Hermann Franke, *Handbuch der neuzeitlichen Wehrwissenschaften* (Berlin and Leipzig, 1937), II, 205; see also Maude, *Attack or Defence*, pp. 1–48 *passim*.

that time. The attempt to overrun the weak Confederate battalions in their intrenchments with concentrated masses miscarried repeatedly, despite the tenacious energy of the high command and the commendable sacrificial courage of the troops.

The Civil War taught one lesson that had remained "entirely disregarded": there was no basic difference between *Feld* and *Festungskrieg*, between operations in the field and those against fortifications. The Americans' experience indicated that the field commander should also have a rudimentary knowledge of military engineering and artillery in order to make intelligent decisions in the likely event that his troops should encounter fortifications or intrenched positions.[47] Freytag-Loringhoven concluded that fortifications constructed in peacetime, such as the Danish works at Düppel, had a greater power of resistance than the improvised works of the Civil War—a statement doubtless intended to refute the arguments of those who, like Scheibert and the Frenchman Auger,[48] believed that earthworks were preferable to permanent fortifications on both military and financial grounds. Like Scheibert, Freytag-Loringhoven was impressed by Lee's defensive use of intrenchments, but he shared the opinion prevalent among German soldiers that defensive battles alone could not win wars. Modern weapons offered much more in the way of firepower to an attacking force than had been the case in the Wilderness, at Düppel, or even at Plevna (1877). While the tactical lessons of Spotsylvania and Cold Harbor had been outdated by modern weapons, they "did bring clearly to view the nature of . . . position warfare," and in this sense, at least, the study of these campaigns was "not without value," even in Freytag-Loringhoven's day.[49]

These views were echoed two years later in a publication of the German General Staff. Operations in the field and against fortifications no longer could be treated as two different and distinct problems; permanent fortifications almost always were superior to improvised works, although the latter could serve a useful purpose in supplementing fortified strongholds and in providing shelter for inexperienced troops. Improvised works required many troops to defend them. Armies should not be bound to such works (which often had been the case in the Civil War) but must remain free to

---

[47] *Studien über Kriegführung*, III, 60, 104-5.

[48] See below, pp. 166-68.

[49] *Studien über Kriegführung*, I, 91; II, 146; III, 61-62, 68-69.

maneuver and assume the offensive. Wherever possible, border fortifications should be of a permanent nature. Earthworks were of less value in 1905 than in 1865 because they offered insufficient protection against the greatly improved howitzers and mortars.[50]

Freytag-Loringhoven's remarks on cavalry are also tempered by the conviction that, useful as the Civil War might appear in illustrating fundamental principles, it contained no tactical lessons that could be applied directly to twentieth-century warfare. Dismounted tactics, like the use of intrenchments, grew out of the uneven and overgrown terrain. If fighting on foot had yielded the best results on occasion, "the lance is and remains the chief weapon" for cavalry.[51] He did not believe that cavalry would undertake many raids in Europe like the much-publicized expeditions of Jeb Stuart. True, armies by 1900 had grown enormously; they were more dependent for supplies upon railroads than had been the case in the Civil War, and they were more sensitive in their rear areas than in 1870; consequently, the destruction of a major railroad would be a "real calamity." Nevertheless, in view of the numbers of cavalry in modern armies,[52] Freytag-Loringhoven considered that it would do well to fulfil its proper functions of reconnaissance, security, and pursuit after battle. Conditions in 1870–71 had not encouraged the use of cavalry in strategic raids, and while he admired Jeb Stuart as a dashing leader of cavalry, Freytag-Loringhoven did not suggest that the Germans imitate his spectacular forays behind enemy lines.[53]

Freytag-Loringhoven and the handful of other German soldiers who wrote about the Civil War after the turn of the century accepted the tactical deductions of those who had analyzed the American campaigns in the 1870's: they minimized the effect of intrenchments and dismounted cavalry tactics; they dismissed the idea of the cavalry raid; and they were firmly convinced of the ineptness of improvised armies. They continued to overlook the basic reason for the change in tactics, increased firepower, and all were agreed that

[50] Prussia, Grosser Generalstab, *Studien zur Kriegsgeschichte und Taktik*, IV: *Die Festung in den Kriegen Napoleons und der Neuzeit* (Berlin, 1905), pp. 202–4, 317–18. Chapter xii of this volume is entitled "Vicksburg und Richmond."

[51] *Studien über Kriegführung*, I, 130; II, 100.

[52] In 1893 a German officer wrote that the cavalry "is the only branch of the German army which has not been increased since the Franco-Prussian War ended" (Lieutenant Colonel Exner, "The German Army," *The Armies of Today: A Description of the Armies of the Leading Nations at the Present Time* [London, 1893], pp. 121–32).

[53] *Studien über Kriegführung*, I, 128–29; II, 29, 74–75.

the tactical lessons of the war had long been outdated. At the same time they had come to regard the war in a slightly different light than had those who wrote in the wake of the Franco-Prussian War. These later writers showed a greater interest in fundamental principles. They looked upon the Civil War as a great industrial and economic struggle, the "first truly modern war" in the sense that matériel and manpower resources had ultimately determined the outcome.[54]

This interest in the Civil War was confined to a handful of individuals, however, for the American campaigns were never taught at the Kriegsakademie, nor did they ever receive special study by the General Staff. The campaigns of Frederick, Napoleon, and Moltke remained the favorite topics of study for German officers, and with good reason. They were well documented, and most of the battlefields were accessible for staff rides. As a rule, the basic military texts slighted the Civil War or else failed to mention it altogether.[55]

The underlying reason for ignoring the Civil War is that however fascinating it may have been from a technical point of view, it did not seem to contain answers to vital military questions of the day. Scheibert and his followers had failed to mention any worthwhile military lessons of the war, and as time passed the feeling grew that "when it becomes a question of obtaining practical hints for our own strategy and tactics . . . we must not go farther back than 1866," when the needle gun and Moltke's strategy had began a new era in warfare. General principles could always be learned from earlier campaigns, but none other than Clausewitz had stated that "the latest military history must always be the most natural field from which to select examples. . . . The farther we go back, the less useful military history becomes."[56] Unless an earlier campaign could contribute to the solution of a particular problem, German theorists

[54] This is Freytag-Loringhoven's position, which was fortified by the experience of World War I. *Krieg und Politik*, pp. 206–16; *Deductions from the World War* (New York, 1918), pp. 15–16; *Politik und Kriegführung* (Berlin, 1918), pp. 138–41.

[55] Von der Goltz, *The Nation in Arms* (London, 1887), and Prince Kraft, *Letters on Cavalry* (London, 1893), *Letters on Artillery* (London, 1890), *Letters on Infantry* (London, 1889), give the Civil War passing mention. It is ignored altogether in Prince Kraft, *Letters on Strategy* (London, 1897), W. von Scherff, *Kriegslehren in kriegsgeschichtlichen Beispielen der Neuzeit* (Berlin, 1894–97), W. Rüstow, *Strategie und Taktik der neusten Zeit* (Zürich, 1892), Oberst Krebs, *Kriegsgeschichtliche Beispiele der Feldbefestigung und des Festungskrieges* (3d ed.; Berlin, 1901), and *Generalfeldmarschall Graf Alfred v. Schlieffen, Gesammelte Schriften* (Berlin, 1913).

[56] Bernhardi, *On War of Today*, I, 49; Karl von Clausewitz, *On War* (Washington, 1950), p. 113.

preferred to concentrate on events more directly connected with the present.

The overriding problem facing German military leaders after 1879, when Germany became allied with Austria, was how best to meet the growing threat of a two-front war involving Russia and France. And on this issue German theorists were agreed on two fundamental points. They were convinced that only an offensive would bring military victory, and they believed in the necessity— on economic as well as military grounds—of a short war. To obtain quick victory, the Germans concentrated on the study of "the mobilization and strategical concentration of armies." For, as the well-known military writer Von der Goltz explained, "the difference between the great military powers is in these days almost reduced to one of hours." He stated the problem well when he described the essential elements of modern war as peacetime preparation and training, rapid mobilization, and "a ceaseless and untiring prosecution of the campaign until the organized resistance of the enemy is broken in decisive battles."[57]

Manifestly, in looking for some "encouraging precedent" to aid in the solution of the problem, the Germans had little time for a war that had begun without peacetime preparation of any sort and was singularly lacking in decisive battles. Having early rejected such tactical lessons as the Civil War might offer and feeling no need to study the strategy of the American campaigns or the over-all conduct of the war, the Germans turned elsewhere for guidance. They were aware, many of them, that the Civil War, with its naval blockade and mobilization of industry and manpower, was a war of attrition, but they were dedicated to the idea, and therefore committed to the strategy, of a short war and a decisive victory. A war of attrition was precisely what the Germans were anxious to avoid. They might have learned something from the Confederates about conducting a war on two fronts, for such were in effect the operations on each side of the Allegheny Mountains, but the Germans knew very little about the campaigns in the West. Besides, Frederick the Great had also waged war simultaneously on two or more fronts, and his battles were much more suitable garb for German theorists.

Occasionally some German writer would try to fit an isolated battle or campaign of the Civil War into some preconceived theory. (Lee, it was once stated, was actually trying to achieve a Cannae on

[57] *The Conduct of War* (London, 1899), pp. 21, 158.

the second day of Gettysburg.)[58] General Friedrich von Bernhardi more than any other important theorist gave lip service to the lessons of the Civil War. Perhaps his theories on the dismounted use of cavalry and the value of the strategic raid were, in part, the outgrowth of his study of the Civil War—certainly Sheridan and Stuart provided suitable documentation for his theories. But there can be no doubt that Bernhardi, like many other military theorists, selected examples from history that seemed to bolster his own arguments. He was one of the few, for example, who still believed in the feasibility of the frontal attack. Schlieffen and most ranking German military leaders were of the opinion that envelopment rather than frontal assault was the key to modern battle; the much-discussed Schlieffen Plan was their blueprint for victory.

To help prove the validity of his theory, Bernhardi cited the battle of Chattanooga (November 24–25, 1863), where Grant "by a frontal assault successfully pierced the centre of the hostile army. A splendid victory," Bernhardi claimed, "was the result of this ingeniously planned battle." To anyone familiar with the battle of Chattanooga, Bernhardi's interpretation is a travesty. This particular battle was fought under irregular conditions and apparently was not conducted exactly according to Grant's original plan. Grant had intended to attack on both flanks; when these attacks had been blunted, his troops stormed the Confederate center and luckily succeeded in reaching the top of Missionary Ridge. But a theory influenced by this battle rested upon a foundation of sand: Fredericksburg, Gettysburg, Cold Harbor, and Nashville would have led to a different conclusion, and again a phrase from Clausewitz comes to mind: "From this sort of slovenly, frivolous treatment of history, a hundred false views and attempts at the construction of theories arise."[59]

Bernhardi was on firmer ground in his interpretation of Civil War cavalry. Since the death of Von Schmidt in 1875, there had been a decided swing back to shock tactics in the German cavalry. An English officer wrote in 1882 that "the idea of shock action is now dominant" in the German cavalry—"hence the tendency to discourage all dismounted action, and the introduction of the lance as an offensive weapon."[60] By the end of the century the lance had be-

---

58 Von Golsler, "Die Schlacht bei Gettysburg," p. 256.

59 Bernhardi, *On War of Today*, II, 73–74; Clausewitz, *On War*, pp. 112–13.

60 Robert Home, *A Précis of Modern Tactics* (London, 1882), pp. 71–72.

come uniform equipment for all German cavalry. According to one German writer, "its superiority over other weapons when used in pursuit or single combat is generally admitted."[61] Bernhardi took exception to this trend, contradicting his own statement that one should not seek tactical lessons from wars waged before 1866 by asserting that the Civil War was "the most interesting and instructive . . . for the service of modern cavalry." An experienced cavalry officer, Bernhardi thought that cavalry should be taught to fight on foot as well as mounted, following the "brilliant examples" of Stuart and Sheridan. He alone among the Germans placed much emphasis upon the strategic raid, arguing that if modern weapons had limited the tactical action of cavalry, its strategical importance had if anything increased. Departing from the conservative theories embodied in the official Cavalry Regulations, Bernhardi urged his fellow officers to be "neither dazzled nor spellbound by the glamor of a past which can never be recalled. Let us rather turn our eyes towards the dawn . . . [of] a new era of fresh demands, new resources, and wider spheres of action." But his was a solitary voice; by his own admission these views received wider attention abroad than in Germany, where they "remained all but unnoticed until the [First] World War."[62]

The other instructive tactical lesson of the Civil War, the use of spade and ax in conjunction with the rifle, also went unheeded. The intrenchments constructed by the American soldiers as a matter of course reappeared at Plevna in 1877–78, during the Boer War at the turn of the century, and in the Russo-Japanese War. Most German military writers could see the defensive value of intrenchments—they were not blind—but as the need for quick, decisive victory in the event of war became increasingly apparent, less was said about the use of trenches and improvised works except as pivot points for maneuver. M. Bloch, a Polish banker, proved to be more perceptive. Generally credited with being the first to foresee that modern inventions would revolutionize war, he predicted that artillery and machine guns had become "so deadly that flesh and blood must evade them by some means, and would probably take to trenches."[63]

61 Exner, "The German Army," pp. 146–47; Ludwig Renn, *Warfare: The Relation of War to Society* (New York, 1939), pp. 154–55.

62 Bernhardi, *Cavalry in Future Wars* (London, 1909), pp. 38–42, 49–55, 62, 90, 124–69, 248–62; *Cavalry in War and Peace* (London, 1910), pp. 5, 367; *Denkwürdigkeiten aus meinem Leben* (Berlin, 1927), pp. 213–14.

63 Quoted in J. Holland Rose, *The Indecisiveness of Modern War and Other Essays* (London, 1927), p. 34. See also Fuller, *War and Western Civilization*, pp. 161–64; Liddell Hart, *Thoughts on War* (London, 1944), pp. 26, 103; and Hoffman

Curiously enough, it was another civilian who most accurately predicted the warfare of 1914–18 from a study of the Civil War. Karl Bleibtreu, novelist and son of a famous painter, had an abiding interest in military matters. He wrote a series of novels about the Franco-Prussian War, a provocative treatise on tactics and strategy, an imaginative book entitled *Weltbrand*, "a vision of the next world war,"[64] and a history of the American Civil War, which he portrayed as the prototype of wars to come.[65]

Bleibtreu took issue with Freytag-Loringhoven's condemnation of improvised armies. He thought it "inexpressibly funny" that an officer of the General Staff should regard the Civil War as a war of amateurs. "The old lesson that war is the only true *Kriegsschule*—a truth which does not sound pleasantly to standing armies—was manifested also . . . in the war of Secession." The American soldiers had "attained the highest grade of martial perfection"; in marching ability and the handling of weapons, as well as in many technical and engineering skills, they were superior to most regular armies of their day. No professional army, Bleibtreu asserted, could have withstood trial any better than Grant's men in 1864, many of whom were relative newcomers to the ranks.[66] Unlike Freytag-Loringhoven, Bleibtreu was familiar with the writings of G. F. R. Henderson;[67] perhaps his appreciation for the American soldier came originally from this source, for he shared the opinion of those British officers who interpreted the Civil War as proof that in addition to "the small professional army the English Volunteers and Territorials would suffice to ward off the strongest invasion." It was "only a question of time" before similar reserves would be required to supplement the regular armies of the Continental powers as well.[68]

Nickerson, *The Armed Horde, 1793–1939: A Study of the Rise, Survival, and Decline of the Mass Army* (2d ed.; New York, 1942), pp. 231–36. Bloch's sixth and final volume has been translated into English and published under the title *The Future of War* (New York, 1899). It refers only occasionally to the Civil War; Bloch evidently got his ideas from European sources.

[64] Diedrich Diederichsen, "Bleibtreu," *Neue deutsche Biographie* (Berlin, 1955), II, 298. This series of *Schlächtenbüchern* began in 1882 with the publication of *Dies irae*.

[65] *Vor 50 Jahren: Das Volksheer im amerikanischen Bürgerkrieg: Eine Zeitgemässe Historie* (Basel, 1912), pp. vii–ix.

[66] *Ibid.*, pp. 3, 193, 202–12 *passim*.

[67] No other German writer listed Henderson's books as a source, although they used the *Official Records* occasionally and even were acquainted with the works of the American novelist John Esten Cooke. For the most part they were dependent upon the writings of Scheibert, Von Borcke, Mangold, Sander, and a smattering of American sources. The Comte de Paris and DeChenal are also quoted sparingly.

[68] *Vor 50 Jahren*, p. 221.

Not only would the war of the future be fought by armies numbering millions; modern firepower would force the armies to disperse and intrench in order to survive. "Lee's trenches, running for many miles along the river banks or through the forests, anticipate . . . what can well make its appearance in the war of the future." Civil War cavalry, "a true model for that arm under present conditions," had also learned to respect firepower. "Exemplary" in reconnaissance and screening, "extremely active" in the attack, the American mounted infantry had succeeded in fighting on foot "without losing the true character of cavalry."[69]

Thus the Civil War appeared to foreshadow the character of the next European war. Whole populations under arms, the duration and fierceness of the conflict, and the lines of trenches that ran unbroken from the Swiss Alps to the English Channel must have given Bleibtreu moments of grim satisfaction. In light of the events of 1914–18, he alone among the Germans who had studied the Civil War had learned the important lessons.

[69] *Ibid.*, pp. 210–12; *Zur Geschichte der Taktik und Strategie* (Berlin, 1901), p. 70.

7

The View from France
1861-1914

In England the Civil War had captured the attention of Hamley, Chesney, and other distinguished military writers as early as 1863; soon afterward in Prussia it had been studied by Stosch and others of the General Staff. In France, however, the Civil War was virtually ignored at the time by soldiers and military writers alike. When it appeared that the French intervention in Mexico might lead to war with the victorious North, the reports of Guzman and DeChenal were analyzed and brought up to date, but the need for an intelligence estimate of the United States Army quickly passed, and little interest was shown in the Civil War for the next decade. As the guns quieted along the Potomac, ominous sounds came from beyond the Rhine; and in the search for a weapon to meet the Prussian needle gun and the watered-down attempts to reorganize the army in order to redress the shifting balance of military power, French soldiers turned their backs on the Atlantic and the strange war that had just ended three thousand miles away.

From the contents of the reports submitted by DeChenal and Guzman, it is apparent that the French authorities were predominantly interested in the organization and administration of the Union forces. This is indicated also by a lengthy study written in 1862 and entitled *Constitution et organisation de l'armée des États-Unis*. La Frustron described in detail the Articles of War of the United States Army, the functions of the Secretary of War, the price of uniforms, the pay of officers, even the daily rations of the private soldier.[1] Replete with elaborate charts and tables of statistics,

[1] Fr. de la Frustron, *Constitution et organisation de l'armée des États-Unis de l'Amérique septentrionale* (Paris, 1863), pp. 79–115 *passim*. This work appeared originally under the same title in the *Journal des sciences militaires*, Vols. VI–IX. La Frustron also wrote "Coup d'œil sur la guerre de l'Amérique septentrionale," *ibid.*, VIII (1862), 132–53, 479–97; IX (1863), 442–62; "Notice historique sur la guerre d'Amérique en 1863," *Le spectateur militaire*, XLVI (May, 1864), 195–206. These writings were of a general nature and contain no additional information on the organization and tactics of the American armies.

this work was intended to give French officers a general understanding of the Union army. It was based almost exclusively upon outdated sources and contained little information on the United States Army after 1861. La Frustron was not interested in tactics or strategy. Perhaps the war was too young for him to generalize on these subjects; possibly he dismissed them because he felt no need to study them. The infantry manuals, both North and South, had been "faithfully copied" from the French regulations; the mounted infantry had clear antecedents in the dragoons and light cavalry that had fought Indians on the western plains; and there seemed to be little in the use of either arm that could be applied in France.[2]

In 1865 the French Minister of War requested a professor of military administration at the Staff School to prepare a study of the American army based upon the official reports submitted by De-Chenal and Guzman. Writing with an eye to possible events in the future, Vigo Roussillon dutifully covered all the information available on the Civil War: he combed the reports of the French military observers, the writings of De Joinville, Lecomte, and others who had visited America, even congressional reports and pertinent American books.[3] The result of his painstaking research was a balanced and impressive study of the Union army, its organization and administration, problems in recruitment and discipline, and the personnel and function of the various army departments. He discussed clothing, encampments, soldiers' pay, remounts, military transport, hospitals, ambulances, army barracks—anything, in fact, that would help to explain the Union army's successes or failures in the recent war.

Like most French soldiers of his day,[4] Vigo Roussillon was concerned primarily with military organization and administration. Of the major departments in the Union army, he was most favorably impressed by the signal corps, which had "rendered excellent service" in the use of the field telegraph, captive balloons, and photography. He thought less of the medical corps than did most of his

---

[2] *Constitution et organisation de l'armée des États-Unis*, pp. 163–65. La Frustron seemed to think well of the Civil War cavalry. He noted especially the advantages of the Sharp's rifle and the Colt revolver, the latter arm being, in his view, "the favorite and perhaps the most powerful arm of the cavalry" (*ibid.*, pp. 165–66, 171, 189).

[3] F. P. Vigo Roussillon, *Puissance militaire des États-Unis d'Amérique d'après la guerre de la sécession, 1861–1865* (Paris, 1866), pp. v, 3–4, 24–25, 161, 261–62, 286.

[4] Dallas D. Irvine, "The French Discovery of Clausewitz and Napoleon," *Studies on War: A Military Affairs Reader* (Washington, 1943), p. 23.

contemporaries, and he found fault with the organization of the quartermaster corps. Insofar as organization and military spirit were concerned, Vigo Roussillon rated his own army superior to that of the United States in every respect. The American system was outdated and wasteful of both men and resources.[5]

This did not mean that nothing was to be learned from the Civil War. The Americans, Vigo Roussillon pointed out, had experimented with many European inventions that were still not fully developed. Taking these and adding new wrinkles of their own, they had made great strides in weapons, military transport, signal and engineering devices, developments which "could have a positive interest for the European armies." Vigo Roussillon recommended the adoption of certain "interesting accessories" such as the McClellan saddle, the camp latrine, and the quartermaster's wagon, and he praised the services of transport and supply, which had functioned "in the most remarkable manner."[6] He especially admired Sherman, whose Atlanta campaign showed what could be accomplished with only one single-track railroad as a line of supply, and he cited numerous examples of important services rendered by the fleet in provisioning as well as providing tactical support to land forces.[7]

A proponent of the long-term professional army, Vigo Roussillon found fault with the American military system. He did not believe that a small regular army swollen by volunteers and militia, most of them untrained, would be adequate in times of emergency. The American militia had not been an efficient military organization, having had no real military instruction prior to the war, and many units were organized on paper only; consequently, the Americans had entered war without sufficient reserves and were dependent upon untrained volunteers to fill the ranks. The French military observers had presented convincing evidence that by 1864 these once undisciplined mobs had, despite poor recruiting practices, become formidable fighting organizations.[8] Isolated and having no powerful neighbors, the United States perhaps could afford such a system, but Vigo Roussillon contended that it would not suit the needs of a Continental power, where time was a vital factor. And

---

[5] *Puissance militaire des États-Unis*, pp. 68–94 *passim*, 284–85, 399, 434.

[6] *Ibid.*, pp. 24, 406–10. This quartermaster's wagon had seen limited service with the French Expeditionary Force in Mexico, and the reports from there had been equally favorable (*ibid.*, pp. 190–95).

[7] *Ibid.*, pp. 63, 157–88, 309, 411.   [8] *Ibid.*, pp. vii, 53–66, 286.

even if the American army had become for all practical purposes "professional" after three years of hard knocks in the rough school of war, it was still, in his opinion, inferior to the French army, which maintained permanent cadres and a trained reserve. The Americans, after all, had had only each other to contend with; they did not have to face anything remotely resembling that army standing poised on the east bank of the Rhine.[9]

As for the tactics of the American armies, Vigo Roussillon recognized that modern firepower had altered the capabilities of at least one of the three arms. No longer could cavalry employ shock tactics against infantry save in exceptional circumstances; henceforth the tactical value of cavalry "appears reduced to combat with other cavalry." But if the tactical value of cavalry had diminished with the introduction of the breechloader, its strategical value had increased with the advent of the railroad, which was highly vulnerable to destructive raids. Because the next European war would likely be fought under conditions somewhat similar to those of the Civil War, Vigo Roussillon believed that the experiences of the American cavalry could lead "to some useful applications," particularly in the attack and defense of railroads. He also maintained that cavalry could still perform valuable services in reconnaissance, foraging, and escort duties.[10]

Like Lecomte, DeChenal, and Von Meerheimb, Vigo Roussillon grasped the real significance of the Civil War. It was not merely a contest between amateur armies; it was a major war of almost unprecedented dimensions, fought under conditions which, however peculiar to America, were nonetheless bound to exert some influence upon the character of future wars in Europe. The Civil War was the first of the modern wars insofar as equipment and military technology were concerned. From the outcome it was evident that the United States could become a "very formidable military and especially a naval power."[11]

Most French soldiers agreed with Vigo Roussillon's basic interpretations of the military lessons of the Civil War. General Joachim Ambert, whose interest in the Civil War was accentuated by large investments owned by the family in Louisiana, likewise condemned the militia and volunteers of 1861. Ambert interpreted war news from America as proof of the advantages of permanent over impro-

[9] *Ibid.*, pp. 383–85, 392–93.

[10] *Ibid.*, pp. 125, 139–40, 159, 316, 388, 400–401.   [11] *Ibid.*, p. 373.

vised armies.[12] Lieutenant Colonel de Coynart, a retired officer and frequent contributor to military journals, was another professional soldier who questioned the worth of improvised armies. Such soldiers tended to shy away from the offensive and were less likely than regular troops to exploit a tactical success. True, the American armies eventually had achieved some remarkable results, but the military system of the United States was "too expensive" to be practical in the conditions then existing in Europe.[13] Most French soldiers, in fact, were convinced of the virtues of a long-service army. One of the reasons they were shocked by the Prussian victory of 1866 was that they had been taught that the German army, composed of short-term conscripts, "was by definition deficient in military spirit and, hence, in fighting ability."[14] In their view, the Civil War armies were too unwieldy, too undisciplined. "Discipline cannot be secured or created in a day," wrote Ardant du Picq, a young theorist who fell in 1870 but whose ideas later were to have a profound influence upon French military thought. "It is an institution, a tradition."

The Americans have shown us what happens in modern battle to large armies without cohesion. With them the lack of discipline and organization has had the inevitable result. Battle has been between hidden skirmishers, at long distance, and has lasted for days, until some faulty movement, perhaps a moral exhaustion, has caused one or the other of the opposing forces to give way. In this American War, the mêlées of Agincourt are said to have reappeared, which merely means a mêlée of fugitives. But less than ever has there been close combat.[15]

There were also many who shared Vigo Roussillon's opinions about American cavalry. Coynart noted that in the Civil War the horse had been used essentially to shift mounted infantry to "a menaced point": the Americans had "invented a new species of dragoon."[16] According to another writer, the long range of fire-

12 J. de la Faye, *Le général Ambert: Sa vie et ses œuvres* (Paris, n.d.), p. 223; Ambert's article entitled "Permanent and Improvised Armies," which appeared in the June 1, 1864, issue of the *Moniteur de l'armée*, is summarized in the *Army and Navy Journal*, June 25, 1864.

13 Lieutenant Colonel E. de Coynart, *Précis de la guerre des États-Unis d'Amérique* (Paris, 1867), pp. 5–6, 99, 180, 210, 344. Coynart's views are inferred rather than stated specifically.

14 Richard D. Challener, *The French Theory of the Nation in Arms, 1866–1929* (New York, 1955), p. 15.

15 Colonel Ardant du Picq, *Battle Studies: Ancient and Modern Battle* (Harrisburg, 1947), pp. 111–12.

16 *Précis de la guerre*, p. 156.

arms, railroads, and the telegraph had combined to alter the tactics of cavalry and at the same time to increase its strategic importance. While cavalry could no longer charge en masse and ride down opposing infantry, it could now fulfil the more valuable service of destroying enemy communications and lines of supply.[17] Several French writers showed especial interest in the strategic cavalry raid: one suggested to his fellow officers that they "read and ponder the works that discuss this matter, and especially what has been written on the war of Secession, in which the Americans have employed this kind of tactic on a very large scale, with much success." Another cited the Civil War raids to show what could still be accomplished by way of seizing enemy convoys, destroying vital railroads, and cutting telegraphic lines. In Europe, "populated, cultivated and civilized as it is," it might not be possible to emulate the raids of Stuart, Stoneman, Sheridan, and Morgan, but this did not mean that independent cavalry could not perform many useful strategic services in future wars.[18]

Occasionally some writer would mention other lessons of the Civil War. Gillmore's *Engineer and Artillery Operations against the Defences of Charleston Harbor* was well publicized in France and prompted other writings on the subject.[19] French writers differed little from their German contemporaries in their evaluation of the power of rifled artillery. "A. F.," to cite one example, wrote that earthworks had held up better under heavy bombardment than forts constructed of masonry: "The old principle, that permanent works can not resist indefinitely a properly led attack by land, but that they can still hold their own against ships and even be superior, is still applicable today." He predicted that defenses would soon catch up with the power of the new artillery: "In theory there is no limit, and in practice there is none other than the consideration of

17 M. A. Brulin, "Étude sur la cavalerie légère:—Partisans," *Le spectateur militaire*, O.S. XLI (March, 1863), 382. Brulin wanted the creation of French cavalry similar to that led by Morgan and Stuart, and to that end he urged lighter equipment for cavalry and a greater dependence upon the revolver. "We must now have light cavalry, capable of fighting as well on foot as on horse, I would even say, better on foot than mounted."

18 E. Erdnegle, "La cavalerie en présence des nouvelles armes à feu," *ibid.*, N.S. XIV (October–December, 1868), 6–7; L. Adé, "De l'emploi de la instruction de la cavalerie," *ibid.*, XVI (April–June, 1869), 58, 374.

19 See "Explosion des canons Parrot," *Journal des sciences militaire*, XVII (1865), 396–450; and "Les deux expéditions contre le fort Fisher . . ." *ibid.*, XVIII (1865), 161–240. Other selections from Gillmore's reports can be found in *ibid.*, XVI (1864), 420–22; XVII (1865), 132–40, 223–67.

expense, to the strength of armor plate destined for forts and land batteries." On the other hand, "the weight and force of armored plates used on ships has a theoretical and practical limit that we have perhaps already reached today."[20] In the main, however, there was considerably less interest in coast defense and related problems in France than in either England or Prussia.

A few French soldiers became interested in the use of railroads during the Civil War. In 1869 Coynart, writing of the Construction Corps in the Union army, thought it significant that in Europe "the organization of such a corps is the order of the day . . . [and] is all but achieved in Prussia."

If one bears in mind the nature of the operations executed by the American Federal troops before Richmond and Petersburg in 1864 and 1865, he will attribute to the railroads an absolute preponderance on the actions of the war, because these operations have had for their principal object the conquest of railroads coming in from the South, in order to occupy or destroy them.

Railways, he predicted, "will play a great part in the wars to come."[21] Another writer went so far as to state that the history of the Civil War "lies completely in those works accomplished by the Railroad division." Pointing to the accomplishments of the Construction Corps, he emphasized the fact that Prussia was benefiting from the experiences of the Americans and urged the prompt creation of a similar body in France.[22] These warnings went unheeded, however, and France went to war in 1870 with her military railroads still governed by regulations adopted as far back as 1851 and 1855. When in 1875 Field Railway Sections and Railway Troops were created to construct, repair, destroy, or operate railroads in war, France modeled this organization after the German *Feldeisenbahnabteilung*, just as the Germans a decade earlier had followed the example of the United States.[23]

Nor did the French take advantage of the tactical lessons of the Civil War. French infantry marched into battle in 1870 trained according to the infantry regulations of 1862, which have been de-

[20] A. F., "L'artillerie rayée au siège de Charleston," *Le spectateur militaire*, VII (January–March, 1867), 179–80.

[21] E. de Coynart, "Les places fortes et les chemins de fer," *Le spectateur militaire*, XVIII (October–December, 1869), 350–51.

[22] *Le spectateur militaire*, XVIII, 231–33, 237–39, 252–53, 260.

[23] Edwin A. Pratt, *The Rise of Rail-Power in War and Conquest, 1833–1914* (London, 1915), pp. 138, 152–53.

scribed as a "faithful reproduction" of the regulations of 1831 varying little in spirit from the Ordinance of 1791, and French cavalry in 1870 was guided by regulations compiled more than forty years earlier.[24] It has been asserted that the Emperor Napoleon III, "having a deep conviction of the utility of hasty intrenchments, ordered a trial of them to be made at the camp of Châlons." Supposedly two Civil War generals had convinced him of the importance of intrenchments, but there is no evidence to confirm this story.[25] Marshal Bazaine, who commanded the expeditionary force in Mexico and who, within a few years, was to surrender an army at Metz, was also supposed to have grasped the importance of shelter trenches from the American campaigns. Bazaine had in fact been closer to the Civil War than most French officials, and it is quite possible that he did learn what was, according to his biographer, "its chief military lesson,"[26] but this, too, is largely a matter of conjecture. The fact remains that no tactical lesson of the Civil War penetrated official doctrine.

It is curious that the French, whose observers had supplied solid information about the armies that fought the Civil War, should ignore the military lessons of that conflict. There are probably several reasons for this neglect. First, it is significant that no prominent French soldier wrote about the Civil War or even demonstrated an interest in it before 1870. Most of them probably agreed with General Trochu, who admitted that while the American campaigns

---

[24] Commandant le Thiry, *Histoire de la tactique de l'infanterie française de 1791 à 1905* (Paris, 1905), pp. 1–2, 12; Major G. T. M. Bridges, "The French Cavalry School," *Cavalry Journal*, III (July, 1905), 301; Colonel T. Bonie, *Étude sur le combat à pied de la cavalerie* (Paris, 1877), p. 150.

[25] Alexis Henri Brialmont, *Hasty Entrenchments* (London, 1872), p. 12; G. F. R. Henderson, *The Battle of Spicheren: A Study in Practical Tactics and War Training* (2d ed.; Aldershot, 1909), p. 27. Lieutenant General John M. Schofield and former Confederate General P. G. T. Beauregard are the persons mentioned in connection with this episode. Schofield did visit France late in 1865 but was never granted an interview with the emperor. He did, however, meet several times with the Prince Napoleon and various high-ranking army officials, and his host during his stay in France was the same Captain Guzman who had accompanied DeChenal to America. Schofield was sent to France "to make known . . . the views and purposes of the government and people of the United States in respect to Mexican affairs" (John M. Schofield, *Forty-six Years in the Army* [New York, 1897], pp. 388, 392). Beauregard visited France the following year on business. It was rumored that he sought an interview with Napoleon III "so that he could tell him about the latest advances in the use of naval mines and small arms." More probably he was interested in obtaining a commission in the French army (T. Harry Williams, *P. G. T. Beauregard, Napoleon in Grey* [Baton Rouge, 1954], pp. 262–63).

[26] Phillip Guedalla, *The Two Marshals: Bazaine–Pétain* (New York, 1943), p. 130.

were "very striking," they had nevertheless occurred "at a distance and in the midst of special circumstances, where the element of the unknown was too great to enable us to judge well."[27] Had there been someone in France of the stature of Hamley and Chesney in England, or had several officers of the General Staff written about individual Civil War campaigns as they did in Prussia, perhaps more junior officers in France would have developed an interest in the subject. It must also be remembered that Vigo Roussillon, whose study was the most influential of all French books on the Civil War, had concluded that the French army was superior to that of the United States in nearly every respect. While appreciating many things about the Civil War, he had actually found little to recommend for adoption in the French army, which before 1866 remained imperturbably complacent.

Prussia's victory at Sadowa soon caused all eyes to turn nervously to the Rhine and led directly to a series of military reforms. A breech-loading rifle was adopted, new siege artillery added, the military transport system improved, and in 1868 legislation enacted which, if implemented, would have brought about a drastic reorganization of the army itself.[28] But it was too little, too late. When war came, France discovered that her army was no match for the Prussians.

French military leaders reacted sharply to the defeats of 1870–71. After this convincing proof that an army composed of short-term conscripts and large reserves need not sacrifice quality for quantity, France set about to create a new army, remodeled—like every major army in Europe save that of England—"along lines roughly paralleling the German system of compulsory military service" and schooled in the tactics of the recent battles. In 1872, legislation was passed creating an army based upon obligatory military service; between 1873 and 1875 further laws were enacted dealing with organization and recruitment,[29] while in the army itself an intellectual movement sharpened interest in the study of military subjects. In October, 1871, less than six months after the Treaty of Frankfort was signed (May 10, 1871), the French War Ministry founded the *Revue militaire de l'étranger*, soon to become one of the most im-

[27] *L'armée française en 1867* (2d ed.; Paris, 1870), pp. 6–7.

[28] General Thoumas, *Les transformations de l'armée française: Essais d'histoire et de critique sur l'état militaire de la France* (Paris, 1887), I, 24; II, 98, 225, 230. See also Challener, *The French Theory of the Nation in Arms*, pp. 10–27.

[29] *Ibid.*, pp. 33–45, 48.

portant of all European military journals. The Réunion des Officiers was formed to stimulate more serious interest in military affairs; many noteworthy papers, among them the notes of Ardant du Picq, were published in the *Bulletin* of this society.[30] In 1878 the École Militaire Supérieure was established, becoming the École Supérieure de Guerre in 1880—the same year that the General Staff was overhauled. The tactical regulations of 1875 and 1876 incorporated some of the lessons of 1870 for infantry and cavalry, respectively, and revealed a new awareness of the firepower of modern weapons.[31] It was a different army, with a new outlook.

Gone were the days when Ardant du Picq had to abandon the publication of his *Studies on War*, when Trochu aroused the angry astonishment of the High Command by the publication of some observations on military institutions, or when MacMahon declared: "I shall remove from the promotion list any officer whose name I have read on the cover of a book."

Thanks to a new group of military writers, "the events of recent wars, technical and tactical problems were enthusiastically studied and discussed" both within the army and without.[32]

This activity naturally was dedicated to an examination of the causes for failure in the late war. French officers refought the battles of 1870, studied the campaigns of the war, analyzed Moltke's strategy and the tactics of his armies, and sought to familiarize themselves with the German philosophy of war. In the 1880's they became acquainted with the writings of Clausewitz, which in turn led to a re-examination of the Napoleonic wars, the source of many of Clausewitz's ideas.[33] As in England, the German victories eclipsed for a decade the war that had been fought across the Atlantic. French soldiers wrote with serious purpose: the key to future victories obviously was to be found in the war that had just been concluded, and it was an inaudible voice that urged the Minister of War to sponsor

[30] Maréchal Franchet d'Esperey, "Du Directoire à la guerre de 1914," in Gabriel Hanotaux (ed.), *Histoire de la nation française*, Vol. VIII: *Histoire militaire et navale* (Paris, 1927), p. 439; Colonel John Frederick Maurice, *War* (London, 1891), p. 113; Irvine, "French Discovery of Clausewitz and Napoleon," pp. 23-25.

[31] Thoumas, *Les transformations de l'armée française*, I, 204-26 *passim*; II, 460-65, 498-506; Thiry, *Histoire de la tactique de l'infanterie française*, p. 15; Commandant J. Colin, *The Transformations of War* (London, 1912), pp. 41-42.

[32] Charles de Gaulle, *France and Her Army* (London, n.d.), pp. 78-79.

[33] Irvine, "The French Discovery of Clausewitz and Napoleon," pp. 28-32.

a work which would be so very useful to the army in calling its attention to the immense progress accomplished by the Americans, especially in improvised fortifications, which would destroy numerous legends still in vogue, even within the ranks of the army, and . . . would describe all of the machinery . . . that constitutes the mechanism of an army. Why doesn't the Second Bureau of the General Staff attempt this task?[34]

The voice was that of P. Poullet, a frequent contributor to military magazines. In a lengthy review article of recent Civil War books, notably the early volumes of the Comte de Paris' *History of the Civil War in America*, Poullet explained why he believed the American campaigns should not be ignored. The Americans, he pointed out, had had four years in which to develop special techniques. He reminded his readers that the Germans, for all their recent successes, were still studying the operation of railroads during the Civil War in the school for engineers at Berlin. He was struck by the "practical character" of the instruction at West Point, particularly in the field of military engineering, where the Americans "had shown themselves to be our masters."[35]

Poullet regarded the widespread use of field fortifications and mounted infantry as the most significant tactical developments of the Civil War. To those who maintained that the use of cover would be likely to damage the "natural élan" of the French soldier, Poullet argued that, on the contrary, the use of trenches could enable a general to withhold substantial reserves until the time had arrived to deliver a counterattack. To those who professed the belief that the importance of cavalry had decreased with the general introduction of the quick-firing rifle, Poullet pointed out that whenever Lee had been without his cavalry, he had usually "found himself in the greatest difficulty." Asserting that the French cavalry in 1870 had often been inept both in fighting and in reconnaissance, particularly in wooded areas, he emphasized the success of Civil War cavalry under comparable conditions. Cavalry in the future, he predicted, would have two primary functions: reconnaissance and independent action against enemy communications and supplies. Because of the repeating rifle, "the arm of the future," the American cavalry had performed well in both tasks, and Poullet urged the formation in France of cavalry fashioned after the "legendary dragoon" that had been "dreamed of but not realized" until the Civil

[34] P. Poullet, "Les enseignements de la guerre d'Amérique," *Le spectateur militaire*, 3d ser., XXXIX (April–June, 1875), 464.

[35] *Ibid.*, XL (July–September, 1875), 387–93; XLI (October–December, 1875), 83–89.

War. If the French were to eliminate all superfluous instruction and parade-ground drill, they, too, might be able to produce what most cavalrymen still regarded as a myth—a dragoon who could fight equally well on foot and on horse, equipped to perform whatever task was necessary to the fulfilment of his mission. Poullet, for one, felt that the Civil War could not "be too closely studied."[36]

Similar convictions were expressed a few years later by Lieutenant Colonel Frédéric Canonge in a survey of military campaigns from 1854 to 1871. Alloting the Civil War an appropriate place in his general work, Canonge claimed that it was a "fertile mine" of information, "disdained by some, unknown by most," but nonetheless deserving of study. Because of the "variety and extent of the resources employed . . . the special character of the battles fought; the new employment of cavalry and railroads . . . [and] of improvised fortifications," the Civil War contained information "which can be neither ignored nor disregarded." Furthermore, because it had been fought under unique conditions, it afforded a fine opportunity to determine whether the general principles of war would remain valid under all circumstances.[37]

The Civil War also offered a good opportunity to gain insight into some of the problems of modern war. In the military use of railroads, for example, several principles had become apparent. To defend a railroad line adequately, it was necessary to fortify and occupy all important points along the line. To keep the line in good repair, it was desirable to establish large and readily available depots of materials for the construction corps. To destroy a railroad line, it was essential for raiding cavalry to tear up long stretches of track, or else the line would be only temporarily out of commission.[38]

Canonge did not attach much value to the tactical lessons of the war—the campaigns of 1866 and 1870–71 spoke with greater authority. He could detect nothing fundamentally new in the handling of infantry or artillery, but he did comment upon the use of intrenchments, claiming that they had given confidence to inexperienced troops and had served to compensate for inferior numbers; in this regard Fredericksburg was "certainly one of the most remarkable defensive battles ever fought," for it illustrated the value

36 Ibid., XL, 406–18; "Le général Lee: Sa vie et ses campagnes," ibid., XXXIX, 152–56.

37 Frédéric Canonge, Histoire militaire contemporaine, 1854–65 (Paris, 1882), I, 209–10, 291–94.

38 Ibid., p. 299.

of preparing the terrain and the impossibility of even good infantry carrying a position thus strengthened.[39]

Canonge's most interesting remarks concern cavalry, for he interpreted the Civil War as proof of what cavalry could accomplish in the new era of rapid-fire, precision weapons. He approved of dismounted tactics on occasion, but his preference was for the *arme blanche*. In America, he contended, unique terrain had placed a false premium on the rifle. But Canonge realized that modern weapons had limited the tactical action of cavalry, and he entertained no glamorous notion of the thundering cavalry charges that had often won the day for Frederick the Great and Napoleon. Every time that cavalry had been thrown against infantry in the Franco-Prussian War it had failed. Canonge expected cavalry to re-establish itself by accomplishing more than it had done previously in other duties such as reconnaissance, and because of the growing dependence of modern armies upon railroads, he believed that Sheridan's and Stuart's raids provided "remarkable models to imitate."[40] Thus Canonge was one of the first to sense the possibilities of the strategic cavalry raid in Europe. Support for his views was soon forthcoming.

In the 1880's French soldiers began to take a lively interest in the cavalry of the Civil War.[41] The reasons are not altogether clear, but the inadequacies of the French cavalry in 1870 must have provided a strong motive. Trained according to outmoded regulations, to which had been added a few wrinkles suggested from experiences in Algeria, the French in 1870-71 had been decidedly inferior to the Prussian cavalry. Immediately following the war, a commission had been established to study the cavalry question, but the resulting Regulations of 1876 were revised periodically until the end of the century, and the fundamental tactical issue remained unsettled. Some maintained that the old-style charge was still feasible, others that the *arme blanche* would have to yield to the rifle. The regulations of 1876 prescribed shock tactics as "essential conditions for success,"[42] but many continued to believe in the future of dismounted tactics.

[39] *Ibid.*, pp. 210, 239, 294-97.   [40] *Ibid.*, I, 295-96; II, 488.

[41] This interest is even indicated in Ernest Grasset's purely descriptive history of the Civil War. While refusing to pass judgment on the merits of mounted infantry, Grasset was favorably impressed by the Civil War cavalry raids, and he accused the Germans of borrowing this feature from the Americans in 1870 (Ernest Grasset, *La guerre de la sécession, 1861-65* [Paris, 1886-87], I, 273-74, 276-80).

[42] Colonel George T. Denison, *A History of Cavalry from the Earliest Times with Lessons for the Future* (2d ed.; London, 1913), pp. 402-14; Commandant Gérôme,

Colonel T. Bonie was one of these. He maintained that cavalry must be able to fight dismounted to hold its place on the modern battlefield. "Cavalry that cannot fight on foot as well as on horse," he insisted, "is backward cavalry, unequal to its mission and fatally dedicated to defeat." Bonie did not arrive at this conclusion by his study of the Civil War alone, for his book commenced with the Greeks and treated the American campaigns as but one phase in the evolution of cavalry. Nevertheless, it was the Civil War that had convinced him of the need for further emphasis on dismounted tactics. Long-range weapons had enabled the other arms to progress rapidly; "must cavalry alone," he asked, "be overlooked by this evolution and remain content with the power possessed by the horse?"[43] Bonie hoped fervently that it would not.

More emphatic still was the author of a provocative article on Civil War cavalry raids that appeared in the *Revue militaire de l'étranger*. This anonymous writer was "absolutely convinced that in combat, cavalry acting as cavalry, that is to say on horse, is today without effect against infantry." Even in instances when cavalry opposed cavalry, the revolver was superior to the saber. As evidence he cited the official statistics of the German Medical Corps: of better than 65,000 Germans killed or wounded in 1870–71, the saber had accounted for only 212 wounded and 6 dead. By contrast he mentioned a brief skirmish in 1864 between two squadrons of Civil War cavalry in which one side alone lost 36 of 100 effectives, most of them casualties of small-arms fire.[44] Better informed on the details of the Civil War campaigns than Bonie, who derived most of his information from Lecomte's book, this writer concentrated on the tactics of mounted infantry as applied to raids, particularly in the West.[45] He claimed that the Civil War was the first modern war in

---

Essai historique sur la tactique de la cavalerie (Paris [1896]), pp. 296–361, 386. For a useful discussion of the cavalry question in France after 1870, see Thoumas, *Les transformations de l'armée française*, II, 498–506.

43 Colonel T. Bonie, *Étude sur le combat à pied de la cavalerie* (Paris, 1877), pp. 36–37, 40–41, 165 ff.

44 F., "Les raids aux États-Unis," *Revue militaire de l'étranger*, No. 530 (July 1, 1881), pp. 9–10.

45 "F." distinguished between the Confederate cavalry of Jeb Stuart, a West Pointer, and the so-called mounted infantry of Morgan and Forrest, an interpretation that can be traced to Denison's *History of Cavalry*. He also made a somewhat similar distinction between Stuart's cavalry and that led by Sheridan, which possibly shows the influence of Scheibert and Von Borcke ("Les raids aux États-Unis," pp. 7, 10).

which mounted infantry predominated, and while he did not necessarily advocate a complete change to mounted infantry in Europe, he nevertheless was of the opinion that

if it is still impossible to agree with General Sheridan and other distinguished officers of the New World that "the *arme blanche* has had its day," it is however necessary . . . to issue to all cavalry a revolver along with a long-range carbine . . . and to dress the cavalryman in such a fashion that, being as free in his movements on foot as an infantryman, he can at the very least perform the role of infantry when the occasion presents itself.

And this, he speculated, "will be often, perhaps, in the next war."[46]

This article prompted another study of Confederate cavalry in the West. Writing about Forrest, Pierre Lehautcourt likewise stressed the fact that Forrest's cavalry had generally fought dismounted and had preferred the revolver to the saber even when in the saddle, but he saw less merit in these tactics than had preceding writers. Mounted infantry, he explained, was really the natural offspring of rough terrain and improvised cavalry consisting of men who already knew how to ride and shoot:

The frequent use of dismounted fighting and the suppression of the *arme blanche* are today considered as heresies, doubtless with good reason. . . . Raids such as the Americans put into practice would be difficult to execute in those theatres of operations in western Europe where our cavalry will in all probability be called upon to operate in the future.[47]

Lehautcourt may have admired Forrest as a leader of cavalry, but he was no proponent of the mounted infantry doctrine.

A more balanced view is found in the writings of General Jules Louis Lewal. Chief of the historical statistical bureau, organizer of the École Militaire Supérieure, prolific and influential student of war, Lewal was reputedly "one of the most brilliant staff officers in the French army,"[48] and in his numerous books on tactics and strategy he displays substantial knowledge of Civil War cavalry.

Lewal distinguished between the troops of Forrest and Morgan and those led by Stuart. The former, indeed the greater part of all Civil War cavalry, he considered mounted infantry. On the other hand, Stuart, while he eventually had renounced the saber, a "cum-

---

[46] *Ibid.*, p. 11.

[47] Pierre Lehautcourt, "Le général Forrest," *Revue de cavalerie*, XVI (October, 1892–March, 1893), 257.

[48] Irvine, "The French Discovery of Clausewitz and Napoleon," p. 23; D'Esperey, "Du Directoire à la guerre de 1914," p. 484.

bersome instrument," in favor of the carbine, had usually fought his command mounted and so had fulfilled the functions of regular cavalry. Lewal thought that there was use for hybrid cavalry of the type bred in America. Sheridan's campaigns had demonstrated the versatility of such a force—his men had been known even to attack intrenchments. Mounted infantry could be transferred from one location to another swiftly and on occasion could supplement the regular cavalry. Above all, American cavalry leaders had been able to utilize firepower without sacrificing mobility. Lewal, however, was by no stretch of the imagination a champion of mounted infantry; he much preferred regular cavalry to any other, and he advocated dismounted tactics only when other means were inadequate to the occasion. He regarded the strategic raid as a legitimate function of cavalry provided it was not carried to excess and was executed by moderate numbers of regular cavalry rather than partisans. Stuart and Sheridan were the leaders to study, and Lewal hoped, in fact believed, that in the future French cavalry "will find occasion to be inspired by the examples of the Americans."[49]

At the cavalry school in Saumur, Major L. Picard, professor and prolific writer, also studied the Civil War cavalry.[50] At first Picard had reservations about the American hybrid, believing, like Lehautcourt, that because cavalry was more difficult than the other arms to improvise, the Americans—particularly the Union forces—had been forced to resort to dismounted tactics. Given the "special conditions" that existed in America, he did not wonder that the Civil War cavalry had preferred dismounted tactics to the *arme blanche*. Picard did not disapprove of mounted infantry, but he thought that its importance had been overrated and that, with the conditions then prevailing in Europe, it "would be reduced to nothing." This was not necessarily true of the raid, which Picard thought could have succeeded in 1870 and might still be used in Europe. Picard was not

---

[49] General Lewal, *Études de guerre: Tactique des renseignements* (Paris, 1883), II, 61, 66, 70–71, 107, 137, 158, 166, 184, 358; *Strategie de combat* (Paris, 1896), II, 71, 73, 142.

[50] Although the emphasis was upon cavalry, Picard wrote of other aspects of the Civil War as well. He comprehended the special problems in logistics and their effect upon strategy; he respected the ingenuity and energy of the American people; and he thought well of the technical services that had exploited the military possibilities of the railroad and telegraph. Like most European officers, he criticized the Civil War armies for their lack of anything resembling a general staff, and he regarded the war as the best proof of the need for a nation to maintain an adequate standing army. Cf. L. Picard, *Leçons d'histoire et de géographie militaire* (Saumur, 1887), I, 147–49, 169, 251–59.

one of those "enthusiastic partisans" in the 1880's who advocated the suppression of cavalry in favor of mounted infantry.[51] Actually, his original views did not differ greatly from official doctrine, for although the cavalry regulations of 1882 were revised in 1899 "because of the progress realized in the construction of firearms" to place greater emphasis upon dismounted tactics, still the *arme blanche* was regarded as the "principal mode of action."[52]

The Boer War caused many to change their views. According to an English war correspondent,

the cavalryman in South Africa has been deprived of much of the brilliancy and picturesqueness which were invariably his on previous battlegrounds. He has not been able to rejoice in the tumult of the charge, to over-ride in close-knit masses the opposing squadrons of his enemy, to thunder with loose rein and bloody spur upon disorganised and shaken infantry, nor to descend like a thunderbolt upon his foeman's guns, and sweep triumphantly through disordered ranks. The only part of the recognised duty of the horseman which has fallen to his lot has been . . . reconnaissance . . . the extended patrol and . . . the swift and hazardous flank movements. . . . On the battle-field itself he has ordinarily fought on foot. . . . We began to perceive that the mounted rifleman of the veldt, simple farmer though he might be, was in reality a formidable enemy, and that he could be met and defeated only by troops able to move with equal rapidity [and] to fire with equal accuracy.[53]

While most cavalrymen would not have agreed that mounted infantry had replaced the old-style cavalry, the war in South Africa brought home to many the need for more adequate training with firearms. Civil authorities, too, occasionally were tempted to jettison cavalry and replace it with mounted infantry, which had the obvious political virtue of being cheaper to equip and maintain.[54]

Picard's later writings reveal the effect of the Boer War. In particulars he was prone to repeat his original views, but his over-all interpretation had changed. He now asserted that the mounted infantry of 1861-65 should be considered cavalry because it had fulfilled all the functions expected of cavalry proper. While admitting that the Americans had shown a decided preference for "*le combat*

51 *Ibid.*, I, 148, 230-36, 248. Picard was aware that the regular army cavalry had consisted mostly of dragoons and light cavalry.

52 Gérôme, *Tactique de la cavalerie*, pp. 426-27. The substance of the Regulations of 1899 is contained in pp. 426-40.

53 Charles Sydney Goldmann, *With General French and the Cavalry in South Africa* (London, 1903), pp. viii-ix.

54 Cf. Général H. Langlois, *Enseignements des deux guerres récentes: Guerres Turco-Russe et Anglo-Boer* (Paris, n.d.), pp. 160-70.

à pied," he pointed out that this applied usually "under circum-
tances . . . which are planned by our regulations for the use of dismounted fighting." The Civil War cavalry could also fight mounted,
but with the revolver and carbine rather than lance and saber, when
the occasion demanded, and it was capable of making long, rapid
marches and of performing all the duties required in reconnaissance
and security.[55]

This new interpretation was not merely an exercise in semantics,
for it signified that the "special conditions" of the Civil War were
no longer universally looked upon as unique. The more recent experience of the British in South Africa suggested to Picard and to
others as well that the mounted infantry of the Civil War might
well be the parent rather than a bastard offspring of modern cavalry.
He still retained some faith in shock tactics, but he was now willing
to grant priority to the rifle and machine gun.[56] The trend of his
thought was that cavalry was in an evolutionary stage, headed in
the direction of greater firepower and employment "in large masses
and . . . emancipation for independent operations."[57]

The best and most original study of American cavalry by a
French soldier is Captain de Thomasson's *Les procédés d'exploration
de l'armée de Nord Virginie*, which appeared in 1901. De Thomasson
deplored the fact that most French soldiers who wrote of Civil War
cavalry made no attempt to deduce lessons applicable in Europe.
He attempted to measure the French cavalry regulations of 1895
and 1899 against the methods and accomplishments of one of the
South's greatest cavalry leaders, Jeb Stuart. He selected a Civil War
subject because he believed this conflict to be the forerunner of the
next European war; he limited his study to the eastern theater because it most nearly resembled the terrain of western Europe, and
he chose Stuart because that officer had performed for Lee "almost
exactly what a commander-in-chief would demand of his cavalry in
a European war." He concentrated upon four episodes: Stuart's
raid around McClellan's army in June, 1862, his reconnaissance
against Pope that August, his raid into Pennsylvania after the battle

[55] Commandant Picard, "Cavalerie ou infanterie montée," *Journal des sciences
militaires*, IX (March, 1901), 425.

[56] This is the burden of Picard, *L'armement de la cavalerie*, as summarized in
Cavalry Journal, I (January, 1906), 80–81.

[57] "Cavalerie ou infanterie montée," X, 118. Picard now believed in the practicality
of the cavalry raid, which "could have the greatest influence" on the result of a
campaign" (*Journal des sciences militaires*, IX, 427).

of Antietam, and his controversial movements during the Gettysburg campaign.[58] This was a fresh approach, and because De Thomasson was the first French military writer to dip into the *Official Records*, his study far surpassed in thoroughness, originality, and scholarship the writings of the majority of French officers before him.

De Thomasson's analysis of the tactics of Stuart's cavalry did not differ substantially from the accepted interpretation, although he credited Stuart with the same technique that Lehautcourt and others had associated with Forrest and Morgan—a combination of dismounted tactics and shock action, with skirmishers being used to pin down the enemy while mounted cavalry charged on one or both flanks. But De Thomasson was not so much interested in the tactics of Stuart's cavalry as he was in their application in the performance of other duties, particularly reconnaissance. Stuart had succeeded in fulfilling this function by observing three elementary principles: frequent use of dismounted tactics combined with the fire of horse artillery, the use of firepower both in combat with cavalry and in reconnaissance against infantry, and the employment of his entire command in seeking information rather than the detachment of splinter groups for this purpose. Above all, Stuart had rarely allowed himself to be distracted by enemy cavalry when information was his main objective.[59]

Stuart's methods, De Thomasson contended, were "not so bizarre, so extraordinary, so distant from our own ideas as one might think." It was not necessary to turn every cavalryman into an expert marksman; all that was required was that the cavalry be proficient enough with the rifle to force infantry to deploy and reveal its position. This accomplished, it could break off the engagement before it became seriously involved. The trouble with the French cavalry was that it was "still haunted" with the exploits of Napoleon's cavalry; it clung to the theory of the decisive combat between immense bodies of cavalry in which the loser was reduced

[58] Capitaine de Thomasson, *Les procédés d'exploration de l'armée de Nord Virginie dans la guerre de sécession américaine* (Paris, 1901), pp. 3–4. This work was originally published under the same title in the *Revue de cavalerie*, XXXI (April, 1900), 81–96, 145–77. All citations refer to the published volume.

[59] *Ibid.*, pp. 41–42, 77; cf. Lehautcourt, "Le général Forrest," p. 255, and F., "Les raids aux États-Unis," pp. 4, 9. According to the most authoritative biography of Forrest, this was the maneuver Forrest "practised so frequently and with such signal success in nearly all of his encounters" (John Allan Wyeth, *Life of Lieutenant-General Nathan Bedford Forrest* [New York, 1908], p. 31).

to an ignominious role for the remainder of the campaign. This was, to say the least, "a little oversimplified" and was not sanctioned by the wars of the nineteenth century in either Europe or America.[60]

Instead of the cavalry duel anticipated in French regulations, which stressed locating and defeating the enemy cavalry in battle before making contact with his main force, De Thomasson would give absolute priority to reconnaissance, using regiments especially prepared in peacetime for this purpose, well mounted, lightly equipped, and practically dressed. They would be grouped in detachments varying in strength according to the nature and difficulties of the particular mission, but they would not be so weak as to diminish their offensive power, nor would they be too large to be easily led and concealed. He recommended a brigade of three regiments and a battery or two of horse artillery, well enough drilled in mounted tactics to enable them to contend with enemy cavalry and at the same time trained for long, fast marches and skirmishing. In brief, in place of cuirassiers and other cavalry trained exclusively for mounted combat, De Thomasson would substitute a modern version of the gray-clad troopers who had served as the eyes and ears of Lee's Army of Northern Virginia.[61]

De Thomasson's book was followed by an anonymous study of Civil War cavalry in general. Based upon the standard French sources, the author of *La cavalerie américaine dans la guerre de la sécession* contributed little that was new to the interpretation of Civil War cavalry. He did not detect any basic differences in the tactics of the various cavalry organizations, but looked upon Union and Confederate cavalry alike as direct forerunners of the mounted infantry the British had employed recently in the Transvaal. Like De Thomasson, this writer was impressed by the way in which the Civil War cavalry had utilized cover to delay the advance of enemy infantry, and he agreed with De Thomasson that the first duty of cavalry was to locate and report on the enemy's main army rather than to seek out and destroy his cavalry. While reluctant to indorse raids of the type that had succeeded in America, he was at least convinced that in the next war cavalry would frequently be assigned strategic missions. Both contestants in 1870–71 could have learned something about cavalry from the Americans, and nearly half a century later Civil War cavalry still deserved to be studied with care because, making proper allowance for the special character of

[60] *Les procédés d'exploration,* pp. 66 n., 85–90.　　　[61] *Ibid.,* p. 94.

the war, "it accomplished great things worthy of being meditated and imitated on occasion by the cavalry of Europe."[62]

There were, of course, many others who displayed an interest in Civil War cavalry. The subject occasionally was discussed in lectures at the École Supérieure de Guerre[63] and mentioned in general works on cavalry.[64] In studying the more recent French views about Civil War cavalry, several significant facts emerge. The first is that French soldiers seemed far more interested in tactics than they had been before 1870, when, secure in the belief that they possessed the finest fighting machine in the world, they had been interested primarily in the organization and equipment of the American armies. Now primarily concerned with the operational side of the war, cavalrymen paid particular attention to reconnaissance, for here the French cavalry had been weakest in 1870.[65]

Moreover, in contrast to what was written in Germany after 1870, there was no unanimity in the French interpretation of Civil War cavalry. Bonie emphasized the importance of dismounted tactics; Lehautcourt virtually repudiated the mounted infantry doctrine in his study of Forrest. Lewal regarded the bulk of American cavalry as "infantry on horseback"; Picard decided that the term "mounted infantry" was misleading. De Thomasson recommended the application of specific principles in reconnaissance; the author of *La cavalerie américaine dans la guerre de sécession* was satisfied

---

[62] *La cavalerie américaine dans la guerre de la sécession* (Paris, 1903), pp. 12–13, 21, 77, 124. Like De Thomasson's work, this book first appeared in the *Revue de cavalerie*, XXXIV (November, 1901–January, 1902), 151–203, 346–84, 517–53.

[63] De Thomasson refers to a lecture given by Commandant Dubois at the École Supérieure de Guerre concerning American cavalry operations (*Les procédés d'exploration*, p. 14), and a United States government publication on the battle of Brices Cross Roads mentions that Marshal Ferdinand Foch made this battle the subject of a lecture at the "general staff college" of France. See United States Department of the Interior, National Park Service, *Brices Cross Roads National Battlefield Site, Mississippi* (Chicago, March, 1946). Although Foch ignored the Civil War in his theoretical works, he may have delivered such a lecture, for Forrest's successful tactics at Brices Cross Roads, "namely, the fierce onslaught from the front, with a charge upon both flanks and in the enemy's rear" (Wyeth, *Life of Forrest*, pp. 416–17), corresponds to Foch's conception of the role of cavalry in battle. He wrote of battle being decided by squadrons of cavalry suddenly appearing "out of a cloud of dust or of smoke, on the flank or in the rear of the position" (Marshal Foch, *The Principles of War* [London, 1918], pp. 348–49).

[64] Cf. Gérôme, *Tactique de la cavalerie,* pp. 233–52. Gérôme seems to have been most influenced by Scheibert, whom he quotes frequently. See also Maurice de Maere d'Aertrycke, *Aperçu historique sur la cavalerie* (2d ed.; Gand, 1899), pp. 103–4.

[65] Spenser Wilkinson, *War and Policy* (New York, 1900), p. 143.

with the "tactical science" of French cavalry and was interested more in "the spirit of adventure and initiative and the tenacity of the Americans."[66] Some asserted that there was a fundamental difference in the tactics and organization of Stuart's cavalry and that of Morgan and Forrest; others professed to see a similar variance between Confederate and Union cavalry, while De Thomasson claimed that it was all mounted infantry.

These different interpretations would seemingly indicate that the French were not at all certain how cavalry should be used and that those who turned to the Civil War did so in the hope of discovering some clues to the problem. They also illustrate some of the practical difficulties involved in studying the Civil War from Europe. The sources used by most writers were often extremely limited; only one, De Thomasson, gives evidence of having actually used the *Official Records*. Moreover, the Civil War examples themselves were so varied that there was a battle to suit every theorist. By selecting unrelated incidents it was possible to arrive at almost any conclusion and to support any theory.

Possibly the views of De Thomasson, Picard, and others of that school had some slight influence upon official doctrine, although the cavalryman's nightmare of being converted to mounted infantry predominated in France as elsewhere. The regulations of 1904 placed greater emphasis upon firepower than earlier regulations, but shock tactics remained the preferred mode of fighting. Most French cavalrymen probably believed in some combination of the two—shock tactics whenever practicable, dismounted tactics if necessary; they differed, naturally, over what was practicable for the *arme blanche*, but most of them would have considered De Thomasson's theories extreme. In France, indeed in most of the Continental armies prior to the First World War, "the employment of cavalry as a means of mobile fire-power was overlooked . . . musketry was neglected, dismounted action practised very little, and . . . training was almost entirely devoted to reconnaisssance duties and shock action against opposing cavalry." Looking back after the war, De Thomasson could find good cause for criticizing the French cavalry that had gone to war in 1914 dominated by "senseless ideas . . . relative to its use."[67]

Aside from the cavalry issue, the French showed little interest in

[66] *La cavalerie américaine*, p. 123.

[67] "Comparison of French and German Cavalry," *Cavalry Journal*, II (1907), 484–86; Lieutenant Colonel M. C. Lowther, "The French Cavalry," *ibid.*, IV (1909),

the Civil War. For practical lessons they studied the Franco-Prussian War; for fundamental principles they felt they could do no better than to study the campaigns of their national hero, Napoleon. As one prominent theorist explained,

Napoleon lays down the principles and shows us the models of modern war; in the war to come we shall assuredly have new weapons, larger masses, more efficient means of transport; it will not be possible to apply the procedure of Napoleonic war without modification . . . [but] it will still be in the Napoleonic war that . . . [we] will find the models that should inspire, the subjects that should be meditated, and the ideas that should be applied in the 20th century. There are operations more recent than Napoleon's, but they were executed under conditions very remote from those in which we shall find ourselves in a future European war.[68]

French military thought prior to 1914 was dominated by what De Thomasson described as "the passionate cult of the offensive." Those who had formulated the infantry Regulations of 1875, remembering the experiences of the late war, had stressed the effectiveness of rifle fire, but as the impression of 1870 faded, "the heroism of military writers showed itself on paper in a firm determination to achieve the impossible." Closer formations as prescribed in the revised regulations of 1884 were the result, with offensive action being considered more in keeping with the "national temperament" of the French soldier.[69] The regulations of 1895 stated: "Only the offensive permits the obtaining of decisive results. The passive defense is doomed to certain defeat; it is to be rejected absolutely."[70] Ferdinand Foch, "the most important and influential figure in molding the intellectual outlook of the French officer before the first World War," preached that "the *offensive* form alone, be it resorted to at once or only after the *defensive*, can lead to results, and must therefore always be adopted."[71]

200; Lieutenant Colonel H. V. S. Charrington, *Where Cavalry Stands To-day* (London, 1927), p. 20; De Thomasson, *Le revers de 1914 et ses causes* (Paris, 1920), pp. 24, 68-72.

[68] Colin, *The Transformations of War*, p. 227.

[69] De Thomasson, *Le revers de 1914*, p. 47; Colin, *The Transformations of War*, p. 42; Thoumas, *Les transformations de l'armée française*, II, 461-65.

[70] Quoted in Irvine, "The French Discovery of Clausewitz and Napoleon," p. 35.

[71] Stefan T. Possony and Étienne Mantoux, "Du Picq and Foch: The French School," in Edward Mead Earle (ed.), *Makers of Modern Strategy: Military Thought from Machiavelli to Hitler* (Princeton, 1943), p. 218; Foch, *The Principles of War*, p. 283. A critical analysis of Foch's theories is contained in Captain B. H. Liddell Hart, *Foch: The Man of Orleans* (Boston, 1932), pp. 21-49; *The Ghost of Napoleon* (London, 1933), pp. 132-39.

This doctrine of the offensive was carried to even greater extremes by Colonel Grandmaison and the so-called Young Turks, who asserted that "the French army, returning to its traditions, no longer knows any other law than the offensive. . . . All attacks are to be pushed to the extreme . . . to charge the enemy with the bayonet in order to destroy him. . . . This result can only be obtained at the price of bloody sacrifice. Any other conception ought to be rejected as contrary to the very nature of war."[72] The Civil War, conspicuous for battles that illustrated the strength of the defensive, was all but ignored in French military writings in the decade preceding the First World War. Even a scholarly soldier like Major Colin devoted but three pages to the Civil War in his study of the evolution of war in the nineteenth century, and then he was interested primarily in cavalry.[73] Only one French soldier dared to swim against the current, but he wrote an important book in the process.

This writer was Captain L. Auger of the engineers, whose history of the Civil War was published in 1895. Auger maintained that the French could still benefit from a study of army organization and administration during the Civil War. He did not think that much could be gained from studying the strategy of the American campaigns except in the use of railroads,[74] but he was enthusiastic about the tactical lessons of the Civil War that were, in his opinion, still valid.

Auger was among the first to comprehend the meaning of Civil War intrenchments. Treating the evolution of trench warfare as "an affair of circumstances, experience and improvisation," Auger did not accept the standard explanation for its causes. Certainly Lee had used trenches to help compensate for lack of numbers, but what about the Confederate field works at Manassas in the winter of 1861 and on the Peninsula the following spring? And what about the battles in the West? To credit Lee with the introduction of trench warfare was to ignore some of the conditions peculiar to the war in America—the emphasis at West Point upon artillery and engi-

[72] Liddell Hart, *Foch*, p. 67. See also Challener, *The French Theory of the Nation in Arms*, pp. 81–82; De Thomasson, *Le revers de 1914*, pp. 46–56; and Major General J. F. C. Fuller, *War and Western Civilization 1832–1932: A Study of War as a Political Instrument and the Expression of Mass Democracy* (London, 1932), pp. 151–64.

[73] See Colin, *The Transformations of War*, pp. 136–37, 163.

[74] L. Auger, *La guerre de sécession* (Paris, 1895), pp. 105–35 *passim*.

neering, the fact that volunteers were inclined to resort to cover, and the influence of terrain.[75]

Moreover, these "exceptional conditions" should not be permitted to obscure the fact that the rise of intrenchments was due above all to the increased rate of fire of modern weapons. The breechloader had "profoundly modified" the conditions of combat, leaving infantry only two alternatives if it was to withstand this fire: dispersed order and protection. And if the legendary charges of Napoleonic warfare had not succeeded in 1861–65, what would be the result half a century later, when the density of fire "has increased more than tenfold." Modern firepower made the defensive "the true mode of combat of the future," indeed "the only one possible in the presence of the probable hetatomb of future war." Such a war would surely "approximate to a certain extent the battles fought before Richmond, and . . . the attack, instead of placing all confidence in numbers and elan, will have to proceed with slowness, gain ground gradually, and consolidate each step."[76]

French infantry regulations for 1895 prescribed that

as soon as the battalion has arrived within 400 metres of the enemy, bayonets are fixed, and individual fire . . . of the greatest intensity delivered. The portions of the reserve that are available are advanced. . . . The battalion in second line in the meantime gradually advances closer. The advance is made by successive rushes followed by a quick fire of short duration. The fighting line reinforced by the reserves . . . gradually reaches to within 150 or 200 metres of the enemy. At this distance magazine fire is commenced, and all available reserves . . . close up for the assault. At a signal from the Colonel the drums beat, the bugles sound the advance and the entire line charges forward with cries of *"en avant, à la baionette."*[77]

This, according to Auger, was pure folly; Lee's methods were far more realistic:

As soon as he had selected a position, he deployed there his first line in order of battle and had it take shelter immediately behind improvised intrenchments; the rear echelons were often covered in the same way and the flanks were protected by strong works. At intervals passages were prepared for the return to the offensive and the fire of artillery. Thus intrenched, Lee awaited the shock of his adversaries and received them with a terrible fire. . . . Then, with the help of his reserves . . . and mobile detachments placed on the flanks, he assumed the offensive, seek-

[75] *Ibid.*, pp. 142, 156–59.   [76] *Ibid.*, pp. 146, 238–40.

[77] Quoted in Fuller, *War and Western Civilization*, pp. 152–53.

ing to overrun the weak side of the enemy line by a turning movement. If he was repulsed himself, he found a new point of support on his second intrenched line, where the battle recommenced under the same conditions.[78]

Such use of intrenchments had enabled Lee to ward off repeated attacks by Grant's larger forces, and Auger maintained that intrenchments could serve a similar purpose should France be invaded again by Germany. Earthworks were durable enough and cheaper than permanent fortifications, and more important still, they need not rob the French soldier of his dash. Lee's troops, after all, had not used intrenchments because they lacked bravery, nor had Grant's men lost their courage as a result of a winter in the lines before Petersburg. The campaigns of Grant and Sherman even demonstrated how intrenchments might be used for offensive purposes. Surely it was as important for French infantry to learn the rudiments of military engineering in order to throw up a defense line quickly as it was for them to master drill evolutions on the parade ground. The next war would be "a duel of nations rather than armies," in which intrenchments were bound to be a determining factor.[79]

Auger was no prophet, merely an observant army officer. He was clearly out of step with official doctrine and accepted military theory, so his book never received the attention it deserved. Yet it is one of the most remarkable books ever written about the Civil War —remarkable not only for its insight but because it was written at a time and place when such ideas were considered heresy. Even those who wrote about the Civil War after 1918 did not state their case any better than Auger. According to Liddell Hart, if Foch "had examined the American Civil War he would have seen clear evidence of the growing power of defense over attack, and renewed evidence that fighting was not the only means to victory."[80] Auger's book proves at least that it was possible to see this evidence before it was made conspicuous by the First World War.

On the eve of the outbreak of war in 1914, another French book about the Civil War was published that deserves brief mention, not so much for the quality of the book as for the subject treated. Captain Boucherie, an officer on the General Staff, became interested in the relationship between various generals and civilian leaders dur-

[78] *La guerre de sécession*, pp. 145-46.

[79] *Ibid.*, pp. 183-84, 239-48.   [80] Liddell Hart, *Foch*, p. 31.

THE VIEW FROM FRANCE, 1861–1914

ing the Civil War. As a work of history, *Les rapports du haut commandement et du pouvoir civil dans un démocratie* is superficial, and Boucherie arrived at no particular conclusions about the general problem of military-political relations.[81] But he did understand that this had been, and doubtless would continue to be, a major problem in a democracy at war, and he was one of the first to sense the value of studying this neglected aspect of the Civil War.

[81] Boucherie decided that McClellan had failed in 1862 because he had lacked the confidence of the administration and that Grant had succeeded because he had enjoyed the trust and support of the government (Commandant M. Boucherie, *Les rapports du haut commandement et du pouvoir civil dans une démocratie* [Paris, 1915], pp. 81–181). Boucherie was a captain when this book originally appeared as a series of articles in *Le spectateur militaire*, XCIV (January–March, 1914), 372–400, 442–61; XCI (April–June, 1914), 59–80, 151–60, 230–40, 298–320, 374–400, 460–78; XCVI (July–September, 1914), 64–80.

8

The Henderson Legacy

In 1886 there appeared in England a small volume entitled *The Campaign of Fredericksburg*, written by an anonymous "Line Officer." To the average soldier this book was probably just another campaign history, better written than most tactical studies but otherwise no different from many similar volumes in the regimental library. But to those concerned with the education of the British officer this book had a unique appeal. Written with an intelligence and insight unusual for such literature and filled with thoughtful observations on the military significance of the campaign, it represented a skilful blending of personal knowledge of the terrain, careful study of the available sources, and a lively, readable style. Colonel (later Sir Frederick) Maurice, then professor of military art and history at the Staff College, reviewed the book enthusiastically and, recalling that Sir Garnet Wolseley, by this time adjutant general, had once visited the Confederate army, forwarded his copy to Wolseley. Wolseley read it, liked it, and made inquiries about the identity of the author. He was charged with the military education of British officers and could use an able instructor.[1]

"Line Officer" proved to be Captain George Francis Robert Henderson, York and Lancaster Regiment. Henderson, then thirty-two years of age, had been at Oxford with a scholarship in history before entering the army in 1877. In the Egyptian campaign of 1882 he had distinguished himself by rushing an enemy redoubt at Tel-el-Kebir. Assigned to garrison duty in Bermuda the following year, Henderson had subsequently been transferred to Halifax, where he had spent his leave tramping over many of the battlefields in Virginia and Maryland. Upon his return to England, Henderson had applied for and received assignment to the Ordnance Depart-

---

[1] Lieutenant Colonel F. Maurice, *Sir Frederick Maurice: A Record of His Work and Opinions* (London, 1913), p. 64; Major General Sir F. Maurice and Sir George Arthur, *The Life of Lord Wolseley* (New York, 1924), p. 236.

ment, duty that provided him with sufficient time and income to continue his study of the Civil War.[2]

Wolseley was so impressed with Henderson that he appointed him to the staff of the Cadet School at Sandhurst. An elaborate tactical study of the battle of Spicheren, published in 1891,[3] led to another advancement, and in the following year Henderson was named Maurice's successor at the Staff College. Rarely has publication led to such rapid promotion, even in an academic atmosphere.

Henderson was one of a new generation of military writers which became active in the closing years of the nineteenth century. Proud of the traditions of the British army, these writers made new studies of its past campaigns and stimulated interest in contemporary military problems. These were the years when Sir Charles Dilke and Spenser Wilkinson[4] were writing their disturbing books about problems relating to colonial defense, when scholars such as Sir Charles Oman, Sir John Fortescue, and Sir Charles Firth had begun to examine many episodes in the history of the British army. All these men with the exception of Dilke were born in the same decade as Henderson; together they were largely responsible for a renaissance in British military thought.

The first English officer after 1870 to undertake a serious study of the Civil War, Henderson intended *The Campaign of Fredericksburg* to serve as a tactical text for officers of the Volunteers. This organization, a sickly child of repeated invasion scares, was assigned an important role in existing plans for home defense. Unfortunately the Volunteer regiments varied greatly in training and quality, and little machinery existed whereby they might be swiftly

2 Information on Henderson's career is found in E. M. Lloyd, "Henderson," *Dictionary of National Biography*, Suppl. II, pp. 240–41; Lieutenant Colonel R. M. Holden, "Lt. Col. G. F. R. Henderson, C.B., In Memoriam," *R.U.S.I. Journal*, XLVII (April, 1903), 375–82, and an obituary, probably by the same author, in the *Times*, March 7, 1903. A biographical appreciation by Field Marshal Earl Roberts in Henderson, *The Science of War*, ed. Captain Neill Malcolm (London, 1906), pp. xiii–xxxviii (cited hereafter as Roberts, "Memoir") is also found in Lieutenant Colonel Ralph Henderson, *Records of My Family* (Carlisle, 1926), pp. 90–111. Many letters from Henderson to Major Jedediah Hotchkiss, onetime Confederate staff officer, are included in the Jed Hotchkiss Papers, Library of Congress.

3 G. F. R. Henderson, *The Battle of Spicheren, August 6th, 1870, and the Events That Preceded It: A Study in Practical Tactics and War Training* (Aldershot, 1891).

4 Spenser Wilkinson, a young journalist who was beginning to make a name for himself as an authority on military subjects, was among those who urged a new appraisal of the Civil War. Spenser Wilkinson, *War and Policy* (New York, 1900), pp. 3–58.

mobilized in time of war.[5] Aware that if the Volunteers were ever called into active service they might have to face a Continental army superior both in manpower and in training, Henderson wished to improve the practical and theoretical training of Volunteer officers. He maintained that a sound knowledge of military history was the best substitute for actual combat experience, that if Volunteer officers would only study past campaigns with intelligence they would find themselves "instinctively doing the right thing."[6]

Unlike the majority of those who had studied the campaigns of the Franco-Prussian War in minute detail, Henderson was not looking for any new or specific military information. While he frequently mentioned the "lessons" to be derived from a study of the Civil War, he used the word to mean "instruction." Napoleon himself had stated that the only way to learn the science of war was to read and read again the campaigns of the Great Captains. Henderson, too, preferred this system to "the tabulated maxims and isolated instances of the text-books," and he considered the battle of Fredericksburg especially suitable for his purposes because both armies had been composed mainly of non-professional soldiers similar to the Volunteers. Surely the experiences of the Americans in 1862, he reasoned, would give Volunteer officers some insight into the problems they were likely to face.[7]

The "lessons" this thoughtful soldier tried to communicate in his account of Fredericksburg all center in his conception of the role of the officer in modern battle. Contemporary observers like Scheibert and Fremantle had noticed that battles tended to escape the effective control of the field commander. Henderson also recognized this trend, which left greater tactical independence in battle to the subordinate, and he pointed out that at Fredericksburg Lee, having brought his troops to the selected positions, first notified his lieutenants of his general plan "and then gave frankly into their hands the conduct of the fight." The lesson was obvious. Henderson advised officers of every rank:

[5] Colonel John K. Dunlop, *The Development of the British Army, 1899–1914* (London, 1938), pp. 55–56.

[6] *The Campaign of Fredericksburg* (3d ed.; London, n.d.), p. 126. This book, together with four essays on the Civil War contained in *The Science of War* and an appreciation of Stonewall Jackson written especially for Mary Anna Jackson's biography of her husband, is found in Jay Luvaas (ed.), *The Civil War: A Soldier's View* (Chicago, 1958). Most of the observations about Henderson contained on this and succeeding pages are taken directly from chapters i, iii, and ix of this work.

[7] *Campaign of Fredericksburg*, pp. vii–xi.

Make up your mind clearly as to the course you intend to pursue. Let your plan be as simple as possible; . . . take care that it is prosecuted with the utmost determination, and, if your subordinates are qualified to command, leave them to themselves, and beware of unnecessary interference. Be determined at the same time . . . to enforce prompt cooperation towards the end in view.[8]

The use of intrenchments at Fredericksburg helped convince Henderson that "good infantry, sufficiently covered . . . is, if unshaken by artillery and attacked in front alone, absolutely invincible." He recommended a well-directed fire by volleys as the best defense against frontal attacks, and he considered a movement against the enemy flank or rear the most likely to succeed against fortified positions. These views harmonized with official British doctrine, for in the years immediately preceding the South African war, volley firing was the "backbone of all musketry training."[9] Yet it is doubtful that even Henderson, at this date, fully respected the value of modern firepower. He thought Lee's comments on the use of the breechloader "worth consideration." "What we want," he quoted Lee as saying, "is a firearm that cannot be loaded without a certain loss of time; so that a man learns to appreciate the importance of his fire."[10] He also attributed the use of intrenchments to "the wooded nature of the country" and explained that cavalry so often found it necessary to fight on foot with the rifle because the terrain afforded "few facilities for cavalry manoeuvres on a large scale."[11]

According to Henderson, the object lessons of the battle of Fredericksburg, at least insofar as the English Volunteers were concerned, could be summarized in two words—leadership and discipline. The conditions of modern battle made it necessary for junior officers to assume greater responsibility; flank marches and volley firing could be successfully executed only through strict discipline.

[8] *Ibid.*, pp. 72–73, 125.

[9] *Ibid.*, pp. 85, 124; Major General J. F. C. Fuller, *The Army in My Time* (London, 1935), pp. 69–70; Dunlop, *Development of the British Army*, p. 37.

[10] *Campaign of Fredericksburg*, p. 131. It is curious to note that never once in all his writings does Henderson mention Scheibert, who certainly wrote more about the Civil War than any other contemporary foreign military observer, including Lord Wolseley. Yet this quotation would suggest that he was familiar, either directly or indirectly, with the opinions of the Prussian observer, for it was to Scheibert that Lee had expressed—in words of which Henderson's quotation is a direct translation—his misgivings about the breechloader. Cf. Justus Scheibert, *Der Bürgerkrieg in den nordamerikanischen Staaten: Militairisch beleuchtet für den deutschen Offizier* (Berlin, 1874), p. 27. Lee's views, incidentally, were not uncommon among Civil War officers.

[11] *Campaign of Fredericksburg*, p. 28.

Henderson admired "the splendid fighting qualities" of the American soldiers, and he saw no reason why the Volunteers, *"if knit together by strict discipline and led by well-trained officers,"* could not "excel even Lee's battalions in mobility and efficiency."[12]

The successive appointments to Sandhurst and the Staff College following publication of *The Campaign of Fredericksburg* afforded Henderson greater opportunity for research and writing, and in the ensuing years the amount of work he accomplished was "enormous." In addition to preparing and delivering "most carefully thought-out lectures" at the Staff College, he appeared frequently before military societies throughout the United Kingdom and contributed numerous articles to the *Times,* the *Edinburgh Review,* and the various military journals. He received more offers from publishers than he could possibly accept, the new *Military Magazine* offering him a guinea a page for anything he cared to write.[13] During the 1890's Henderson also devoted whatever time he could afford to the preparation of his major work, *Stonewall Jackson and the American Civil War.*

Henderson's articles and speeches during this period reveal a growing conviction that the tactical lessons of the Franco-Prussian War had been overrated. He continued to take students on periodic tours of the battlefields of 1870,[14] but he himself became increasingly absorbed in the study of the Civil War. In 1891, the same year that his study of Spicheren was first published, Henderson wrote:

Despite the absolute ignorance of war and its requirements which existed amongst the mass of combatants, despite the lack of experience, the tactics of the American troops, at a very early period, were superior to those of the Prussians in 1866. . . . The success with which from the very first the cavalry was employed on the outpost line puts to shame the inactivity of the Prussian horsemen in Bohemia; and, whilst the tactics of the Prussian artillery . . . were feeble in the extreme, the very contrary was the case in the Secession War. . . . Nor were the larger tactical manoeuvres even of 1870 an improvement on those of the American campaigns. . . . Flank attacks and wide turning movements were as frequent in one case as in the other; and not only were the victors of Sedan anticipated in the method of attack by successive rushes, but the terrible confusion which followed a protracted struggle, and for which

12 *Ibid.,* p. 147.

13 Roberts, "Memoir," pp. xxvi–xxix.

14 "I go off to-morrow to Germany with a class of officers to visit the battlefields of 1870, and shall be away a fortnight." Henderson to Jed Hotchkiss, May 9, 1895, Hotchkiss Papers, Library of Congress.

Prussian tacticians still despair of discovering a remedy, was speedily rectified by American ingenuity. . . . [The American tactical] formations were far better adapted to preserve cohesion than those of the Prussians.

To those who were still inclined to discount the lessons of a war waged before the universal introduction of the breechloader, Henderson pointed out that the Americans, compared with the Prussians in 1870, "made more careful preparations for the attack, were far more zealous to re-form the ranks after every phase of battle, and, whilst developing a broad front of fire, kept within proper bounds the initiative of their company commanders."[15]

From Major Jed Hotchkiss, Jackson's old topographical engineer, Henderson continued to learn details of the campaigns and battles of the Civil War. His letters to Hotchkiss reveal some of the problems that still concerned him. When he learned that Hotchkiss was working on a book about the Civil War, Henderson urged his American correspondent not to make the book too short. "Remember," he cautioned,

What may seem trivial details to you will be exceedingly interesting to soldiers and also to our large army of enthusiastic volunteers. I am now going to be impudent, and suggest what points we should like to hear about particularly.

1. The characters, demeanours, and appearance of your generals.
2. The character of the troops and of their fighting, and of their discipline.
3. The nature of the entrenchments and breastworks constructed.
4. The way in which the fighting in woods was carried out and the precaution taken to maintain order and direction.
5. The way intelligence of the enemy was obtained, and the country mapped. I would suggest you give an example or two of the . . . maps. . . .
6. The methods of the Confederacy [sic] marksmen—the efficiency of their fire and the manner in which it was controlled by their officers —or otherwise. The more military your book is the better it will go down over here, as, owing to our number of volunteers and our constant little wars, the people generally understand and enjoy all details connected with the grand art of killing one's fellow man.[16]

Meanwhile Henderson labored to improve his own knowledge about the details of the Civil War. He was interested in nearly every phase of the military operations. His first book had been written when, as a company officer, Henderson had been concerned prima-

[15] *Science of War*, pp. 129–30.
[16] Henderson to Jed Hotchkiss, October 13, 1895, Hotchkiss Papers.

rily with what he later termed "Minor Tactics," a phrase used to describe "the formation and disposition of the three arms for attack and defence." But after teaching for a few years at the Staff College, his outlook had naturally broadened to include more general problems of military policy, organization, and especially that "higher art" of generalship known as strategy or "Grand Tactics," which Henderson defined as "those strategems, manoeuvres, and devices by which victories are won, and concern only those officers who may find themselves in independent command."[17]

His interest in the Civil War was at once professional and historical. No matter what the occasion, Henderson could see lessons in the Civil War of special significance to the British army. In an article reviewing *Battles and Leaders of the Civil War*, for example, he devoted considerable attention to the special problems of a volunteer army. Two lectures on the Civil War delivered before the Aldershot Military Society in 1892 gave him an opportunity to air his views on modern cavalry. In a subsequent lecture on the battle of Gettysburg he developed his ideas on leadership and staff duties, while a speech he gave about the Wilderness campaign almost predicted the nature of wars to come. On virtually every matter of current speculation or controversy, then, Henderson could point to exemplary lessons from the experiences of the Americans in 1861–65.

One of the main military questions of Henderson's day continued to revolve around the Auxiliary forces, the Volunteers and Militia. There was general and perhaps justifiable concern about the efficiency and capabilities of these organizations, for while much attention had been given to their assignment in time of war, there remained many who doubted that untried soldiers such as these could stand up against a large professional army from the Continent.

Henderson's writings and speeches reflect that concern. Unlike his patron Wolseley, who had been content merely to state that "the armies of raw levies" ought to be taken into consideration when one was evaluating the generalship of the Civil War, Henderson pleaded for a better understanding of the special problems of the American armies. After all, the Civil War had been fought by elements comparable to the Auxiliary forces, so "their experience . . . will help us to anticipate the shortcomings likely to occur amongst

17 *Science of War*, pp. 310, 168.

our own volunteers and may enlighten us as to the measures by which these shortcomings may be most readily corrected."[18] While admitting that the Civil War armies had suffered at first from lack of discipline, Henderson also noted that they had improved steadily as the war progressed, until by 1863 they were "in very many respects . . . superior and more advanced in military knowledge than even the Germans in 1870." The Volunteers, he believed, could be trained to the point where they would be "fully equal" to the Continental armies; in fact, he anticipated that the next great war would be fought largely by armies comprising just such soldiers. Henderson's remarks to a military audience in 1894 seem almost prophetic:

If I see in the future an English general at the head of an army far larger than that which drained the life-blood of Napoleon's empire in the Peninsula, if I see our colours flying over even a wider area than in the year which preceded Waterloo, you may think that I am over-sanguine; but to my mind the possibility exists, and with it the probability that the forces which are employed . . . will be constituted, at least in part, as were the armies of the American Civil War. Our men will not all be regulars. They will come straight from civil life, and to civil life they will return. The habits and prejudices of civil life will have to be considered in their discipline and instruction, and officers will have to recognise that troops without the traditions, instincts, and training of regular soldiers, require a handling different from that which they have been accustomed to employ.

The experiences of the Americans in raising, equipping, and training their volunteer armies in the 1860's was, to Henderson's way of thinking, "one of the most important lessons" to be learned from the Civil War by British soldiers.[19]

Much could also be learned from the American campaigns about the handling of cavalry. The controversy over the weapons and tactics best suited to cavalry was still raging in the 1890's, and Henderson approached this issue with the same objectivity and thoroughness that characterized his examination of the qualities of volunteer soldiers. He neither condemned Civil War cavalry for its new tac-

18 *Ibid.*, p. 190; Wolseley, "General Sherman," *United Service Magazine*, N.S., III (July, 1891), 304.

19 *Science of War*, p. 190. Henderson expressed this opinion in 1891, three years after General Sir Henry Brackenbury's memorandum on the subject of "French Invasion," two years after plans had actually been drawn up for the defense of London against such an invasion, and the same year in which the *Stanhope Memorandum*, defining the role of the Volunteers and Militia in the defense of England, was issued. Dunlop, *Development of the British Army*, pp. 12-14.

tics nor accepted blindly the arguments of the young hotheads who shouted that the old-style cavalry was dead. When he wrote *The Campaign of Fredericksburg*, Henderson evidently still believed that, in fighting dismounted, the American cavalry was not "exercising its proper functions."[20] For several years thereafter he continued to think that unfavorable terrain had been the primary reason for the emergence of dismounted tactics,[21] but further study, supplemented by the experiences of the Boer War, sufficed to convince him that the rise of mounted infantry was due instead to the increase in firepower, which as early as 1861 "had already become the predominant factor in battle." Although he appreciated the value of mounted infantry and personally was convinced that cavalry "armed, trained and equipped as the cavalry of the Continent, is as obsolete as the crusaders," Henderson nevertheless refused to side with those extremists who asserted that regular cavalry had no place in modern war. Rather, he believed that the key to the success of Civil War cavalry was the fact that it had been able to strike "the true balance between shock and dismounted tactics."[22]

However, Henderson was not of the opinion that the Civil War brand of cavalry could fight dismounted as well as regular infantry or could hold its own with European cavalry in "manoeuvring power" and "cohesion." He agreed with Wolseley that little faith could be placed in "the military Jack-of-all-arms." Both men hoped instead that a force of mounted infantry comparable to that which rode under Stuart and Sheridan could be provided in England by the Volunteer cavalry, the Yeomanry. Such a force would supplement the regular cavalry and was needed because the English countryside afforded "even fewer opportunities for purely cavalry combats than Virginia."[23] However, such hopes for converting the Yeomanry into mounted infantry did not materialize. In 1888 two schools for the instruction of mounted infantry had been established for the training of regular army units, principally infantry, but on the eve of the Boer War the Yeomanry were still trained as cavalry proper and retained the sword as an essential part of their armament. Henderson always regretted that British soldiers, by failing to realize the potentialities of mounted infantry, "had overlooked at least one of the lessons of the American campaigns."[24]

[20] *Campaign of Fredericksburg*, p. 132.

[21] *Science of War*, p. 266.

[22] *Ibid.*, pp. 55, 57, 372.

[23] *Ibid.*, p. 278.

[24] *Ibid.*, p. 108. See also A. H. Godley, "Mounted Infantry Training at Home," *Cavalry Journal*, I (January, 1906), 52–55; Dunlop, *Development of the British*

Henderson also discussed another significant development in tactics hastened by the Civil War—the use of intrenchments. Unfortunately, little attention was paid to this subject in most European armies. The Franco-Prussian War had been fought along more or less traditional lines, and while the Turks had made skilful use of field fortifications in the defense of Plevna in 1877, those operations were regarded as the exception rather than the rule. At any rate they did not have much influence upon Continental doctrines. Attack, not defense, was the accepted military maxim, for there was a prevalent belief that troops sheltered by earthworks—just like cavalry fighting on foot—somehow lost their spark. Auger had tried to combat this tendency in the French army, and while they were less extreme, most English military theorists also preached the doctrine of the offensive, a doctrine that deliberately played down the use of intrenchments as partial compensation for the increased power and rate of fire of modern weapons.

In the light of subsequent events it would have been better for the British had they heeded Henderson's remarks, for here he was years ahead of his time. Although preferring offensive action, he was realist enough to see that trench warfare strengthened the defensive. He had already made this point in *The Campaign of Fredericksburg*. Convinced that "the importance of the spade is often overlooked in peace," he warned repeatedly that intrenchments "as a tactical expedient and precaution, and especially as an essential adjunct to attack, do not receive, at field-days and manoeuvres, the attention they deserve." The Boer War further confirmed his contention that intrenchments "play as great a part in modern campaigns as in those of 1861–65 or 1877–78." Henderson considered mobility the best antidote to intrenchments. Sudden seizure of key tactical points, outflanking maneuvers, and marches against the enemy's line of retreat had frequently enabled the Americans to overcome the natural advantages of the defensive. The ability to maneuver had enabled Grant to pry Lee out of successive defensive positions in the Wilderness, for example, and Sherman's campaign for Atlanta offered additional proof that "against troops which can manoeuvre earthworks are useless." Henderson did not formulate any special

---

Army, pp. 52–55. The *arme blanche* was abolished for Yeomanry in 1901, the sword being retained for ceremonial purposes only, and in 1909 it was further decreed that the Yeomanry were to be armed only with rifles. Some of the Yeomanry regiments evaded these orders, and at least one, the Northumberland Yeomanry, arrived in France in 1914 with the lance and sword as part of its equipment (information obtained in correspondence with Captain B. H. Liddell Hart).

theory based upon these observations, nor did he advocate unlimited use of intrenchments; but he did appreciate the significance of this phase of Civil War military operations, and he earnestly advised officers of all ranks to study Grant's operations in the Wilderness because, in his view, they provided a "better clue to the fighting of the future than any other which history records."[25] Within twenty years many of Henderson's former pupils at the Staff College—Haig, Allenby, Robertson, and Wilson, to name only a few—would have occasion to ponder the wisdom of this forecast.

In August, 1898, Henderson completed his major work, *Stonewall Jackson and the American Civil War*. For over a decade he had worked on this labor of love, studying the *Official Records*, corresponding with former Confederates, scrutinizing every source he could lay his hands on. Hotchkiss had proved indispensable, not only in providing him with a picture of the way the Confederate army had lived and fought but also in supplying maps and unpublished reports and in answering Henderson's innumerable queries. Did Jackson, Henderson would inquire, in planning his maneuvers depend upon maps or his memory of the terrain? What sort of books did he have in his library? (The answer to this question, Henderson thought, would be "a very interesting point to all thinking soldiers over here.") Had he studied the campaigns of Napoleon? How did he look in combat? "What is the truth of the delay on June 25 (night) and 26th?"[26] To these and many similar questions Hotchkiss was generous in his answers, and he put the inquisitive Englishman in touch with other old Confederates who could add personal touches to the portrait of their esteemed leader. "Never was a biographer better served than by these men."[27] From these varied sources Henderson was able to capture the spirit of Stonewall Jackson and his men as no foreign writer and few American writers—before or since—have succeeded in doing. Stonewall came to life, and his campaigns acquired a new significance.

Greeted with enthusiastic acclaim both in England and in the United States, *Stonewall Jackson* was soon indorsed by such prominent soldiers as Lord Wolseley and Field Marshal Earl Roberts (who later claimed that the book had provided him with inspiration

[25] *Campaign of Fredericksburg*, p. 123; *Science of War*, pp. 68, 308, 340–41; *Stonewall Jackson and the American Civil War* (London, 1906), II, 347.

[26] Henderson to Jed Hotchkiss, April 24, 1892; April 11, 1895; April 28, 1895; June 27, 1895; Hotchkiss Papers.

[27] Douglas Southall Freeman, *The South to Posterity* (New York, 1951), p. 161.

and guidance in his campaigns against the Boers[28]). Sir Henry Brackenbury praised the book as a military biography, an authentic campaign history, and a general treatise on the art of war, and ended a laudatory review with a deep bow: "As an old Professor of Military History, I uncover my head to the author, and tender him my grateful thanks."[29]

Both as history and biography *Stonewall Jackson* deserves a place among the military classics. But it is something more than a vivid and accurate account of a great captain and his campaigns. Its pages contain Henderson's cogent observations on virtually every phase of military activity, from problems of a purely technical nature such as tactical formations for infantry, the position of artillery in attack, and fire control to the more general problems of discipline, morale, and the sensitive relationship between soldier and statesman in a democracy at war. Here it might be pointed out that Henderson shared Wolseley's suspicion of all things political, agreeing that politics must necessarily exercise a supreme influence upon strategy yet at the same time stressing the dangers which often accompanied the domination of the army by civilian leaders. He was critical of the civilian interference with the army in Washington, but it must be remembered that Henderson was primarily concerned with but one phase of the war and that the least fortunate of Lincoln's administration. In most of his writings Henderson was weakest in his treatment of the political-strategical aspects of the war.[30]

There is concrete evidence to prove that Henderson actually intended his biography of Jackson to serve as a treatise on the art of war. He was critical of Hamley's *Operations of War*, at that time probably the best-known military text in the English language. Hamley, he felt, had "deliberately omitted all reference to the spirit of war, to moral influences, to the effect of rapidity, surprise and secrecy"—those vital intangibles so essential to good leadership and, incidentally, so characteristic of Jackson. Speaking before the Royal United Service Institution in 1894, Henderson explained his views on the need for a new textbook in strategy:

28 Roberts, "Memoir," pp. xxxiv–xxxv. See also *The Civil War: A Soldier's View*, p. 304.

29 "Stonewall Jackson," *Blackwood's*, CLXIV (December, 1898), 722.

30 See *Stonewall Jackson*, I, 13–16, 205–16 *passim*; II, 289, 489; *Science of War*, pp. 240–61 *passim*.

The methods by which the great generals bound victory to their colours are scarcely mentioned in the tactical text-books; and in Hamley's "Operations of War" the predominating influence of moral forces is alluded to only in a single paragraph. In short, the higher art of generalship, that section of military science to which formations, fire, and fortifications are subordinate . . . has neither manual nor text-book.[31]

There can be no doubt that Henderson, in writing his biography of the great Confederate captain, had in mind also the need for filling this gap in military literature.

Instead of outlining campaigns and expounding principles, Henderson wrote from the eye level of Jackson, describing each situation as he thought Jackson himself would have viewed it and focusing his attention upon the commander's methods and psychological reactions. This technique enabled Henderson to inject his own philosophy of war so skilfully into the narrative that on occasions where the facts were not known—or did not appear to reflect the usual credit on the Confederate general—Jackson's actions are explained and justified by Henderson's own strategical concepts.[32] While this practice occasionally led to minor distortion of fact, it did not necessarily detract from the value of the book as a military study. On the contrary, as Liddell Hart has suggested, it probably even enriched it as a military treatise, since the genius of Jackson was supplemented by the theories of a profound student of war.[33]

The year after *Stonewall Jackson* was published war broke out in South Africa. After British forces had suffered a series of setbacks, Lord Roberts was called to assume command. He had previously heard Henderson lecture before the Dublin Military Society, and by coincidence he had just finished reading the biography of Jackson. Convinced that Henderson "would be able to turn his knowledge to practical account," Roberts in January, 1900, appointed him to his newly formed staff as Director of Intelligence. On the long sea voyage out, the two spent hours together walking up and down the decks of the "Dunottar Castle," discussing strategy and its application to the coming campaign. During the days of preparation at Cape Town, Henderson's "fertile suggestions and

---

31 A. R. Godwin-Austen, *The Staff and the Staff College* (London, 1927), p. 114. See also *Science of War*, p. 169, and Henderson, "Strategy and Its Teaching," *R.U.S.I. Journal*, XLII (July, 1898), 767.

32 See *The Civil War: A Soldier's View*, p. 303 n.

33 *The British Way in Warfare* (London, 1932), p. 76.

sober criticisms . . . played no small part in confirming the native intuition and strengthening the resolution of his chief."[34] He performed useful service in obtaining maps of the theater of operations, and, doubtless guided by Jackson's dictum, "always mystify and mislead" (a phrase that has become idiomatic in English military parlance), he even took pains to plant misleading newspaper articles to camouflage the British plan of campaign. Lord Roberts has recorded that during the campaign former students of Henderson at the Staff College would file into his tent at odd hours, "eager to discuss those actual problems which they had so often studied in theory, glad of the chance given them of referring their doubts and difficulties" to their esteemed teacher.[35]

But ill health soon caused Henderson to relinquish active campaigning and return to England, where he was assigned the task of writing the official history of the war. In the fall of 1901 he again visited South Africa, this time to study the battlefields and gather material for his book. He soon suffered a relapse, and although he continued with his research for another year, he did not recover. Never in robust health, Henderson died in 1903 in Egypt, where he had been sent to avoid the rigors of another English winter. He was not quite fifty.

"The influence of such a man must bear good fruit." Lord Roberts expressed his hope that Henderson's writings would have as much influence on British military policy as the books of Captain A. T. Mahan had had in naval matters.[36] The obituary that appeared in the *Times* likened Henderson's influence in the British army to that of Von Moltke in Germany,[37] and while this statement is doubtless an exaggeration, Henderson did have a wide following, and his views on military subjects were well received. Through his lectures and numerous publications he reached a large audience, and for years he served as the special military correspondent for the *Times* in covering foreign military maneuvers. In 1901 Lord Roberts ordered him to revise and bring the old *Infantry Drill Book* up to date. Henderson died before completing this task, but the manuscript he left behind was found to be so meaty in doctrine common to all the arms that the committee designated to complete the work

[34] L. S. Amery, *My Political Life*, Vol. I: *England before the Storm, 1896–1914* (London, 1953), p. 126.

[35] Roberts, "Memoir," pp. xxxvi–xxxviii.

[36] *Ibid.*, p. xxxiii.   [37] *Times,* March 7, 1903.

issued it under a new title, *Combined Training* (1902). The "fore-runner of a new conception of military textbooks," *Combined Training* represented a definite break with the past. Until "all works and regulations which had hitherto dealt with the subject contained in this manual" were revised, Lord Roberts instructed that it was to be regarded as "authoritative on every subject with which it deals."[38]

From the nature of his writings, however, it seems probable that Henderson left his deepest mark not so much upon tactical and material reforms as upon military thought in general. His writings, like his lectures, were inspirational. *Stonewall Jackson*, "an admirable exposition of the generalship of small semiprofessional armies," became a popular military text. Lord Wolseley stated that he knew of no book that could add more "to the soldier's knowledge of strategy and the art of war," and General Fuller has testified that "its influence was enormous."[39]

If Henderson has not become identified with any specific school of military theory, there are good reasons. He died before his thoughts on war had crystallized. *The Science of War*, regarded by some as Henderson's most important military work,[40] was after all a collection of representative essays rather than a carefully thought out synthesis of Henderson's views, and in all his writings he was interested primarily in providing "a clear insight into the innumerable problems connected with the organisation and the command of an armed force."[41]

It must be kept in mind, too, that while Henderson may have envisaged a war fought by a British army far larger than that which Wellington had commanded, he was writing for an army designed primarily to police the empire and protect the country against the old bogy of invasion. In Germany and France the military leaders could anticipate every detail of mobilization beforehand and shape their strategy accordingly. But in England it was not so simple. As Henderson himself pointed out:

[38] Dunlop, *Development of the British Army*, pp. 225–26, 291. In 1905 *Combined Training* became Part I of *Field Service Regulations*, which was superseded in 1909 by a new manual. Sir James E. Edmonds (comp.), *Military Operations, France and Belgium, 1914* (London, 1922), I, 9.

[39] Wolseley, "Introduction," *Stonewall Jackson*, I, xvi; Fuller, *The Army in My Time*, p. 122.

[40] See Ralph Henderson, *Records of My Family*, pp. 114–15.

[41] *Science of War*, p. 395.

It is as useless to anticipate in what quarter of the globe our troops may be next employed as to guess at the tactics, the armament, and even the colour . . . of our next enemy. Each new expedition demands special equipment, special methods of supply and special tactical devices, and sometimes special armament. . . . Except for the defence of the United Kingdom and of India, much remains to be provided when the Cabinet declares that war is imminent.[42]

In his writings Henderson was as flexible as the military situation confronting Britain. Strategical principles were to be obeyed "rather in the spirit than in the letter." According to Henderson, the successful strategist is a man like Jackson, who, knowing "exactly how far he can go in disregarding or in modifying" the so-called principles of war, was at the same time "ingenious enough to bring those into adjustment which are apparently irreconcilable."[43] Henderson's students faced a more rigid situation. The shift in British foreign policy signified by the Anglo-French Entente in 1904 meant not only the abandonment of a policy of isolation but, ultimately, commitment to France. It became increasingly clear, therefore, that the army these men had to raise, train, and equip was destined for use on the Continent. Henderson had indicated where answers to some of the questions might be found, but he never attempted to devise any specific formula for victory.

Henderson also left his mark on military education. As one of the team sent by Wolseley to the Staff College in the 1890's to make the British officer a more serious student of his profession, Henderson made a major contribution in elevating the reputation of that institution. Previously the courses there had often been dull and formal. Sir George Aston, who attended the Staff College in 1889, recalls that one of the best students in his class, a Royal Engineer "who had earned great fame by his surveys of large areas on the North West Frontier of India," had had one of his maps returned by the instructor with the comment, "You should practise gravel-pits."[44] But with the arrival of the new regime such pedantry was discouraged. "We want officers to absorb, not to cram," insisted Colonel H. T. H. Hildyard, who became commandant in 1893, and Henderson's teaching was in line with this policy. He broadened the course in

[42] [Henderson], "The War in South Africa," *Edinburgh Review,* CXCI (January, 1900), 251–52.

[43] *Science of War,* p. 42.

[44] Major General Sir George Aston, *Memories of a Marine* (London, 1925), pp. 100–101.

military history to include the Civil War campaigns in addition to the wars for German unification, and, perhaps remembering his days as a history student at Oxford, he gave each student personal attention such as he might receive in a university seminar.[45]

Henderson must have been an unusual teacher, and there is abundant evidence to indicate that he was an effective one. By "the charm of his personality and the inspiration of his teaching," he exercised an influence that was "almost unique" in the history of the Staff College. He was intrusted with some of the best minds in the army, many of his students later attaining positions of high command during World War I.[46] These men, wrote one of Henderson's most prominent pupils, "would readily admit that such successes as attended their leadership were largely due to the sound instruction and inspiring counsel which they received from their old tutor some twenty years or so before." The *Times* had sounded the right note indeed when it had predicted, in 1903, that Henderson's influence would be felt "in the next great war, if that should take place when those who have passed through the Staff College in the nineties are in positions of command."[47]

Henderson's writings, particularly *Stonewall Jackson*, influenced both the quantity and the quality of the literature on the Civil War published in England during the following decade. Most of the books and articles that appeared were written to assist hopeful young officers in mastering the intricacies of Jackson's campaigns in preparation for the promotion examinations.[48] The military history

[45] Godwin-Austen, *The Staff and the Staff College*, pp. 231–33.

[46] The following extract from a letter printed in the *Times* is of interest: ". . . in May, 1897, Colonel Henderson said to a small gathering of whom I was one, 'There is a fellow in your batch who will be Commander-in-Chief one of these days'; and on being asked who it might be, said 'Douglas Haig.' The fulfilment of this forecast came at St. Omer at the end of 1915." Quoted in Ralph Henderson, *Records of My Family*, pp. 111–12. One naturally wonders if this story existed before Haig became famous.

[47] Sir William Robertson, *From Private to Field Marshal* (Boston, 1921), p. 83; Sir Frederick Maurice, *The Life of General Lord Rawlinson of Trent* (London, 1928), pp. 26, 84; *Times*, March 7, 1903.

[48] The Officer Promotion Examinations were instituted in 1850, when it was decreed that ensigns and lieutenants should undergo an examination before being promoted to a higher rank (Sir John W. Fortescue, *A History of the British Army* [London, 1899–1930], XIII, 20–21). In 1871, a system of garrison classes to prepare officers for these examinations was developed, and years later, when these classes were abolished, young officers had to resort to the "crammers" (Colonel Willoughby Verner, *The Military Life of H.R.H. George, Duke of Cambridge* [London, 1905], I, 143–45). Most of the Civil War campaign studies written between 1900 and 1914 were designed to serve this purpose. After 1904, the questions for the promotion

section of these examinations generally included one or more of the Civil War campaigns, and each year that a Civil War topic was selected, new studies appeared about the campaign in question. Both the examinations and the accompanying cram books leaned heavily upon the facts and opinions presented in Henderson's biography of Jackson. In November, 1904, for example, the questions for the promotion examinations were based upon Henderson's treatment of the Virginia campaigns, with special emphasis upon Jackson's operations in the Shenandoah Valley. A similar examination for officers of the Auxiliary forces covered the operations leading up to and including the battle of Fredericksburg, Henderson's books being considered the chief text.[49] The questions for 1908–9 concerned Grant's campaign in Virginia in 1864,[50] but the following year officer candidates were again being tested on their knowledge of the early campaigns in Virginia and Jackson's Valley campaign.[51] In

---

examinations—of which military history formed only one of six categories—were selected by the Army Council and generally included one or more of the campaigns treated in *Stonewall Jackson*. Every candidate for advancement to any rank up to and including that of major was required to pass these examinations (R. J. Grewing, "Officers," *Encyclopaedia Britannica* [11th ed.; New York, 1910], XX, 20). Perhaps it is significant that one of the members of the Army Council, Major General H. C. O. Plumer, had been a close personal friend of Henderson and was himself convinced of the value of studying the Civil War (see *R.U.S.I. Journal*, LV [September, 1911], 1144).

[49] H. M. E. Brunker, *Story of the Campaign in Eastern Virginia* (London, 1904), was specifically written to aid officers in preparing for the Officer Promotion Examination in 1904. Like most books written for this purpose, it was little more than a poor condensation of *Stonewall Jackson* and contained numerous errors. J. H. Anderson, *Notes on the Life of Stonewall Jackson* (London, 1905), suffers the same shortcomings. A third book, Edward Nash, *Jackson's Strategy* (London, 1904), is of higher caliber. Nash showed an independence lacking in most of the campaign studies of the period, and he was one of the few who occasionally criticized Jackson (pp. 10, 11, 16, 18, 26–27).

[50] Cram books written to help prepare British officers for this examination include J. H. Anderson, *Grant's Campaign in Virginia, May 1–June 30, 1864* (London, 1908); Charles Francis Atkinson, *Grant's Campaign of 1864 and 1865; The Wilderness and Cold Harbor* (London, 1908); H. M. E. Brunker, *Grant and Lee in Virginia, May and June, 1864* (London, 1908); and Captain G. H. Vaughan-Sawyer, *Grant's Campaign in Virginia, 1864* (London, 1908). See also T. Miller Maguire, "The Battle of Spotsylvania," *United Service Magazine*, XXXVIII (October, 1908), 63–71; and two thoughtful articles by Lieutenant Colonel J. E. Edmonds: "The Campaign in Virginia in May and June, 1864," *Journal of the Royal Artillery*, XXXV (1908–9), 521–47; and "Lee and Grant in Northern Virginia in May and June, 1864," *Royal Engineers Journal*, VIII (July, 1908), 5–23.

[51] J. H. Anderson, *The American Civil War* (London, 1910), deals only with the Virginia campaigns to June, 1863. See also Major G. W. Redway, "The Shenandoah Valley Campaign," *United Service Magazine*, XL (February, 1910), 522–30, and Redway, "McClellan's Campaign on the Yorktown Peninsula," *ibid.*, XLI (May, 1910), 166–78.

1912 the questions were once again on the Virginia campaigns of 1862 and 1863,[52] while two papers on the Shenandoah Valley campaign—one general and the other covering in detail the events between May 16 and June 9, 1862—were required for the promotion examination in 1913.[53]

Paradoxically, Henderson, whose primary intent had been to develop a flexible and inquisitive attitude in the minds of his students, ultimately became the agent of a dogmatic approach to the Civil War. Official reliance upon his books and heavy emphasis upon facts naturally did not encourage either new research or original thought. Most of the campaign studies of this period, in fact, were little more than abridged—and often mutilated—versions of *Stonewall Jackson*. By writing to drum facts into the heads of candidates for promotion, the authors of these cram books succeeded only in eclipsing the main lessons Henderson had contrived to teach. What had given life to *Stonewall Jackson* was the way in which Henderson had blended his philosophy of war into the narrative. In contrast, the majority of those who followed in his footsteps concentrated on excessive detail and thus ignored the very qualities that had made the biography of Jackson a valuable military text. A few scattered writers stepped out of Henderson's shadow either by conducting independent research or else by concentrating on campaigns not included in *Stonewall Jackson*,[54] but most of the military studies of the Civil War written in England during this period differed little from the earlier treatment of the Prussian campaigns. As all armies were shortly to discover, "to be able to enumerate the blades of grass in the Shenandoah Valley and the yards marched by Stonewall Jackson's men is not an adequate foundation for leadership in a

---

[52] J. H. Anderson, *Notes on the Battles of Antietam and Fredericksburg* (London, 1912); Colonel P. H. Dalbiac, *Chancellorsville and Gettysburg* (London, 1911); Colonel J. E. Gough, *Fredericksburg and Chancellorsville* (London, 1913); "Miles" [Walter E. Day], *The Campaign of Gettysburg* (London, [1911]); Captain E. W. Sheppard, *The Campaign in Virginia and Maryland* (London, 1911); H. W. Wynter, "Artillery Fighting at the Battle of Gettysburg," *Journal of the Royal Artillery*, XXXVIII (1911–12), 51–74.

[53] T. Miller Maguire, *Jackson's Campaigns in Virginia, 1861–62* (London, 1913); Lieutenant Colonel Holmes Wilson, "The Strategy of the Valley Campaign (1861–62)," *Journal of the Royal Artillery*, XL (1913–14), 197–216.

[54] These works include Captain Cecil Battine, *The Crisis of the Confederacy* (London, 1905), a competent tactical study of Gettysburg and the Wilderness obviously intended as a sequel to *Stonewall Jackson;* Atkinson, *Grant's Campaigns of 1864;* "Miles," *Campaign of Gettysburg;* and the writings of Edmonds and Redway.

future war where conditions and armament have radically changed."[55]

Henderson's dramatic portrayal of the colorful Jackson together with the sentimentalism of the dying Victorian era did much to produce that legendary atmosphere which in England was beginning to surround both Jackson and Lee. The former came to be regarded with an awe and admiration quite out of proportion to his genius. One writer, who had sense enough at least to remain anonymous, openly rejoiced that Stonewall "should be placed upon a pedestal. . . . There may be another and perhaps seamier side to Jackson's career, but Colonel Henderson has done well to keep it from our sight. We want no blemishes or infirmities reproduced upon the statue as it is reared for our delight nor should we tolerate dirt to be flung at it in its glorious completeness."[56]

This volley was aimed at Major G. W. Redway, who had been so bold as to suggest that perhaps too much attention was being paid to the Shenandoah Valley campaign—which was, after all, essentially a subsidiary operation and not the decisive campaign of the war. Redway's article was denounced on the ground that it was "bald and dull, paradoxical and misleading, and subversive to one of the tenets of our military faith." Actually Redway was one of the better English students of the Civil War, having both visited many of the battlefields and consulted the *Official Records*. He can hardly be blamed for feeling indignant at the reception of his views. "It seems," he wrote in self-defense, "that I had erred in venturing to descant upon a topic which involved reference to . . . Jackson without first consulting the work of . . . Henderson and squaring my views . . . with those of his disciples." There were others who also dared criticize Jackson, but they managed somehow to escape the abuse that had caused Redway to wonder, with considerable justice, if perhaps Jackson "has not been too fortunate in his biographer."[57]

[55] Liddell Hart, *The Remaking of Modern Armies* (London, 1927), pp. 170–71. General Fuller writes: ". . . in 1913, I remember a Major recommending Henderson's *Stonewall Jackson* to a brother officer, and then, a few minutes later, when this book was being discussed, committing the error of supposing that [the battle of] 'Cross Keys' was a public house in Odiham and Jackson the name of the man who ran it" (*The Army in My Time*, pp. 53–54).

[56] "Hotspur," "Stonewall Jackson: Some Current Criticisms," *United Service Magazine*, XLI (April, 1910), 49.

[57] G. W. Redway, "The American Civil War—A Reply," *ibid.*, XLII (March, 1911), 637–39. The article in question was Redway's "Shenandoah Valley Campaign." Evidently others besides "Hotspur" also attacked this article, for Redway wrote: "I have been continually reminded by my critics of the debt we owe to . . . Hender-

Redway's case doubtless is an extreme example, but it does indicate the extent of Henderson's popularity at the time in England. Enthusiasm for the Civil War may also have been evoked by the experiences of the English in South Africa, for it was frequently noted that the two wars were fought under basically similar conditions.[58]

Henderson died on the eve of the greatest changes in the British army since the Napoleonic wars. The Cardwell Reforms had altered army organization, but the changes that occurred in the decade before 1914 were more fundamental. Some were intended to correct flaws that had contributed to the early military reverses in South Africa;[59] others were designed to create an army that would enable Britain to fulfil her obligations should war break out on the Continent.

These reforms were accompanied by an organized effort to mobilize public opinion and to increase Everyman's knowledge of military affairs. The National Service League, vigorously led by Lord Roberts, demanded compulsory military service as the only means of national survival, while the Navy League, founded in 1895, clamored for the support of all classes in maintaining the fleet "at

---

son. One says, 'The life of Stonewall Jackson is a priceless legacy bequeathed to the British Army'; another thinks that 'there is nothing more remarkable than the way in which . . . Henderson's work has been recommended to officers and set over and over again for examinations'" ("The American Civil War—A Reply," p. 638). Redway's *Fredericksburg: A Study in War* (London, 1906) is one of the best campaign histories of the Civil War written during this period.

[58] Various English writers have compared the Civil War with the war in South Africa. Colonel F. N. Maude was of the opinion that the Civil War "deserves far closer and more attentive study" because it approximated "very closely indeed" the conditions of the current struggle against the Boers ("Military Training and Modern Weapons," *Contemporary Review*, LXXVII [January–June, 1900], 311). "Miles," who later visited the Civil War battlefields and wrote a respectable book about Gettysburg, thought it "worth considering" that Lord Roberts had promoted Henderson to his staff, an action that to "Miles" indicated an opinion on the part of Lord Roberts "that the particular study of the . . . Civil War was the one that was most immediately applicable to the present Transvaal War" ("Lessons of the War," *Contemporary Review*, LXXVII, 156–57). For others who professed to see a parallel between the Civil War and the Boer War, see Spenser Wilkinson, *War and Policy* (New York, 1900), chap. xxx; Major E. S. Valentine, "An American Parallel to the Present Campaign," *Fortnightly Review*, LXXIII (August, 1901), 660–67; T. Miller Maguire, "A Study in Devastation," *National Review*, XXXVII (August, 1901), 901–12.

[59] The Elgin Commission was established in August, 1902, to investigate the Boer War. In April of the following year the Norfolk Commission was appointed to study the condition and function of the Auxiliary Forces, and in 1904 Lord Esher headed a committee charged with the task of reorganizing the War Office. Dunlop, *Development of the British Army*, pp. 121 ff.; Lieutenant Colonel J. S. Omond, *Parliament and the Army, 1642–1904* (Cambridge, 1933), pp. 148–70 *passim*.

the requisite standard of strength"—meaning, of course, to keep
well ahead of Germany in the Dreadnought race.[60] One has but to
scan the pages of any English periodical of this period to appreciate
the extent to which the public was kept informed on military matters. In 1905 the *Times* appointed Lieutenant Colonel Charles
A'Court Repington its first regular military correspondent in the
expectation that his columns "would stimulate thought concerning
the art of war." Soon afterward Oxford established a chair in military history,[61] bringing the study of war within the scope of higher
education. If it was true that before the turn of the century "the
British people took an interest in war rather like a virtuous spinster
takes an interest in wickedness,"[62] clearly such a spinsterhood did
not long survive Queen Victoria.

Within the army itself there were signs of "a great intellectual
awakening." The Manchester Tactical Society was increasingly
active and served as a sounding board for discussion of proposed
army reforms. Inexpensive editions like "The Pall Mall Series,"
originating in 1903, and "The Special Campaign Series," which began to appear in 1907, facilitated publication and encouraged soldiers to try their hand at military history.[63] Obviously there was a
demand for military books, otherwise Gale and Polden, Limited,
would never have stocked better than half a million volumes of
military interest. It was an age of rapidly changing concepts of

---

[60] Fuller, *The Army in My Time*, p. 113; David James, *Lord Roberts* (London,
1954), pp. 411–53; Arthur J. Marder, *The Anatomy of British Sea Power: A History
of British Naval Policy in the Pre-Dreadnought Era, 1880–1905* (New York, 1940),
pp. 49–61; Spenser Wilkinson, *Thirty-five Years, 1874–1909* (London, 1933), pp. 255–
85. A pacifist's view of these proceedings is found in Caroline E. Playne, *The Pre-war
Mind in Britain* (London, 1928), pp. 140–55.

[61] *The Twentieth Century Test* (Vol. III of *The History of the Times, 1884–
1912* [New York, 1942]), p. 462. The *Times* often had had on its staff someone
competent to write on military subjects, and, when the situation demanded, a temporary appointment was made to insure coverage of important military events. Mr.
L. S. Amery, for example, was named Chief of the *Times* war correspondent service
in South Africa in 1900 (Amery, *My Political Life*, I, 115), but not until Repington's
appointment did the *Times* employ a regular military correspondent. It was this same
Amery who managed "to persuade" his college, All Souls, to endow a readership in
military history in 1905, which was converted to a full professorship in 1909. Spenser
Wilkinson, one of the founders of the Navy League, prominent journalist and noted
writer on military subjects, received the first appointment to this chair, possibly at
the instigation of Sir Charles Firth (*ibid.*, I, 221; Wilkinson, *Thirty-five Years*, pp.
312–15).

[62] Arthur, *Wellington to Wavell*, p. 83.

[63] Another publisher, Messrs. Clowes and Sons, helped at least one military writer
publish his books at extremely modest prices. See T. Miller Maguire, *The Campaigns
in Virginia* (London, 1913), p. vi.

warfare, and much energy was also expended in translating the writings of foreign theorists. The views of Bernhardi, Foch, Von der Goltz, and Clausewitz were known to many English readers.[64]

The Civil War, for reasons already explained, was given a disproportionate amount of attention in the decade preceding the outbreak of war in 1914.[65] Crammed as they were with military technicalities and burdened by excessive detail, most of these campaign studies were mediocre, devoid of any new ideas, and lacking in perception and literary ability. They are of interest today primarily for what they reveal about British military thought during the period.

Because of their connection with the promotion examination, the first purpose of these cram books obviously was to emphasize and illustrate accepted military principles. Officers studying for promotion were often required to read about Jackson's Valley campaign, for example, because it provided a correct application of the strategy of interior lines, and in the examinations they were likely to be asked, as were the candidates in 1913, to justify from Jackson's campaigns the position that "the inferior force holding the interior position between its enemies must have the advantage, if it strikes them in detail while separated."[66] Captain H. W. Wynter's articles on artillery at Antietam and Gettysburg furnish a specific case in point. Guided by regulations "preached" by the *Field Artillery Training*, Wynter culled the *Official Records* for incidents "applicable to the conditions of modern warfare and the principles of modern tactics."

> The material of artillery has of course been revolutionized since the year 1862, and there is little or nothing to be learnt by studying the effect of fire in those days. But the co-operation between guns and infantry is an unchanging principle of modern war, and . . . no little advantage can be derived by studying the successes and failures of the Americans in this respect.[67]

[64] For signs of this "intellectual awakening" among British soldiers, see George Arthur, "The Soldier as Student," *Fortnightly Review*, LXXXVIII (October, 1907), 620–29; Lt. Col. Alsager Pollock, "A Military Education," *ibid.*, LXXXVII (February, 1907), 537–47; T. Miller Maguire, "The Military Education of Officers," *National Review*, XXXVI (December, 1900), 507–16.

[65] One-fourth the number of books published in "The Special Campaign Series" were about the Civil War.

[66] Maguire, *Jackson's Campaigns in Virginia*, p. 42.

[67] Captain H. W. Wynter, "Artillery at the Battle of Sharpsburg," *Journal of the Royal Artillery*, XL (1913–14), 177.

Wynter was especially interested in the use of shrapnel during the Civil War, in "the moral and physical effect of artillery" (which did not appear to be very great), in "concentration and centralized control over the guns," the responsibility of artillery officers and their relations with brigade and divisional commanders, "the distribution of artillery in a large army," and other subjects of this nature covered in the *Field Service Regulations*.[68]

Curiously enough, the official texts were slow to incorporate examples from the Civil War. Even the latest editions of Clery's *Minor Tactics* and Home's *Précis of Modern Tactics* continued to stress campaigns in Europe; this was true also of most books on strategy, the one phase of the so-called science of war where fundamental principles were regarded as constant. Hamley, who had drawn upon Civil War campaigns to illustrate his precepts, was still looked upon as the "strategic pedagogue of the British Army,"[69] but more recent studies like James's *Modern Strategy* made less use of the Civil War campaigns.[70]

The Civil War also provided fuel for the burning issues of the day, the most controversial being that over the tactics and armament of cavalry. Technically the question was whether cavalry ought to act solely as mounted infantry, as Havelock had urged years before; whether it should continue as regular cavalry supplemented by a separate force of mounted infantry, as Wolseley and later Henderson had advocated; or whether it should be employed as a combination shock and missile weapon, trained in the use of both rifle and saber and capable of fighting mounted as well as on foot. Basically it was a question of emphasis: was the rifle or the saber to be the chief weapon for cavalry?

The Civil War gave comfort to writers in every camp. Extreme advocates of mounted infantry found their spokesman in Erskine Childers, who had seen the cavalry in action in South Africa and had become convinced of the inadequacy of the *arme blanche* in modern war. Childers had written that volume in *The Times His-*

---

[68] Wynter, "Artillery Fighting at the Battle of Gettysburg, July 1st, 2nd, and 3rd, 1863," *ibid.*, XXXVIII (1911–12), 64.

[69] Cyril Falls, *A Hundred Years of War* (London, 1953), p. 29.

[70] Lieutenant Colonel Walter H. James, *Modern Strategy: An Outline of the Principles Which Guide the Conduct of Campaigns* (London, 1903), *passim*; see especially pp. xi, 79–80. Greater attention was given the Civil War in Colonel C. E. Callwell, *Military Operations and Maritime Preponderance: Their Relations and Interdependence* (Edinburgh and London, 1905), pp. 108–9, 171–72, 273–74, 289–96, 403–5, 408–15.

tory of the War in South Africa which dealt with guerrilla operations,[71] and in subsequent books on the subject of cavalry he had
enlarged his study to include relevant experiences from other wars.
Naturally a good many of his examples came from the Civil War.
Childers wrote with conviction. Where had cavalry first "learnt
reliance on the firearm, though their example passed unnoticed in
Europe"? In the Civil War. What had he himself seen "winning its
way to success in South Africa"? The mounted rifleman. "What
weapon succeeds in Manchuria?" The firearm. England had ignored
the lessons of the Civil War and the teachings of "its most brilliant
English proponent, Colonel Henderson," for the British cavalry
that rode off to war in 1899 little resembled the mounted forces that
had established a "really great and stimulating" precedent in 1861–
65.[72]

Likewise, the Boer War convinced the Earl of Dundonald of the
value of mounted infantry, which he predicted "will be more generally useful to the Empire than the man trained to consider the
sword as his principal weapon. The cavalryman of the future should
be a first-class rifle shot, a first-class walker, and trained in recon-
noitring and outpost work to the highest degree of efficiency."[73] In
the preface to his *Cavalry Training, Canada* (1904), Dundonald
was more emphatic still.

It is said by some that the next European war will show that the
effective use of the sabre and the lance is not over. . . . There will be
occasions, no doubt, when men may run short of ammunition or be too
panic-stricken to offer much resistance to pursuing swordsmen, but such
occasions are likely to be extremely rare, and they will depend for success largely on favourable conditions . . . unlikely often to occur.

The rifle, then, is the weapon for cavalry in the future; especially for
cavalry . . . which has but a short time for training. To make a skilled
swordsman demands a lengthened period; but with coolness, courage
and common sense added to his comparatively limited preparation, the
intelligent Canadian behind a rifle will be more than a match for any
two swordsmen. So, in order that they may be of the greatest possible
service . . . the cavalry of the Dominion should give the utmost attention
to marksmanship.[74]

[71] Erskine Childers (ed.), *The Times History of the War in South Africa, 1899–
1902*, V (London, 1907), xii.

[72] Erskine Childers, *War and the Arme Blanche* (London, 1910), pp. 52, 353;
German Influence on British Cavalry (London, 1911), pp. 11–12, 49, 62–63.

[73] Lieutenant General the Earl of Dundonald, *My Army Life* (London, 1926),
pp. 181–82.

[74] Quoted in *ibid.*, p. 252.

Lord Roberts was another who had faith in mounted infantry. Roberts took care not to repudiate officially the old doctrine, but he wrote a spirited Foreword to one of Childers' books, and he often expressed his opinion that the *arme blanche* alone would never be able to win a decisive victory over a highly trained enemy armed with magazine rifles. Even in his *Memorandum* of 1903 on cavalry armament, Roberts made frequent and favorable mention of Civil War cavalry.[75]

If what they wrote about the Civil War is any criterion, most English soldiers probably preferred some combination of shock and dismounted action. Whereas Wolseley and Henderson had argued for a balanced arm comprising separate regiments of mounted infantry and cavalry, these later writers wanted to make their man "equally efficient with both rifle and cold steel."[76] They accused Childers of slanting his information on the ground that "although a rifle was added to the equipment of the U.S. Cavalry soldier shortly after the war commenced, the sword and revolver for use at short quarters were not discarded, and that this equipment, as a result of the experience gained in the American Civil War has been retained ever since."[77] Captain Cecil Battine, author of a tactical study of Gettysburg, was a typical spokesman for this school: "There is no campaign in which greater error has been taught, or more fallacious views on . . . cavalry expressed, than will be found as regards the . . . American Civil War. . . . It was not until 1864, when Sheridan *first massed his cavalry* [i.e., shock tactics] that the fruits of victory were duly secured. In 1862 and 1863 the American cavalry . . . was employed only as mounted infantry."

Experience had "taught" Sheridan to make greater use of shock tactics, and thus he had become a "worthy rival" of Stuart himself. To Battine, the Civil War proved that no decisive result could be attained "without combination of fire and shock actions; the one is a consummation and necessary complement of the other."[78] Major Legard was another who was convinced that the Americans "struck

[75] James, *Lord Roberts,* pp. 439–41; "Memorandum by the Commander-in-Chief," *R.U.S.I. Journal,* XLVII (May, 1903), 575–82.

[76] "Miles," *Gettysburg,* pp. 179–80.

[77] See the review by General Staff officer of Erskine Childers' *War and the Arme Blanche* in the *Cavalry Journal,* V, 411.

[78] Captain Cecil Battine, "The Use of the Horse Soldier in the Twentieth Century," *R.U.S.I. Journal,* LII (March, 1908), 326; *Crisis of the Confederacy,* pp. 26, 75–78, 272, 273, 391–400; "Cavalry at Sadowa," *Cavalry Journal,* III (April, 1908), 167–74.

the proper mean between shock tactics and dismounted work, and used both in close and effective co-operation." Contrary to what Childers and others had asserted, Civil War cavalry was much more than mounted infantry—"cavalry combats such as Brandy Station, cases of Cavalry charging Infantry such as Chancellorsville and Aldie, are far too numerous to admit of this view being taken by even the most bigoted and prejudiced advocate of Mounted Infantry." According to Legard, the American campaigns showed, first, the power gained by a close combination of shock and fire tactics and, second, the weakness of employing cavalry in small bodies rather than concentrating for a decisive charge.[79] While attaching much importance to the power of the rifle, Legard and others of this school still regarded "lance and sabre" cavalry as being good for something other than providing occasional splendor at military funerals and ceremonial escorts.

The most significant fact about the British views of Civil War cavalry is that they parrot official doctrine. In 1903 it was stipulated that henceforth the carbine or rifle would be considered the "principal weapon" for cavalry, and the *Cavalry Manual* issued under the auspices of Lord Roberts in 1904 stressed the importance of mounted infantry. But Lord Roberts retired from the army that same year, the victim of a reorganization that abolished the office of commander-in-chief, and before long official enthusiasm for mounted infantry began to wane. Within two months Roberts felt sufficiently concerned to solicit the support of his former chief of staff for continued abolition of the lance because he feared "that a great struggle will be made to get that weapon re-introduced now that I have left the War Office."[80]

His concern was justified: the new drill book that was issued in 1906 did not attach as much importance to mounted infantry as previous regulations, and by 1907 not only were two of the three existing schools for mounted infantry abolished but, according to a German observer, "the impression [in England] is once more gain-

[79] Major D'Arcy Legard, "Confederate Cavalry in Virginia," *ibid.*, II (January, 1907), 41, 52. Similar views, with minor variations, are expressed in "Eques," "American Cavalry," *ibid.*, pp. 295–301; Captain J. W. E. Donaldson and Captain A. F. Becke, *Military History Applied to Modern Warfare* (2d ed.; London, 1907), pp. 356, 380; John Formby, *The American Civil War: A Concise History of Its Causes, Progress, and Results* (New York, 1910), I, 484; Colonel E. R. Kenyon, "Some Lessons from the American Civil War," *United Service Magazine*, XLVIII (January–March, 1913), 669; and Redway, *Fredericksburg*, pp. 55, 57, 68.

[80] James, *Lord Roberts*, pp. 430–40; Charles Sydney Goldman, "Cavalry: Its True Functions in Modern War," *Cavalry Journal*, I, 65.

ing ground that even in these days, well trained, well mounted cavalry can still attack with the best results."[81] Despite use made of mounted infantry by the Russians and the apparent ineffectiveness of regular cavalry in Manchuria in 1905,[82] the lessons of this war, like those of the American war before it, were misconstrued. Russian cavalry was weak, it was said, precisely because of its habit of fighting on foot; genuine cavalry, "and plenty of it," was all that was needed to remedy the situation. Russian cavalry had played a subordinate part because "for many years the Russians have been teaching their men to look on the rifle as the principal thing, the horse taking second place as a useful means of conveyance." Critics of this type of cavalry were convinced that such training was detrimental to the so-called cavalry spirit and that therefore "nothing useful and effective is achieved."[83] Clearly this was the underlying philosophy of the *Cavalry Training Manual* for 1907, which stated: "The essence of the cavalry spirit lies in holding the balance correctly between fire power and shock action. . . . It must be accepted as a principle that the rifle, effective as it is, cannot replace the effect produced by the speed of the horse, the magnetism of the charge, and the terror of cold steel."[84]

The speed of the horse, the magnetism of the charge, and the terror of cold steel! Chesney, Havelock, Denison, Wolseley, and Henderson all had become convinced of the need for mounted infantry, for in varying degrees the Civil War had taught each that shock tactics no longer would enable cavalry to rule the battlefield. Yet, significantly, almost every one of the Civil War campaign studies published after 1907, the year in which the new cavalry regulations were issued, advocated some combination of fire and shock tactics. Because these books went hand in glove with the promotion examination, they were expected to represent the official point of view. So it was that "in America, where rifle and sword were used, at first the conditions were looked on as 'quite abnormal'; but now [1909], while American methods are held to be good, great stress is laid on their use of the sword."[85]

81 "German Views on Mounted Infantry," *Cavalry Journal*, II, 347–51.

82 See Lieutenant General Sir Ian Hamilton, *A Staff Officer's Scrap-Book during the Russo-Japanese War* (London, 1908), I, 191.

83 "The Cavalry Lessons of the War," *Cavalry Journal*, I, 56–60; Major G. des Barrow, "The Spirit of Cavalry," *ibid.*, p. 22.

84 Quoted in Childers, *War and the Arme Blanche*, pp. 1–3.

85 "A Rifleman," *The Question of Mounted Infantry* (London, 1909), p. 86.

Any article on the Civil War printed in the *Cavalry Journal* was also certain to agree with the prevailing theories, for this periodical had been founded in 1906 by men who believed it "unwise to discard the sword or lance," and it soon was published under the auspices of the Cavalry School, where it came under the control of General Sir John French, the most prominent exponent of shock tactics as opposed to mounted infantry.[86] During the Boer War, French and his chief of staff, Colonel (later Field Marshal Sir Douglas) Haig had actually used mounted infantry to good effect, Haig even preparing a memorandum to show "the greatly increased power of action possessed by cavalry, now that it is armed with a good carbine,"[87] but after the war both men became militant proponents of modified shock tactics. Haig was convinced that Childers' theories, if followed, would lead directly to the grave, and in an unsigned review of Dundonald's *Cavalry Training* he defended the old-style cavalry:

Lord Dundonald sneers at the effect produced by sword and lance in modern war; surely he forgets that it is not the weapon carried but the moral factor of an apparently irresistible force, coming on at highest speed in spite of rifle fire, which affects the nerves and aim of the rapidly dismounted rifleman?

I ask those who have felt the elation of a successful charge or who have known the despondency which attacks those who have been ridden over by the horsemen whom they have fired at in vain, whether magazine fire, which makes the shooting so erratic, hurried, and much less easily controlled, and spends the ammunition so quickly, has really so very much changed the conditions of 30 years ago?[88]

Significantly, in his book on the strategical and tactical use of cavalry, Haig made no mention of Civil War cavalry despite the story that he was an avowed admirer of the Confederate cavalry leader Forrest. Seemingly forgetting all their South African experiences and ignoring or distorting the lessons of history, Haig and

[86] One of the original promoters of the *Cavalry Journal* was Charles Sydney Goldman, who contended that the Boer War did not signify the end of the *arme blanche*. See Goldmann, *With General French and the Cavalry in South Africa* (London, 1903), p. 411. In 1908 the editorship passed to Colonel W. H. Birkbeck and the staff of the Cavalry School, and in 1911 the Army Council made the editorship a part of the regular duties of the commandant of the Cavalry School (information derived from editorial notes in successive issues of the *Cavalry Journal*).

[87] This memorandum, dated November, 1899, is reprinted in Duff Cooper, *Haig* (London, 1935), I, 377–82.

[88] Quoted in Dundonald, *My Army Life*, pp. 252–53, where Haig is identified as the author of the unsigned review.

French convinced themselves "that only the old knee to knee cavalry charge with lance or sword would decide the wars of the future"; it would take the machine gun and trench of the first World War to prove conclusively that they had placed their bets on the wrong type of horse.[89]

The far more important problem of field fortifications attracted less attention. Those who studied the Civil War, even the early campaigns, were not blind to the value of intrenchments. They realized, most of them, "that one good man behind an earthwork was equal to three good men outside it,"[90] that "the length and intensity of these engagements" offered a clue to future campaigns,[91] but with one exception they did not attempt to synthesize the American experiences to discover fundamental operating principles. On the contrary, the author of the most detailed study of the Wilderness campaigns decided that the "one tactical lesson of all these battles was that attacking entrenchments was a matter not of principles, but of particular cases."[92]

The solitary exception was Lieutenant Colonel J. E. Edmonds, of the Corps of Royal Engineers; of all English authorities on the Civil War, Edmonds perhaps came the closest to comprehending Henderson's prediction that the Wilderness campaign was characteristic of wars to come. The Russo-Japanese war had "proved the correctness" of this forecast, for "many of the main characteristics of the two campaigns are the same:—There are the battles of many days duration; the continued use of night operations; the universal use of the spade both in the attack and in the defence, making the war one of what may be called siege operations in the field; and the

---

[89] Major General Douglas Haig, *Cavalry Studies, Strategical and Tactical* (London, 1907), *passim.* Haig reportedly considered Forrest "one of the greatest . . . of English-speaking commanders of mounted troops." Robert Selph Henry, *First with the Most Forrest* (New York, 1944), pp. 463–64. Haig's changing views toward cavalry are discussed in Amery, *My Political Life*, I, 132. A useful summary of the cavalry controversy, written by one who sympathized with the Haig-French school, is Lieutenant Colonel V. S. Charrington, *Where Cavalry Stands Today* (London, 1927), pp. 17–26.

[90] Redway, *The War of Secession, 1861–2*, pp. 145–46. Apparently the British *Official History* arrived at the same conclusion from the experiences of the First World War: ". . . in a conflict between foes of the same standard of skill, determination and valour, numbers approaching three to one are required to turn the scale decisively." Quoted in Liddell Hart, *Thoughts on War* (London, 1944), p. 292.

[91] Battine, *Crisis of the Confederacy*, pp. 386–419.

[92] Atkinson, *Grant's Campaign of 1864*, p. 327; "American Civil War," *Encyclopaedia Britannica* (11th ed.; New York, 1911), I, 826.

employment of all available troops in the front line without retaining a general reserve."

Edmonds did not venture to predict whether the next war would resemble "the rapid movements of a Stonewall Jackson" or "the deliberate hammerings of a Grant," but he believed in preparing for either eventuality. If he felt that the use of intrenchments had been overdone during the Civil War and that offensive maneuver was preferable to a war of sieges, he nonetheless recognized the instructive value of the Wilderness campaign. Specifically, it taught "the difficulty of reconnaissance in a close country," the value of "hasty fortifications constructed on the battlefield as opposed to positions prepared in advance," and the need to hold an enemy in front while outflanking him in his defensive positions. He learned that most of the attacks made by the Americans had "failed because they were made over too great a distance, without proper reconnaissance, and . . . because the force making them was not sufficiently strong," that "without proper artillery preparation . . . even in 1864 an attack on an entrenched position had little chance of success."

The Civil War also

repeatedly proved that even when the night march had succeeded, it was difficult to get the troops into attacking formation unobserved, and that the advantage gained was quickly lost. The records show that the troops were reported too tired to attack without rest and . . . a pause for food, and that those who went into action after a night march suffered more than usual from shock when they were wounded. The case is different when, as so often happened in Manchuria, troops already in position are led forward *short* distances in the darkness, or use the cover of darkness to advance a short distance to a fresh position.[93]

Edmonds also collaborated with W. Birkbeck Wood, an officer of the Volunteers, to write an informative and readable history of the Civil War, a book that stemmed from "the stimulating influence" of Henderson at the Staff College. Edmonds' book, in fact, remedied the main weakness of Henderson, who had concentrated on the campaigns in the East to the neglect of those in the West: English soldiers had always manifested greater interest in the eastern campaigns, but never before Henderson's time had the campaigns in the West been so completely ignored. Fletcher had given them

[93] Edmonds, "The Campaign in Virginia in May and June, 1864," *Journal of the Royal Artillery,* XXXV (1908–9), 541–47; "Lee and Grant in Northern Virginia in May and June, 1864, Some Notes on the Operations of," *Royal Engineers Journal,* VIII (1908), 19–20.

proportionate space in his history, and Hamley, Chesney, and Wolseley had all appreciated the genius of Sherman; but the campaign histories that flooded the market after Henderson's death contained little or nothing about the war in the West. Edmonds studied the war as a whole and concluded that the "military genius" of Lee and Jackson, the "unrivaled fighting capacity" of the armies they led, and the close proximity of Richmond and Washington had caused "disproportionate attention to be concentrated upon the Eastern theatre of war." Edmonds, therefore, advocated a reappraisal of the western campaigns, where, in his view, the "decisive blows were struck."[94] It is significant that the only other English officer to write a general history of the Civil War likewise regarded the western campaigns as "the most important in a military sense."[95]

From Chesney to Henderson, British officers had been interested in the performance of volunteer armies, and in the decade preceding the First World War this interest was intensified by the reorganization of the Volunteer and Reserve forces and by growing agitation for some form of conscription. Compulsory service was "actively canvassed" by a number of people; reviews and service journals "were full of articles advocating various remedies for the military problems." Some saw the solution in a more effective Volunteer establishment; others, like Roberts, believed that only conscription would give England enough soldiers to enable her to meet commitments.[96] Many British soldiers opposed conscription, and the great majority of those who wrote on the Civil War during these years agreed with Chesney, Fletcher, and Henderson. Civil War armies, they wrote, had ultimately attained a high state of efficiency, and the conscript—as distinguished from the volunteer—was "usually of inferior quality," providing the army with "only the worst and most unsoldierly elements of the population."[97] Few seemed to listen to the dissenting voices of two civilians—T. Miller Maguire, whose investigations of this problem had led him to conclude that "conscripts and obligatory men are better than volunteers in war," and

[94] W. Birkbeck Wood and Major J. R. Edmonds, *A History of the Civil War in the United States*, p. 527.

[95] Formby, *The American Civil War*, I, 72.

[96] Dunlop, *Development of the British Army*, p. 151; Theodore Ropp, "Conscription in Great Britain, 1900–1914," *Military Affairs*, XX (Summer, 1956), 71–76.

[97] Atkinson, "American Civil War," p. 826; *Grant's Campaign of 1864*, p. 46; Battine, *Crisis of the Confederacy*, pp. 43–49, 115, 412–13; "Miles," *Gettysburg*, pp. 22–24; Redway, *Fredericksburg*, p. 166, and *War of Secession*, p. 161.

H. W. Wilson, who feared that England might one day repeat the mistake of the Union by "not resorting to conscription at once" and thereby spill the cream of British youth in the first rush of volunteers to the colors.[98]

The Civil War literature written in England during the years 1904–14 bears the imprint of Henderson. Intense interest in the Civil War, requirements of the Officer Promotion Examinations, and undue concentration upon the Virginia campaigns all attest to his influence. But it is equally apparent that with few exceptions these writers saw what they wanted to see, nothing more. Their vision was limited not only by the one-sided interest in the Virginia campaigns but by self-imposed blinders as well. Some, it is true, had no particular ax of their own to grind and endeavored merely to illustrate fundamental principles for the convenience of studious officers. Others used examples from the Civil War to "prove" that shock tactics were still practicable and that conscripts were inferior to those who had volunteered for duty. Only a few, notably Edmonds and Redway, approached Henderson in objectivity and understanding, and their voices were not heard above the tumult.

These few men were to be vindicated only by a new turn of history, a new war which swept away all the old tactical questions that had cluttered the military literature of the pre-1914 era. Attention was now to be concentrated on war as a whole, on great questions of strategy and politics, and thus on the neglected aspect of the Civil War. Those British officers who studied the Civil War after 1918 turned to the campaigns of 1864 and the decisive campaigns in the West for instruction, studying Grant and Sherman as the preceding generation had concentrated upon the great leaders of the eastern armies—Lee and Henderson's Jackson.

[98] T. Miller Maguire, "Improvised Armies of the Nineteenth Century: A Historical Analysis," *R.U.S.I. Journal*, LV (September, 1911), 1131; H. W. Wilson, "The Human Animal in Battle," *Fortnightly Review*, LXVI (July–December, 1898), 280.

9

The Postwar View
A New Approach

In August, 1914, Europe was plunged into war. Successful in their initial moves, the German leaders were forced to abandon the much-publicized Schlieffen Plan after their right wing was first contained, then thrown back, by the Anglo-French forces in the battle of the Marne (September 6–9, 1914). Then followed a desperate scramble for possession of the Channel seaports, after which the rival armies burrowed into the ground and for the next four years waged a sanguinary, unimaginative war of attrition. Millions were incorporated into the gigantic armies that grappled over a barren earth landscaped only by miles of twisting trench and tangled barbed wire and pimpled by countless shell craters and ruined villages. New weapons—the tank, airplane, and poison gas—were used in a fruitless effort to break the trench deadlock, but they were still largely in the experimental stage when the war finally ended. All the theoretical study in the Kriegsakademie, the École de Guerre, and the Staff College had not prepared the military leaders to expect a war such as this, nor had it instructed them how to fight under these new conditions.

The years following this holocaust witnessed an unprecedented interest in military affairs. "We live in a time," Liddell Hart wrote in 1933, "when 'war' is on everyone's lips, when everything contemporary is dated in relation to the last war."[1] Soldiers of all nations studied the revolutionary changes in warfare, explained the mistakes of 1914–18, and suggested avenues to victory in a future war. In each country there was a reappraisal of military doctrine, as soldiers tried desperately to keep pace with the swift, unpredictable march of the times.

The war provided new lenses through which the Civil War could

[1] *The Ghost of Napoleon* (London, 1933), p. 145.

be viewed, with the result that the events of 1861–65 were brought into sharper focus; new angles of vision opened up areas that hitherto had gone unnoticed, and some of the favorite subjects could be seen in proper perspective. Before 1914, when there had been a lively controversy over the proper tactical and strategical use of cavalry, virtually every European soldier who wrote about the Civil War paid close attention to cavalry operations; now the old issue of shock tactics versus firepower was dead, and serious military thinkers were concerned instead with a new knight in armor, the tank. Similarly, before 1914 the significance of intrenchments had been a matter of speculation; now, for the time being at least, the question had been decided by the experience in France, and that nation, which previously had been the most dedicated to the doctrine of the offensive, in time came to place her faith in the protection of the most elaborate "trench system" ever constructed. So, too, the war had practically eliminated the earlier distinction between regular armies and those comprised of citizen-soldiers. All nations had been forced to resort to conscription of one kind or another, and the massed guns which for four years had thundered almost ceaselessly on the western front had not been able to distinguish between career soldier, volunteer, and conscript. The postwar generation faced different problems, and those who studied the Civil War looked for new lessons altogether.

Most of them were not interested in tactics except to explain a campaign or evaluate generalship. They recognized that the Civil War had given birth to tactical forms that had been misunderstood or ignored in Europe, but they stressed those aspects of the Civil War which had not been outdated by the recent revolution in warfare. Morale and leadership, logistics and strategy, the mobilization of industry and the economic consequences of the blockade—these were the subjects which after 1918 appealed to most foreign students of the Civil War. Now it appeared obvious that the Civil War, far from being unique, had been in fact the forerunner of the type of war Europe had recently experienced. It, too, had been a war of attrition in trenches, a struggle between peoples rather than armies and fought on economic, moral, and political as well as military battlegrounds. In both wars the "law of numbers" and the "law" of the dollar had prevailed. Both had commenced with a general belief in a short war; both had lasted four years and had ended abruptly, the result of complete exhaustion.[2] In France, particularly, new importance was attached to the role of Union sea power in winning the war, an interesting development in view of the fact that before 1914 French strategists had virtually ignored the navy.[3] After 1918, French soldiers manifestly had come to appreciate the fact that the British navy had contributed substantially to the victory.

This new attitude toward sea power is best seen in a recent book by a French naval officer and well-known authority on naval matters, Captain A. Lepotier's *Mer contre terre*. Lepotier regarded the Civil War as the prototype of the First World War in that both of them had been military stalemates in which sea power had proved the decisive factor. Command of the sea had enabled the North to avoid "irreparable defeat" in 1861–62, for while the Confederates were victorious on land the Union forces had managed to seize most of the southern seaports. The Union navy had made possible the blockade of the Confederacy and the eventual conquest of the Mississippi, both of which had contributed to the downfall of the South. It had also supplied tactical as well as logistical support to the Union armies along the coast and on inland waters. "The sea had conquered the land." Comparing the Confederacy with the Central Powers in 1914–18, Lepotier pointed out that both had won initial victories on land only to lose finally to superior sea power: "We have seen in Antietam a battle of the Marne, and in Gettysburg a Verdun." A generation later, "Antietam and Gettysburg were played at El Alamein and Stalingrad," while Allied air and naval forces reopened the Mediterranean much as the Federal navy had reconquered the Mississippi. Frenchmen could not afford to forget that liberation in 1944 had come from the sea.[4]

[2] See Hans Delbrück, continued by Emil Daniels and Otto Haintz, *Geschichte der Kriegskunst im Rahmen der politischen Geschichte* (Berlin, 1936), VII, 4, 168, 301, 348–49; Gaston Roupnel, *Une guerre d'usure: La guerre de sécession* (Paris, 1916), *passim*; Lieutenant Colonel Daille, "Une leçon de la guerre de sécession," *Revue militaire française*, XIV (October–December, 1924), 8, 9, 11, 14, 171–73; "Une seconde leçon de la guerre de sécession," *ibid.*, XVI (July–September, 1925), 326; René Sauliol, *Une autre guerre de nations: La guerre de sécession* (Paris, 1929), pp. 3, 4, 43–57, 383.

[3] In 1913 Sir Henry Wilson, then Director of Military Operations, noted in his diary that whereas he did not consider the British navy "worth 500 bayonets" in a war with Germany, "Castelnau and Joffre did not value it at one bayonet! Except from the moral point" (Major General Sir C. E. Callwell, *Field-Marshal Sir Henry Wilson: His Life and Diaries* [London, 1927], I, 122.)

[4] Capitaine de Vaisseau A. Lepotier, *Les leçons de l'histoire (1861–1865) Mer contre terre* (Paris, 1945), pp. 58, 93, 182–83, 333–36, 347.

Lepotier's book is typical in another respect. Endowed with rare insight, it nonetheless represents little or no original research. Lepotier and indeed most French writers continued to draw most of their facts from Lecomte, Grasset, the Prince de Joinville, and the Comte de Paris. Their interpretations were different because, having lived through four years which, on the surface at least, closely resembled the earlier conflict in America, they were better prepared to understand and appreciate those features of the American campaigns which the previous generation had been inclined to dismiss as unique. In Germany, too, those who wrote about the Civil War fell back upon the old sources—Von Borcke, Scheibert, Sander, and Von Freytag-Loringhoven—and neglected the more recent findings of American scholars.[5] Neither in Germany nor in France, however, was any widespread interest manifested in the Civil War, certainly nothing to compare with the popularity of the subject in England. In Germany, for example, Field Marshal von Hindenburg and several other high-ranking officers were acquainted with the Civil War,[6] but the official fare for officers remained the wars of Frederick the Great, Napoleon, Moltke, and, above all,

[5] See, for example, Hauptman George Friemel and Oberleutnant Koehler, "Lee," in Generalmajor von Cochenhausen (ed.), *Führertum: 25 Lebensbilder von Feldherren aller Zeiten* (Berlin, 1930), pp. 347–63, 399–400. Even Emil Daniels and Otto Haintz, students of the famed military historian, Hans Delbrück, were careless in their use of American sources; how else could they have made the mistake of asserting that at Gettysburg, "field fortifications formed an integral ingredient of the Union battle plan"? (*Geschichte der Kriegskunst*, VII, 257).

[6] Lieutenant General Friedrich von Boettischer, military attaché of the German embassy in Washington in the 1930's, asserts that Hindenburg, "when about 80 years old . . . once discussed with me for more than an hour the most important operations of General R. E. Lee. He knew every detail, and, without having a map, he remembered the names of every place where Lee had been operating and fighting." According to Hindenburg, the Civil War was "the only war where an officer can learn everything, strategy and tactics"; therefore "that is the war for us to study." General Friedrich von Boettischer to the writer, March 4, 1955; Douglas Southall Freeman, *The South to Posterity: An Introduction to the Writing of Confederate History* (New York, 1951), pp. 166–67. Hindenburg told Von Boettischer that the Civil War had been "the foundation of all his teachings" at the Kriegsakademie when he was an instructor there in 1885–89; if so, it is curious that one of his pupils, Baron von Freytag-Loringhoven, does not mention the Civil War when describing the course of instruction there (*Menschen und Dinge wie ich sie in meinem Leben sah* [Berlin, 1923], pp. 55, 109–10). Another and more recent German general has written that during his entire military career, including fifteen years on the General Staff and several years on the instructional staff of the Kriegsakademie, he heard "precious little" about the Civil War officially, although he and several others studied it on their own initiative. General Gunther von Blumentritt to the writer, October 6, 1954.

the recent conflict.[7] In France, too, interest in the Civil War was confined to a few individuals.

On the other hand, enthusiasm in England for the Civil War was if anything more intense than before 1914; certainly it was more positive. No longer was it fashionable to concentrate on one or two of the Virginia campaigns and memorize the detailed tactical maneuvers of battles. Now there was greater interest in the later campaigns, which, as Henderson had predicted, more nearly resembled twentieth-century warfare. More attention, too, was paid to the operations in the West, where it was generally believed the decisive blows had been delivered.[8] Henderson would have been pleased to observe that the postwar studies in England stressed strategy and the psychology of generalship, factors which in military history have remained relatively constant, in contrast to the earlier overemphasis upon tactics. Even those books written especially to prepare officers for examinations in military history were free of the professional pedantry and the superficial detail typical of the prewar campaign studies. The outlook of these later writers, several of whom enjoy international reputations,[9] was far broader than that of the company officers who had summarized Henderson for the convenience of those studying for the promotion examinations.

[7] This is apparent in an official study by an officer of the General Staff in which, out of twenty-four battles selected, only one was not from the wars of Frederick, Napoleon, and Moltke—the battle of Cannae. Gunther Frantz, *Die Vernichtungs-schlacht in kriegsgeschichtlichen Beispielen: Im Auftrage der Heeresinspektion des Erziehungs und Bildungswesens* (Berlin, 1928). One of the best-known German generals of the Second World War, General Heinz Guderian, taught Napoleon's campaign of 1806 and the German and French cavalry operations in 1914 to future staff officers. General Heinz Guderian, *Panzer Leader* (London, 1952), p. 21. See also Colonel Eugene Carrias, *La pensée militaire allemande* (Paris, 1948), pp. 344–47.

[8] See Eric William Sheppard, *Military History for the Staff College Entrance Examination* (Aldershot, 1933), p. 40; Sheppard, *The American Civil War, 1864–65* (Aldershot, 1938); Lieutenant Colonel Alfred H. Burne, *Lee, Grant, and Sherman: A Study in Leadership in the 1864–65 Campaign* (Aldershot, 1938). This new interest in the campaigns of 1864–65 also induced W. Birkbeck Wood and Brigadier General Sir James E. Edmonds to bring out a second, revised edition of their *History of the Civil War* in which the campaigns of the first two years of the war were telescoped into a seventy-five-page Introduction. See Wood and Edmonds, *The Civil War in the United States with Special Reference to the Campaigns of 1864 and 1865* (London, 1937).

[9] The roll call of the postwar British historians of the Civil War would include two major generals (Sir Frederick Maurice and J. F. C. Fuller), and several others with the rank of brigadier general or colonel. Most of the postwar writers had something original to say, even in those books written specifically for some particular examination.

Moreover, the Civil War was still periodically the set subject for military history in the Staff College and promotion examinations. John Masters, the novelist, recalls that as a young officer of the Fourth Prince of Wales Own Gurkha Rifles he devoted an hour each night to studying Jackson's classic marches for his approaching examinations. Subsequently, during a visit to the United States, he utilized the opportunity to study the Shenandoah Valley campaign on the spot, at which time he was asked to lecture the faculty of the Virginia Military Institute on the subject. His comments are revealing:

Hell, it was no different from the Child Welfare Book really, and they did not know much about that war because it still hurt. The Europeans had started studying it much sooner than the Americans. It snowed hard, and I took Henderson's *Stonewall Jackson* out of the trunk and lay down on my stomach with it in the blizzard at Port Republic, trying to find out where Tyler had put his guns, and where was the forested path along which the Louisiana regiments had marched to turn the tide of battle. . . . I drove up the Valley Pike . . . and since I was an infantryman I could smell the sweat and the dust in the files, and hear the bugles blow. . . . I marched in those long-dead ranks and knew why I did so and where I was going.[10]

The operations in the West and Grant's final campaign against Lee also appeared on the promotion examinations. The Civil War continued to be taught at the Staff College during the period between the two world wars, and it constitutes one of the main historical periods assigned there for individual study.[11]

The difference lay in the approach to the subject. Henderson had used military history as a means to stimulate independent thought rather than to provide specific patterns or lessons; for this reason *Stonewall Jackson* survived the First World War with its value as a military text undiminished, while most of the prewar campaign studies, once considered thoroughly practical, now were casualties of newer concepts in warfare. Henderson would have approved most of the Civil War books written by this later gen-

[10] John Masters, *Bugles and a Tiger: A Volume of Autobiography* (New York, 1956), pp. 240–41, 274.

[11] See A. H. Burne, "Hints on Studying the 1864–1865 Campaign," *Fighting Forces*, XV (June, 1938), 140–45. Books written specifically for the promotion examinations include Lieutenant Colonel Alexander H. C. Kearsey, *Strategy and Tactics of the Shenandoah Valley Campaign, 1861–1862* (Aldershot, 1931); Burne, *Lee, Grant, and Sherman;* and Sheppard, *The American Civil War.*

eration of British officers. For one thing, they seemed to be interested primarily in biography.

Not content with assembling the facts of battle and measuring the success or failure of a campaign by the casualty lists, these later writers endowed Lee, Forrest, Grant, and Sherman with living ideas and explained their achievements in terms of present conditions. Fuller wrote of a Grant whose ideas could be of help in his own day; Major General Sir Frederick Maurice viewed and described the Civil War through the eyes of Lee; Liddell Hart concentrated on the working of Sherman's mind, while Major E. W. Sheppard went so far as to blend fact with fiction that he might present a realistic, lifelike portrait of Forrest.[12]

Moreover, the First World War had established new standards by which to judge generalship. Because many of the problems that had arisen in 1914–18 had had precedent in the Civil War, it was easier for this later generation to appreciate the accomplishments of the American generals, and with these new standards, military reputations changed. Jackson was still admired as he will always be by anyone acquainted with Henderson's biography, but more and more he had to share the stage first with Lee, then with Grant and Sherman. Lee was now praised for his skill in the tactical use of trenches; Sherman emerged as a model strategist who had understood the value of mobility and had fully appreciated the moral factor in war; and Grant at last came into his own. He was now described as a strategist of the highest order who, as commander-in-chief of the Union armies, had skilfully combined all the resources of the North for the final destruction of the Confederacy. Remembering the frightful casualties of Passchendaele and the Somme, the postwar generation could look beyond the butchery in the Wilderness and understand Grant's strategy of attrition, which seemed much more instructive than any recital, however detailed and accurate, of Jackson's exploits in the valley of Virginia.

Even Lincoln, who in Wolseley's day had been harshly criticized as a war leader, was now treated as nothing less than a military genius, a man who, by the "interesting light . . . thrown backwards by the Great War," turned out to be a "born strategist" with a "fine perception of the duties of the Higher Command." At one time blamed for interfering with his generals, Lincoln after

[12] See Sheppard, *Bedford Forrest* (New York, 1930), p. 6.

1918 was applauded by British soldiers for the way in which he had supported Grant during the dark days of 1864–65.[13]

Lee found his most sympathetic biographer in General Maurice, the son of Henderson's predecessor at the Staff College and a well-known military historian in his own right. The Confederate general had long been recognized as a master of maneuver, but Maurice in his appreciation of Lee's generalship paid special tribute to him for his handling of intrenchments in 1864–65. Had the lessons of Spotsylvania been learned, "many a blunder made in the Great War might have been avoided." And like most of his contemporaries, Maurice was sympathetic to Grant, believing his campaign of attrition to be the surest, perhaps the only, way to defeat a determined enemy under siege warfare conditions.

If we consider Grant's performance in the light of recent experience, we will, I think, view it with more kindly eyes than have some of the critics who wrote before the Great War. Cold Harbour was a costly blunder, but it was a blunder in execution as well as in conception, and for the execution Meade, the actual commander of the attacking troops, must take a great share of the responsibility. Despite that blunder, Grant's campaign had brought the war appreciably nearer its end, and that justifies his policy of fighting hard and often.[14]

Maurice's personal experience during the late war interested him in another phase of the Civil War. As a member of the Imperial General Staff he had been witness to the controversy between Britain's civilian and military heads,[15] and he hoped by examining

13 Colin R. Ballard, *The Military Genius of Abraham Lincoln* (London, 1926), pp. 4, 8, 236, 239. The late Field Marshal Earl Wavell was among those who believed that Lincoln's relations with his generals "are well worth study." Wavell, *Generals and Generalship* (New York, 1943), p. 30.

14 Major General Sir Frederick Maurice, *Robert E. Lee the Soldier* (Boston, 1925), pp. 232, 242, 291. Maurice deliberately limited the scope of his study of Lee when he learned that a more complete biography based upon the Lee papers was in process in the United States. His own book, however, was so well done that the descendants of Colonel Charles Marshall, one of Lee's staff officers, invited him to edit and publish the Marshall papers, which appeared under the title *An Aide-de-Camp of Lee: Being the Papers of Colonel Charles Marshall, Sometime Aide-de-Camp, Military Secretary, and Assistant Adjutant General on the Staff of Robert E. Lee, 1862–1865* (Boston, 1927).

15 This struggle over the conduct of the war was personified by the sharp differences which existed between Lloyd George, the Prime Minister, and Field Marshal Robertson, C.I.G.S. Robertson eventually resigned rather than choose between two distasteful alternatives. See Sir William B. Robertson, *From Private to Field Marshal* (Boston, 1921), chap. xvi; Robert Blake, "Great Britain: The Crimean War to the First World War," in Michael Howard (ed.), *Soldiers and Governments: Nine Studies in Civil-Military Relations* (London, 1957), pp. 39–50.

this neglected aspect of the Civil War to learn something of the interrelationship between policy and strategy. Maurice was not the first soldier to investigate this problem; the American General Emory Upton had explored the over-all conduct of the war in the 1870's but had died before completing his study beyond 1862,[16] and just before the war the French General Boucherie had treated superficially the personal relationships between Lincoln and two of his generals. But Maurice was the first European soldier to examine systematically the functioning of the Union high command, "the best example in existence of the coordination of political and military forces in a democracy." In his opinion, the North's achievement of an effective unity of command constituted the most important lesson of the Civil War.[17]

Long dissatisfied with the judgments of Wolseley and Henderson, Maurice set out to re-establish Lincoln as a wartime leader. Too much emphasis had been placed upon Lincoln's earlier mistakes, he felt, and not enough attention devoted to "the processes by which he evolved a system for the conduct of the war." Experience convinced Maurice that in a democracy the direction of a war should be in the hands of one man, the statesman, and that success in war depended ultimately upon the establishment of a proper balance between civilian heads and military commanders. In large measure this proper balance, if it were to be achieved, was dependent upon the important factor of personality. McClellan obviously "did not know how to treat his political chief," whereas Grant impressed Maurice as "fitted by character and mentality to cooperate with the President." If Grant lacked some of Lee's inherent qualities as a field commander, he at least understood the system under which he was working, was aware of his responsibilities to his government, and succeeded in planning his strategy accordingly. Thus he had been able to receive almost unlimited support from the same administration that had repudiated McClellan in 1862.

Maurice considered Lincoln an ideal "model for the statesman in

16 Brevet Major General Emory Upton, *The Military Policy of the United States* (Washington, 1912). Upton's views are summarized in Peter S. Michie, *The Life and Letters of Emory Upton* (New York, 1885), chap. xi.

17 *Lee the Soldier*, p. 223; *Statesmen and Soldiers of the Civil War: A Study of the Conduct of War* (Boston, 1926), p. 151. This book, published originally under the title *Governments and War* (London, 1926), is an outgrowth of Maurice's Lees-Knowles Lectures in Military History at Cambridge University, 1925-26.

the direction of war." He had made mistakes, true, but he had been quick to learn and profit by them. "Modern war demands . . . a partnership between the statesman and his military commanders," and for this partnership to function efficiently "the statesman must have learned from the experience of others . . . what are the essentials of a good system for conducting war." In Maurice's opinion, no better instruction existed than the example of the partnership of Lincoln and Grant during the last years of the Civil War.[18]

The Lee portrayed by Maurice had a message for the twentieth century, but both subject and biographer at heart were conventional soldiers. Lee may have been a bold strategist and a clever tactician, but he was no innovator; if at times he abandoned orthodox strategy, it was simply because desperate odds called for desperate measures, as at the second battle of Bull Run and Chancellorsville. Maurice himself was flexible in his views but unwilling to indulge in speculation. Often critical of the leadership in the First World War, he nonetheless was "mildly surprised at the courage and confidence" of those who predicted the nature of the next war, and he was frankly skeptical of many of the claims made by adherents of air power. Unwilling to commit himself to any particular school of theorists, his written views were at least orthodox enough to be pronounced by the chief of the Imperial General Staff "a very useful adjunct" to the study of the Field Service Regulations.[19]

The new biographers of Grant and Sherman were of a different mold altogether. Without question the two greatest military theorists produced by the British army in modern times, Major General J. F. C. Fuller and Captain B. H. Liddell Hart must be considered revolutionary thinkers. Lifelong students of war, they have been prolific, controversial, and influential writers. Both have drawn many of their arguments from history, and, although occasionally accused of slanting the facts,[20] they both wrote vital books on the Civil War. Their theories on armored warfare, frequently ignored in Britain and the United States, influenced the subsequent

[18] *Ibid.*, pp. 75, 81–83, 97, 115, 121–22; *Lee the Soldier*, pp. 75–76.

[19] Maurice, *British Strategy: A Study of the Application of the Principles of War*, with an Introduction by Field Marshal Sir G. Milne, C.I.G.S. (London, 1929), pp. xvi, 17, 56–62.

[20] See Colonel E. H. Beadon, "Some Strategical Theories of Captain Liddell Hart," *R.U.S.I. Journal*, LXXXI (November, 1936), 747–60.

development of the blitzkrieg technique in Germany;[21] their books, original and dynamic, have reached a vast civilian as well as military audience. No American soldier has written such stimulating books about the Civil War, and, just as no study of twentieth-century warfare would be complete unless their writings are consulted, no interpretive history of the Civil War should be written without taking into account their basic ideas.

Possessing what has been described as "the most brilliant and unorthodox speculative mind" in the British army, Fuller was one of the original exponents of armored warfare. He was instrumental in designing the successful tank assault at Cambrai on November 20, 1917, "a landmark in the history of war." After the war he wrote profusely on the potentialities of the tank and the need for mechanization. One of the most influential textbooks on mechanized warfare was Fuller's *Lectures on Field Service Regulations III*, published in 1932. This book, while virtually ignored in England, attracted wide attention in foreign armies, particularly in Germany and Russia.[22] Fuller left the army in 1933, frustrated in his desire to play a more direct part in the mechanization of the army and too much the "unconventional soldier" to avoid antagonizing his more orthodox superiors,[23] and he has since devoted his time to writing military history.

Like most British officers, Fuller in his younger days "had been fed upon Henderson's *Stonewall Jackson*," and even before the war he had made a study of the battle of Chancellorsville. A decade after the war, following the trend in England, he grew interested in the Civil War as "the first of the modern wars" and in Grant as an example of modern generalship. Like Maurice, Fuller did not attempt to write a history of the Civil War or a detailed account

[21] General Heinz Guderian, a pioneer in armored warfare, writes that "it was principally the books and articles of the Englishmen, Fuller, Liddell Hart, and [Lieutenant General Sir Giffard] Martel, that excited my interest and gave me food for thought. . . . I learned from them the concentration of armour" (*Panzer Leader,* p. 20).

[22] Liddell Hart, *The Defence of Britain* (New York, 1939), p. 342; Cyril Falls, *A Hundred Years of War* (London, 1953), p. 194; Thirty thousand copies of the first edition of *Lectures on F.S.R. III* were sold in Russia alone. Fuller, *Armored Warfare: An Annotated Edition of Fifteen Lectures on Operations between Mechanized Forces* (London, 1943), Preface.

[23] Fuller, *Memoirs of an Unconventional Soldier* (London, 1936), pp. 448–51. Additional information on the career and writings of Fuller are found in Lieutenant General Sir Gifford Martel, *An Outspoken Soldier: His Views and Memoirs* (London, 1949), *passim*, and Walter H. Butler, "A Case in Preparedness," *Armor* (November–December, 1951), pp. 30–35; Liddell Hart, *The Tanks* (London, 1959), I, *passim*.

of a particular campaign. Rather, he believed that "the supreme value of military history is to be sought in the personalities of the generals. . . . At base, seven-eighths of the history of war is psychological. Material conditions change, yet the heart of man changes but little, if at all."[24]

The Civil War personality that most appealed to Fuller was Grant, a misunderstood man who "had not received sufficient credit."[25] Grant was "one of the greatest strategists of any age." Compared with Lee, he was a superior general-in-chief with a firmer grasp of grand strategy—a more typical product of the industrial age. In Lee's place it is unlikely that Grant would have done much better, for "neither . . . was a true revolutionary general. Yet I much doubt whether in Grant's place Lee would have done half as well as Grant, for his outlook on war was narrow and restricted, and he possessed neither the character nor the personality of a General-in-chief."[26] Fuller's comments have caused many admirers of Lee to wince, and not all of his conclusions have gone unquestioned, even by English soldiers,[27] but Fuller's works have gone far to re-establish Grant as a general. Like Henderson, he stressed the psychological aspects of generalship, and, like the author of *Stonewall Jackson*, he occasionally inserted his own thought into the narrative. His biography of Grant is fully as thought-provoking, as interestingly written, and as much alive as *Stonewall Jackson*, and no English officer since Henderson has displayed keener insight into the general nature of the Civil War.

The most valuable military lesson of the Civil War, according to Fuller, was the strength of the rifle on the defensive. The rifle was the key to Civil War tactics:

It was the bullet which created the trench and rifle pit; which killed the bayonet; which rendered useless the sword, which chased away guns and horsemen . . . and which prevented the rapid decision of the

24 Fuller, *Grant and Lee: A Study in Personality and Generalship* (London, 1932), pp. 11–12; *Memoirs of an Unconventional Soldier*, p. 28.

25 Major General J. F. C. Fuller to the writer, September 25, 1950.

26 *Grant and Lee*, pp. 93, 242–44, 256–57, 278; *Generalship of U.S. Grant*, pp. 372–81.

27 See, for example, Douglas Southall Freeman's remarks in his Preface to Burne's *Lee, Grant, and Sherman*. Freeman contends that Fuller had no understanding of many of the problems of the Confederacy. Sheppard writes: "Everything General Fuller writes is well worth reading, even if one disagrees with it. I am afraid I personally disagree with much of what he says" (*The American Civil War*, pp. xv–xvi). Burne, also, cautions readers that criticisms from Fuller "must receive close and careful attention" (*Lee, Grant, and Sherman*, p. 203).

battles of preceding centuries. In 1861–65 the rifle-bullet was the lord of the battlefield as was the machine-gun bullet in 1914–18.[28]

If neither Grant nor Lee had fully comprehended the significance of firepower, Foch and his disciples made the same mistake fifty years later, a fact which Fuller regards as "the supreme tragedy of modern warfare." Like Henderson, Fuller observed that mobility alone could counteract the overwhelming superiority of the defensive. The Civil War clearly demonstrated the futility of frontal attacks; only assaults against an enemy's flank and rear offered much prospect of success. "This does not mean that frontal attacks should be avoided, but that they should be mainly looked upon as holding attacks and not as decisive operations; as . . . tactical bases of operation upon which to pivot outflanking movements."[29]

Fuller's own theories were not directly influenced by his study of the Civil War but grew out of personal experience with tanks in the First World War.[30] As a military historian, Fuller recognized the Civil War as a significant phase in the evolution of warfare, and his understanding of the general military situation enabled him to see Grant in a more favorable light. He was interested in the Civil War primarily for what it taught about generalship, which he considered "brilliant and instructive" largely because it was devoid of the usual professional pedantry.[31] Critical of British leadership in 1914–18 and despairing the lack of imagination and foresight in rebuilding the army in the years that followed, he could appreciate the resourcefulness and adaptability of the Civil War commanders, most of whom had managed to avoid the "professionalism" that "has so often proved itself to be the dry rot of armies." The Civil War

was a war born of steam-power, which changed not only the historical structure of nations, but the traditional structure of armies. Today we are faced by many similar changes; for it may be said . . . that we are

[28] *Generalship of U.S. Grant*, p. 358.

[29] *Grant and Lee*, pp. 250; see also pp. 45–49, 262, 268; *Generalship of U.S. Grant*, pp. 62, 195–96, 204, 357–59, 364–65.

[30] This is evident in Fuller's more technical works, which include *The Reformation of War* (London, 1923); *The Foundations of the Science of War* (London, 1925); *On Future Warfare* (London, 1928); and *Armoured Warfare* (London, 1943).

[31] "Probably no war in the whole of military history produced such a galaxy of generals. In this war, the first of the modern wars . . . the personal factor remained supreme" (Fuller, *Generalship: Its Diseases and Their Cure: A Study of the Personal Factor in Command* [London, 1933], p. 39).

now living in the throes of the second industrial revolution, a most powerful sequel which is daily adding to the might of coal and steam the might of oil and electricity.[32]

So Fuller looked to the Civil War not for incidents to document his theories but for kindred spirits who had been confronted with similar problems created by an earlier industrial revolution.

Although Fuller regarded an appreciation of the Civil War as essential to an understanding of modern warfare, it was Liddell Hart who actually incorporated the teachings of that war into a theory—his much publicized "strategy of the indirect approach." He used examples from 1861–65 to illustrate points in practically all his writings.

Liddell Hart was studying history at Corpus Christi College, Cambridge, when the war broke out. Commissioned in 1914, he fought as an infantry officer until wounded and gassed in the Somme offensive of 1916. While recuperating, he wrote a book describing this battle, an honest account which was refused publication "on the ground that it gave too exact a picture." In 1918 he became known to General Sir Ivor Maxse, Inspector General of Training of the British Armies in France, for his new "Battle Drill" system and other training methods. Through Maxse's good offices he was asked to rewrite the *Infantry Training Manual* soon after the war—he was then only twenty-four—and his views on infantry tactics, indorsed by Maxse,[33] rapidly captured attention. Invalided out of the army in 1924, Liddell Hart became military correspondent for the *Morning Post* (of which Maxse was a director), later the *Daily Telegraph*, and ultimately the *Times*.[34]

As publicist, lecturer, military editor of the *Encyclopaedia Britannica*, and author of numerous books and articles on a wide variety of military subjects, Liddell Hart quickly became recog-

[32] *Generalship of U. S. Grant*, pp. viii–ix, 9, 185.

[33] Liddell Hart's ideas "are not commonplace, and they deserve attention. . . . I hope this lecture will induce many battalion, and brigade commanders to make an effort to put this system into practice" (Maxse, Foreword to Liddell Hart, *The Framework of a Science of Infantry Tactics* [London, 1921]).

[34] Information obtained in correspondence with Liddell Hart. Of the many articles written about Liddell Hart, that dealing most fully with his military thought is Général Chassin, "Un grand penseur militaire britannique: B. H. Liddell Hart," *Revue de défense nationale* (October, 1950), pp. 334–46. See also Colonel Robert J. Icks, "Liddell Hart: One View," *Armor* (November–December, 1952), pp. 25–27.

nized as "the leading military writer in Britain."[35] He was influential in the creation of the first British Mechanized Force in 1927, and frequently he was consulted by civilian and military heads alike in matters pertaining to the organization, training, and equipment of the army. In the late 1930's, with the rearmament of Europe and war clouds growing darker on the horizon, Liddell Hart devoted himself more and more to current problems, at the expense of his historical studies. During the Second World War he contributed frequent military commentaries in the press,[36] and since the war he has been occupied studying the war and contemporary military problems.

Through the years Liddell Hart has been motivated by two forces—the desire, amounting almost to a passion, to avoid repetition of the pointless slaughter of 1914–18, and a belief in mobility as the vital ingredient in war. "Without mobility an army is but a corpse—awaiting burial in a trench."[37] As early as 1921, partly because of the influence of Fuller, Liddell Hart became a "convinced believer in full mechanization,"[38] and in the years following his conversion his main concern was to convince his countrymen of the future of armored warfare and the need for a "new model" army. In the process he gradually formulated his well-known "strategy of the indirect approach," a theory which is woven into the fabric of all his later writings.

The purpose of strategy, according to Liddell Hart, "is to diminish the possibility of resistance . . . by exploiting the elements of movement and surprise." Movement could be achieved through mechanization, surprise by following a strategy of indirect approach. In place of the frontal attacks of 1914–18, colossal assaults that had merely pushed the enemy back upon his reserves and secondary defenses, Liddell Hart advocated a deep movement behind the enemy's flank or a deep penetration of his lines by independent armored columns, an indirect thrust aimed at cutting the enemy's communications and thus causing "the paralysis of the opposing command." The more he studied military history, he wrote, the

[35] Irving M. Gibson, "Maginot and Liddell Hart: The Doctrine of Defense," in Edward Mead Earle (ed.), *Makers of Modern Strategy: Military Thought from Machiavelli to Hitler* (Princeton, 1943), p. 376.

[36] Many of these are reprinted in *This Expanding War* (London, 1942).

[37] Liddell Hart, *The Remaking of Modern Armies* (London, 1927), p. x.

[38] Information furnished by Liddell Hart.

more clearly has the fact emerged that a direct approach to the . . . objective along the "line of natural expectation" has ever tended to negative results. The reason being that the strength of an enemy country or force lies far less in its numbers or resources than in its stability or equilibrium—of control, morale and supply. . . . To move along the "line of natural expectation" is to consolidate the enemy's equilibrium, and by stiffening it to augment its resisting power. . . . The decisive victories in military history have come from the strategy of indirect approach, wherein the dislocation of the enemy's moral, mental, or material balance is the vital prelude to an attempt at his overthrow. The strategy of indirect approach is, indeed, the highest and widest fulfilment of the principle of surprise.[39]

Flexibility and deception were essential to the success of the strategy of the indirect approach, for even a stroke against the enemy's flank or rear, "by the very directness of its progress," would become a direct approach whenever the opposing commander could change front to meet it. Hence it was necessary to pursue "alternative objectives," to threaten two or more points simultaneously in order to force the enemy either to abandon one in defense of the other or else to overextend his forces in an effort to defend both—a move similar to the fork play in chess. To achieve flexibility in execution, Liddell Hart recommended in advance in wide, loosely grouped formations "like the waving tentacles of an octopus," which would distract the enemy and conceal until the last moment the true objective of the campaign. This appeared to constitute a violation of the universally accepted principle of concentration, but Liddell Hart maintained that "Effective concentration can only be obtained when the opposing forces are dispersed; and usually, in order to ensure this, one's own forces must be widely distributed."[40] A premature concentration against the enemy's main army usually resulted in a frontal, direct attack with the advantage resting solidly on the side of the defensive—a repetition of 1914–18 which Liddell Hart was anxious to avoid.

Because he recognized the "great and growing superiority" of the defensive, Liddell Hart suggested the "baited gambit," or combination of offensive strategy with defensive tactics.

Throughout history it has proved one of the most effective of moves, and its advantages have increased as modern weapons have handicapped other types of move. By rapidity of advance and mobility of manoeuvre, you may be able to seize points which the enemy, sensitive to the threat,

39 *Thoughts on War* (London, 1944), pp. 231, 238.
40 *The British Way in Warfare*, p. 107.

will be constrained to attack. Thus you will invite him to a repulse which in turn may be exploited by a riposte. Such a counterstroke, against an exhausted attacker, is much less difficult than the attack on a defended position. The opportunity for it may also be created by a calculated withdrawal. . . . Here is another gambit of future warfare.[41]

Liddell Hart did not claim to have invented the strategy of indirect approach—"alternative objectives," "organized dispersion," and the "baited gambit" simply were his terms for strategems that had been used before in history.[42] But he did organize and blend these techniques into an elevated doctrine adaptable to mechanized war, and many of his theories were successfully employed in the blitzkrieg of a later day.

The strategy of the indirect approach, with its many ramifications, was born of a searching examination of history for signposts to the revival of mobile warfare. Liddell Hart regarded history as a useful supplement to theory rather than as a quarry to provide examples to illustrate fixed ideas. Like Henderson, he had shifted the weight of his thought from tactics to strategy as his interests broadened and his knowledge of military history increased. Above all he preached a doctrine of mobility: in *Scipio Africanus* (1926) he stressed mobility "as an object lesson to modern general staffs, shivering on the brink of mechanicalisation, fearful of the plunge despite the proved ineffectiveness of the older arms in their present form"; in *Great Captains Unveiled* (1927) he urged the replacement of the horse by the tank, "and we might well regain the Mongol mobility and offensive power."[43] In none of his early books, however, does Liddell Hart mention the strategy of the indirect approach as such. The first clear-cut sign of this theory appeared late in 1927,[44] a few months before he undertook to write his biography of Sherman.

First introduced to the Civil War by Henderson's *Stonewall Jackson*, a book "recommended to all young officers," Liddell Hart saw at once that the American campaigns were rich in examples of

41 *Thoughts on War*, p. 241.

42 Cf. Liddell Hart, *The Decisive Wars of History* (London, 1929), *passim;* revised editions of this work have been published periodically, the latest being *Strategy: The Indirect Approach* (London, 1954).

43 *A Greater than Napoleon: Scipio Africanus* (London, 1926), p. 97; *Great Captains Unveiled* (Boston, 1927), pp. 31–32.

44 *Thoughts on War*, pp. 187, 238–39. Liddell Hart, a tidy keeper of files, for years has been in the habit of writing down each thought, dating it, and filing it away for future reference. These were collated in his *Thoughts on War*, making it possible to trace the development of his theories by observing the date of each entry.

surprise and mobility, of unexpected thrusts and skilful strategic combinations. Determined to avoid a repetition of the trench deadlock of 1914–18, he became especially interested in "the ways in which a somewhat similar deadlock had been overcome, particularly in the West, and by Sherman"—campaigns that had "a significant bearing on the problem of the revival of mobile warfare." It was at this point, in 1928, that an American publishing firm approached Liddell Hart about writing a book on one of the great leaders of the Civil War, "preferably Lee." At the risk of some financial sacrifice he wrote instead about Sherman, and the value of what he learned "from that piece of research," he later commented, "was ample compensation."[45]

Sherman had a special appeal to Liddell Hart because he had been the only Civil War general to follow consistently a strategy of indirect approach. True, Grant had employed an indirect approach in his campaign for Vicksburg, but "the underlying lesson had not apparently impressed itself upon his mind," and he conducted his operations in Virginia the following year along the usual "direct overland approach" to Richmond.[46]

Sherman's strategy, too, had been orthodox at first, but the Vicksburg campaign had alerted him to the possibilities of a strategy which minimized fighting by upsetting the opponent—both mentally and physically—and by substituting mobility and deception for force. "Sherman had clearly grasped the truth that to roll the enemy back along their communications means that their resistance will be solidified and expended by accretions like a snowball." And in the Atlanta campaign Sherman, although committed to a direct line of advance because he was dependent for supplies upon a single railroad line, had nevertheless managed to maneuver his wary opponent out of successive defensive positions. The technique here had been to advance "in a wide loose grouping or net," pliable and at the same time sufficiently cohesive to prevent the Confederates from attacking and defeating isolated sections in detail. In the famous March to the Sea and the subsequent northward sweep through the Carolinas, Sherman had made further use of this "strategic net,"

[45] *Reputations* (London, 1928), p. 272; Liddell Hart to the writer, September 7, 1950.

[46] Liddell Hart qualified this generalization by explaining that the 1864 campaign was "in no sense a mere frontal push." Grant had used outflanking tactics and had conducted his campaign according to "all the good military precepts" (*Sherman,* pp. 272–73).

moving on a wide and irregular front—with four, five or six columns, each covered by a cloud of foragers—if one was blocked, others would be pushing on. And the opposing forces in consequence became so "jumpy" that they repeatedly gave way to this moral pressure, and fell back before they felt any serious physical pressure, their minds so saturated with the impression of the uncanny manoeuvring power of Sherman and his men, that whenever they took up a position of resistance they were thinking about their way of retreat.[47]

Sherman's campaigns also first suggested to Liddell Hart the potentialities of the "baited gambit." In September, 1928, his research suggested that

it is advantageous for an armoured force to seek the enemy's rear before seeking battle. Thereby it may even draw the enemy into attacking it to gain relief—and the power of an armoured force to crumple up such an attack, for which it has schemed, has potentialities not yet exploited. Sherman's Atlanta campaign of 1864, when, by manoeuvre, he repeatedly forced a reluctant enemy to attack him, might well be studied by the armoured forces.

Six months later the "baited gambit" had become an important ingredient in Liddell Hart's strategical thinking:

A most striking example of the baited offensive was in the Atlanta campaign. . . . Only once in all these weeks of manoeuvre did Sherman permit a frontal attack, at Kenesaw Mountain, and . . . [here] he did it to save his troops from the strain of a further flank march. . . . This, indeed, was the only occasion during the whole hundred miles advance through mountainous and river-intersected country that Sherman committed his troops to an offensive battle. Instead, he manoeuvred so skilfully as to lure the Confederates time after time into vain attacks, their repulse being ensured by the skill of his troops in rapid entrenching after gaining a vantage point. Thus to force an opponent acting on the strategic defensive, into a succession of costly tactical offensives, was a triumph of strategic artistry.[48]

In the Atlanta campaign Sherman had been forced to adhere to a single objective—Atlanta—and to rely upon the "strategic net" and "baited gambit" to keep his opponent off balance. In his celebrated March to the Sea, however, he was able to advance along a line that threatened several objectives at once, and it was this campaign that gave Liddell Hart his first glimpse of the use of "alternative objectives." Sherman always kept the Confederates in doubt as to his ultimate destination. First it appeared that it might be Macon or Augusta; then, after Sherman's army had passed north of

[47] *Ibid.*, pp. 242, 253, 369.
[48] *Thoughts on War*, pp. 241–42.

Macon, the Confederates had to decide whether he was marching toward Augusta or Savannah. "And while Sherman had his preference, he was ready to take the alternative objective if conditions favoured the change. The need did not arise thanks to the uncertainty caused by his deceptive direction."[49]

After reaching Savannah, Sherman turned northward to the Carolinas, where once again he divided his opponents by compelling them to cover two possible objectives, Augusta and Charleston. Ignoring both cities, Sherman seized Columbia, the center of Lee's best source of supply. Again the Confederates were uncertain whether Sherman intended to march upon Charlotte or Fayetteville, and when he had occupied the latter, they did not know whether Raleigh or Goldsboro would be the next objective. "Sherman had sought and found a solution in variability, or elasticity—the choice of a line leading to alternative objectives with the power to vary his course to gain whichever the enemy left open."[50]

Perhaps the main reason Liddell Hart so admired Sherman was that Sherman had found both "a state of immobility prevailing and . . . a way to overcome it."[51] In 1864, as in 1914–18, increased firepower, the consequent growth of intrenchments, and enormous logistic problems had impeded mobility; armies had grown "stagnant from their own bulk." Sherman had restored mobility "by a ruthless scrapping" of transport and equipment, and when the British army devoted its principal training exercises in 1931 to experiments in the reduction of military transport, the result was appropriately called a "Sherman march." For, as Liddell Hart had consistently pointed out, something had to be "scrapped in the Sherman spirit" if modern armies were "to be capable of moving."[52]

In formulating his theories on armored warfare, Liddell Hart had also to consider the potentialities of mobile operations behind enemy lines. Here again the Civil War had something to offer:

The very limited field of historical study which the British Army has cultivated in the past has given rise to a general impression, largely drawn from some reflections on "Jeb" Stuart's operations in Virginia, that raids on communications rarely repay the effort or detachment of force. A more thorough knowledge, even of the American Civil War, especially in the main Western campaign, would serve as a useful cor-

[49] *Ibid.*, pp. 58–59, 242–43; *Sherman*, p. 315.

[50] *Ibid.*, p. 383.

[51] *The British Way in Warfare*, p. 91; *Thoughts on War*, p. 191.

[52] *Ibid.*, p. 193; *Sherman*, p. 331; *The British Way in Warfare*, pp. 239–41.

rective to such assumptions. Such raids frequently had a crippling effect on the opposing army's plans.[53]

In 1935, as a direct outgrowth of a discussion with the late Field Marshal Earl Wavell on the use of armored forces, Liddell Hart made a study of the Civil War cavalry operations in the West, "with special reference to raids on communications." He concluded that there was no good reason why these mobile raids could not be duplicated on a larger scale against armies whose communications were vulnerable to attack by aircraft, airborne engineers, or tanks.[54] While his concept of "deep strategic penetration" dates from his study of the Mongol campaigns in the mid-1920's, Sherman and Forrest enabled Liddell Hart "to see more clearly its application against modern mass armies, dependent on railroads for supply."[55]

Manifestly Liddell Hart learned from military history and particularly from the American Civil War. Many of his theories were still embryonic when he commenced work on his biography of Sherman; yet within a year his "strategy of the indirect approach" emerged in its mature form, and the "baited gambit" and the principle of "alternative objectives" can be traced directly to this study. In another book, *The Decisive Wars of History*, Liddell Hart examined other wars for confirmation of his theories and became more than ever convinced that "throughout the ages decisive results in war have only been reached when the approach has been indirect."[56] The opening moves in Virginia, Pope's overland advance in 1862, McClellan's Peninsular campaign (a case in which an indirect approach became direct when the Confederates changed their dispositions to meet McClellan's advance), all revealed the ineffectiveness of the direct approach, whereas Lee's maneuvers before the second battle of Bull Run and Grant's campaign for Vicksburg, together with the campaigns of Sherman, testified to the soundness of this new theory.

In 1935 Liddell Hart became the military correspondent of the *Times*, and most of the books and articles he wrote in the next few years concerned England's defenses, recent military developments at home and abroad, and the course England should take if another

---

[53] *Thoughts on War,* p. 55.

[54] This study is reprinted below, Appendix B. It is also summarized in Liddell Hart, *The Strategy of the Indirect Approach* (London, 1941), pp. 199–200.

[55] *Thoughts on War,* pp. 76, 131–32, 267.

[56] *The Decisive Wars of History,* p. 4.

world war were to come. As unofficial adviser to Mr. Hore-Belisha during the latter's first year as War Minister in 1937–38, Liddell Hart became involved in a series of army reforms. Disappointed in the results of these reforms, he soon dissolved this "partnership" in order to be free to "apply the spur of public criticism to the inadequate efforts of the new military regime in the War Office." He also resigned from the *Times* over a difference in foreign policy and drew criticism for his most controversial book, *The Defence of Britain*, "an attempted last-hour warning against courses of action likely to lead to disaster" in the impending war.[57] For many years a controversial figure, Liddell Hart was attacked for urging a policy of limited liability on the Continent as well as for his outspoken preference for the defensive.[58] While a discussion of these disputes is beyond the scope of this study, it should be remarked that most criticisms of Liddell Hart were directed against specific recommendations with respect to England and the international situation before 1940 rather than his earlier and more detached views on mechanized warfare.

Nor has the time come for an objective appraisal of the extent of Liddell Hart's influence. In Britain he has been admired by many soldiers, ignored or viewed with hostility by others.[59] He is still an active writer, and his characteristic impatience for military orthodoxy and unimaginative leadership continues to alienate many professional soldiers. Others are irritated whenever he seems to say, "I told you so"—an attitude bolstered by the fact that some of the most successful among the German generals have publicly acknowledged their debt to Liddell Hart. Field Marshal Erwin Rommel was receptive to his theories on the tactical consequences

[57] Information furnished the writer by Liddell Hart. *The Defence of Britain* (London, 1939) was thrown together in a month's time and published six weeks later; Liddell Hart collapsed from exhaustion while reading the proofs.

[58] See Gibson, "Maginot and Liddell Hart," pp. 381–85; Liddell Hart, *The Current of War* (London, 1940), pp. 180–94.

[59] If Field Marshal Viscount Montgomery was not directly influenced by Liddell Hart, his theories—if correctly stated by his biographer—strike a similar note: "Under Montgomery's theory the old slogging match was out. Stealth and cunning were far more important than the massing of overwhelming numbers. One must never strike directly at important objectives, but go around them. The cutting edge of the Army must consist of strong highly trained and highly mobile columns, capable of making narrow but deep penetrations and then fanning out in the rear of the enemy line" (Alan Moorehead, *Montgomery* [New York, 1946], p. 64). Major General Eric Dorman-Smith has testified that Liddell Hart's theories "influenced the course of events" twice in North Africa between 1940 and 1942. See Liddell Hart, *Strategy: The Indirect Approach*, pp. 373–85.

of motorization and armor; General Heinz Guderian stated that he was "deeply impressed" by his ideas on "the use of armoured forces for long-range strokes, operations against the opposing army's communications," and his proposed "type of armoured division combining panzer and panzer-infantry units"; and General Hasso van Manteuffel, who engineered the Ardennes breakthrough of December, 1944, described him as "the creator of modern tank strategy."[60] Indeed, it almost has become a rule of the publisher's trade for any English translation of the memoirs of a German general to include an introduction by this well-known advocate of mobile warfare. Many of Liddell Hart's books had been translated into German before the war; from his frequent conversations with German generals since, it is obvious that some of them, at least, had been read.[61]

[60] See Liddell Hart (ed.), *The Rommel Papers* (New York, 1953), pp. 203, 299. According to a publisher's note, it was because Rommel had been in basic agreement with Liddell Hart that the Rommel family "was particularly anxious" to have Liddell Hart edit the English edition of *Krieg ohne Hass.* Guderian, *Panzer Leader,* p. 20. In his first conference with Hitler, Guderian read an article by Liddell Hart on the organization of armored forces, past and future (*ibid.,* p. 295).

[61] See Liddell Hart, *The Other Side of the Hill: Germany's Generals: Their Rise and Fall, with Their Own Account of Military Events, 1939–1945* (enlarged and revised ed.; London, 1951), *passim.*

10

Conclusion

Fuller and Liddell Hart constitute an appropriate final chapter. They are not the last of their generation in England to write about the Civil War, but they are more prominent than the others, and their interpretations are as valid today as they were a quarter of a century ago. Fuller's *Grant* and Liddell Hart's *Sherman* have recently been republished, and in his Foreword to a new edition of Sherman's *Memoirs* Liddell Hart once again acknowledges his debt to "the first modern strategist," whose campaigns closely parallel the blitzkrieg of 1940–41 and the final Allied thrusts into Germany. Nor are there likely to be any new pragmatic studies of the war to replace the works of Fuller and Liddell Hart. The Civil War is a field that has been plowed over not once but hundreds of times, and military technology is experiencing such rapid and revolutionary changes that many of the lessons of the last war now seem outdated. The Civil War will always serve to dramatize broad aspects of command and strategy; because of "the romance of it, the chivalry and the supreme heroism,"[1] it will continue to appeal to soldier and civilian alike, but as a course for practical instruction its usefulness has ceased. It is an instructive period in military history, but for today's soldier a knowledge of present conditions is far more likely to provide insight into the events of 1861–65 than vice versa.

Contrary to popular belief, there never was a time when the Civil War exterted a direct influence upon military doctrine in Europe. Foreign soldiers first grew interested in it because they desired to learn more about the performance of new weapons and, in the case of England, the behavior of untried troops. The official observers sent to the American battlefields reported useful, though not always new, information about the strength of various metals, ballistics, the power of rifled artillery, and new wrinkles in fortifications; but this knowledge was of value only for the moment, and much of the data merely confirmed experiments that had been

---

[1] John Buchan, *Memory Hold the Door* (Toronto, 1941), p. 261.

conducted in Europe. Some of the equipment used by the Civil War armies was recommended to authorities in London, Berlin, and Paris, and had there been no major war in Europe for the next decade or so, the value of the Civil War as a testing ground for new weapons and equipment doubtless would have been greatly enhanced. But the Danish war of 1864 offered a still better opportunity to observe the effects of rifled cannon and breech-loading rifles, and the campaigns of 1866 and 1870–71 naturally took precedence over the American campaigns in the minds of most European soldiers. As it was, each of the major European armies found some part of the American experience of special significance. The Prussians profited from studying the maintenance and repair of Civil War railroads; the British probably increased their understanding of the auxiliary forces by observing the volunteer armies in America; and the French were favorably impressed by some aspects of the organization and administration of the Union army. Interestingly enough, nearly all foreign observers expressed admiration for the quality of instruction at the United States Military Academy at West Point.

Failure to take advantage of specific developments in tactics or strategy during the Civil War cannot be attributed to false or insufficient information. There were ample observers and military visitors in America at all times; scarcely a campaign in Virginia and Maryland did not come under the scrutiny of some foreign officer accompanying one or the other of the armies, and even specialized information was easily obtainable in print. Practically all the observers spent their time in the East, however, so the view from Europe became distorted, but the fact remains that the necessary information was available—it simply was ignored or misinterpreted.

Reasons for this vary. Manifestly, events in Europe following on the heels of the Civil War induced most soldiers either to dismiss or at least to minimize American innovations in tactics and strategy. Prussia was preoccupied with the wars for German unification, while France before 1870 was still impressed by the accomplishments of French arms under Napoleon and consequently was in no frame of mind to follow the example of armies of civilians fighting each other in uncleared forests, particularly when those armies had been trained according to French drill regulations. British public opinion was still perturbed by what had happened in the Crimea and in India, and progressive soldiers were working to reform some of the abuses and weaknesses uncovered there.

Then too, most professional soldiers agreed that the Civil War was unlike any campaign which they had seen, or were likely to see for that matter, in Europe. It had been fought entirely by armies comprised of volunteers, militia, and conscripts, and while it was frequently recognized that these armies by 1864 had become hardened veterans, there was no way to know how the Civil War armies would have compared with other armies of their day. To at least one writer, Leon Gambetta's hastily raised Army of the Loire in 1871 was the best militia army that had ever existed; it had fought a professional army, so at least it offered some basis for comparison.[2] Others who maintained that the Civil War armies by 1864 could have held their own against any army from the Continent hastened to point out that few nations in Europe could afford to spend the first two years of war training troops; time was a luxury they could not afford.

Finally, it should be remarked that while European soldiers recognized the distinct logistical problems and the new importance of railroads during the Civil War, with the exception of the Construction Corps there was not much from this side of the Civil War that could be applied directly in Europe, where geography and the density as well as the distribution of population created problems of a different sort altogether from those which had plagued American strategists.

After 1871 it was the Germans who first demonstrated an interest in the Civil War. For a period of about ten years their military journals published numerous studies of individual campaigns and the tactics of the Civil War. The Germans wrote with clarity and intelligence, and almost without exception they repeated the conclusions of Justus Scheibert—as a modern war the Civil War was worth studying, but it contained few military lessons of any intrinsic value. In time German military writers turned their attention to the more pressing problem of preparing for a possible war on two fronts, using as a signpost from history the campaigns of Frederick the Great and Napoleon. Later the French, still searching for explanations for their failure in 1870, grew moderately interested in the American campaigns. Some of the French studies showed pro-

---

[2] Colmar Freiherrn von der Goltz, *Leon Gambetta und seine Armeen* (Berlin, 1877), p. 258 ff.

phetic originality, but official doctrine was determined by those who recently had discovered Clausewitz and rediscovered Napoleon, and no attention was paid to the warnings of those few who cited the Civil War as an example of wars still to come. After 1870 the English lost interest in the Civil War completely and did not regain it until the appearance of Henderson's *Campaign of Fredericksburg* in 1886. By this time a reaction against the imitation of German methods had set in, and Henderson rapidly became a prominent spokesman for a new and vigorous group of military writers and theorists. Through his teaching and writings, the Civil War acquired new significance, becoming so popular among British soldiers that after his death it was the war most often cited to illustrate official doctrine. In the last decade before the First World War, German interest in the Civil War experienced a slight revival, but save for one writer, a novelist, these later studies, too, were barren of any fresh interpretations.

In retrospect it would appear that European armies might have capitalized upon some of the tactical lessons of the Civil War. Prussian cavalry performed poorly in 1866, and in 1870 the French cavalry was inadequate; both could have increased their usefulness had they employed some of the techniques made popular by Stuart, Forrest, or Sheridan. The British found mounted infantry indispensable in South Africa in 1900; yet only a few years earlier Henderson had expressed the opinion that this lesson of the Civil War had been overlooked.

The pre-eminent importance of intrenchments was another misunderstood feature of the Civil War. That intrenchments had been used extensively and with good effect in 1864–65 none could deny, and the reappearance of earthworks at Plevna in 1877 and in Manchuria in 1904–5 should have indicated that this lesson might be repeated in the future. Yet only a few military writers, notably Auger, Bleibtreu, and Henderson, really appreciated the significance of this phase of the Civil War. Again it was Henderson who feared that "the importance of the spade is often overlooked in peace." As for artillery, the Civil War was important only because it represented a transition from smoothbore to rifled cannon, and the foreign military critics undoubtedly were correct in relying more upon later campaigns in Europe. To most European soldiers of that day and age, modern warfare really began in 1870, with the universal introduction of the breechloader and rifled artillery.

But if the European armies did not take practical advantage of the exemplary tactical lessons of the Civil War, it is not quite correct to conclude that they learned nothing of value from it. The nineteenth century was an industrial age: military conditions were constantly changing as new weapons appeared and as transportation and communication facilities improved, and every war was likely to indicate probable trends. After 1862 it was apparent to all that railroads had given new dimensions to strategy and that rifled artillery would make obsolete many existing coastal defenses. In this sense the Civil War did not go unnoticed, even though few American practices were imitated in detail.

Until 1914 most European soldiers writing about the Civil War were absorbed in the study of tactics, many of them becoming embroiled in long-standing controversies. To some the Civil War was an eye opener; to others it was primarily an arsenal of convenient facts, but most writers assumed that Civil War tactics had not been completely outmoded. They were aware of the broader aspects of strategy, to be sure, and in their introductory remarks they frequently mentioned the modern characteristics of the Civil War. But they focused their attention on tactics. Rarely did they describe a campaign fought west of the Alleghenies, and as a rule they confined their treatment of strategy and logistics to one particular campaign. After 1918 the general problems of military policy, grand strategy, and command replaced some of the dead tactical issues. Looking back, the postwar generation could see many things in the Civil War that earlier soldiers had missed. The events of 1914–18 provided fresh insight into the problems that had faced the statesmen and soldiers of 1861–65, and a few, in turn, found in the Civil War clues to the solution of problems arising from the recent global conflict.

Among those European soldiers who studied the Civil War several emerge as key figures. Certainly Scheibert, who wrote largely from personal experience, set the pattern for subsequent studies of the Civil War in Germany. His interpretations were rarely challenged, and because he found little to recommend for adoption by the German army it is scarcely surprising that his successors should likewise fail to do so. In France, DeChenal and Vigo Roussillon provided the basic sources of information, supplementing in technical detail the accounts of Lecomte and the Bourbon princes. Havelock and Denison were the most original English students of the Civil War before Henderson; they were responsible, at least, for Wolseley's and Chesney's partial conversion to the idea of mounted infantry, and their writings fanned the controversy between adherents of firepower and of shock tactics. Henderson's significance cannot be too strongly stated. He reintroduced the study of the Civil War in England; at the Staff College he was in a position to influence a whole generation of British officers; and he comprehended the basic tactical lessons of the war. Unfortunately, his observations often were lost upon his followers, who committed fundamentally the same mistake made by an earlier generation of British officers who had concentrated upon the details of the Prussian campaigns. Of the later writers, only Liddell Hart managed to incorporate lessons from the Civil War into constructive theory, although others wrote equally penetrating studies of the American campaigns. From the standpoint of the development of his military thought, *Sherman* is probably the most important book he has written. For that matter, Sherman seems to have contributed more to European military thought than any other Civil War general.

There are others who, less influential than the above, were no less discerning in their analysis of the Civil War. Auger and De Thomasson are striking examples. From his study of the Civil War Auger was able to predict the trench warfare of 1914–18 twenty years before the event, and De Thomasson's analysis of Stuart's cavalry operations convinced him that those who assumed that the next war would start with a series of mounted combats between cavalry were wrong: by overlooking the value of dismounted action, most theorists minimized the potentialities of cavalry in reconnaissance. Both Auger and De Thomasson were ignored, just as in Germany the novelist Bleibtreu was a prophet without honor. In England, J. E. Edmonds, an Engineer, was the only one of Henderson's pupils to comprehend the significance of intrenchments in modern war.

Considering the number of European soldiers who wrote about the Civil War, it seems at first glance surprising that many of its lessons were advocated by so few. The fact of the matter is that nine out of every ten who wrote about the Civil War simply carried into their books or articles doctrines carefully instilled by years of training. German writers, opposed in principle to improvised armies, invariably stressed the lack of adequate training and a general staff in the American armies. Before 1870 French soldiers were wedded to the idea of a long-term, professional army; it was only after their defeat that they were ready to admit that military lessons could be learned from a war fought by amateurs. British officers looked with favor upon the same volunteer armies that the Germans had criticized. Most European soldiers who wrote about the Civil War were relatively junior officers, and writing, as many of them doubtless did, with an eye on their career, it is not to be wondered that they were inclined to be cautious and would stress views already embodied in the training manuals and military textbooks.

Equally significant is the fact that nearly every European writer who saw something new and valuable to be learned from the Civil War was himself a maverick who had strayed beyond the pale of military orthodoxy. Havelock is a prime example; Denison, a militia officer and a Canadian, is another; Bleibtreu was a creative writer with an interest in military history. Even Scheibert, conventional though most of his interpretations may seem, ran counter to official opinion in the matter of fortifications, where his views in part rested upon his observations in America. Nothing is known of Auger and De Thomasson, but Fuller appropriately entitled his autobiography *Memoirs of an Unconventional Soldier,* and through the years Liddell Hart has stoutly maintained his independence. To a lesser extent this is true of Henderson, whose writings excelled in synthesis rather than originality, for Henderson's brief experience with the official history of the Boer War suggests that he, too, could be independent. He was an accomplished scholar as well—which may account for his keen observations about many aspects of the Civil War. In this connection it is worthy of note that Edmonds, after Henderson the most perceptive English student of the Civil War during the Great Revival at the turn of the century, likewise was a prominent historian. He became the official army historian of the First World War, and the revised edition of Wood and Edmonds' *The Civil War in the United States* has just appeared in a new edition. Outside of popular eyewitness accounts of visits to the campfires and battlefields of the Civil War, this book is one of the few produced by European soldiers in sufficient demand to warrant republication.

Conclusions based upon a survey of the military literature of a single war must be speculative, yet this much appears certain: American developments in military technology were noted and in several instances imitated by the European armies, who also observed that most of the accepted rules of strategy still applied, although the science of logistics was revolutionized by the use of railroads for military purposes. But the tactical lessons of the Civil War were rejected by most European soldiers and recognized by only a few. In every instance when the experience of the American armies conflicted with popular opinion at home or the lessons of more recent wars, the latter prevailed. Most of those who studied the Civil War after 1870 were in reality seeking to confirm accepted principles rather than to discover new information that might lead to a change in doctrine. For this reason the tactical lessons of the Civil War went unheeded, proving again the wisdom of Bronsart von Schellendorf's observation: "It is well known that military history, when superficially studied, will furnish arguments in support of any theory or opinion."[3]

The same might apply to other fields of history as well, but in military history, unfortunately, more than an academic reputation is often at stake.

[3] Quoted in Prince Kraft zu Hohenlohe-Ingelfingen, *Letters on Artillery* (2d ed.; London, 1890), p. 108.

A Work of Fiction

In 1864 a three-volume work was published in Leipzig, entitled *Ein deutscher Landsknecht der neuesten Zeit*. To all outward appearances this was based upon the papers of an anonymous German soldier of fortune whose colorful career had ended abruptly in Virginia in 1863. The editor of these *"hinterlassenen Papieren"* was Julius von Wickede, a popular and prolific military writer.

This work, at least that portion dealing with the Civil War, must be considered fiction rather than fact. Von Wickede never mentioned the name of the anonymous author and failed to explain how the papers came into his possession; moreover, he was in the habit of passing off his own books as memoirs or edited literary remains.[1] The first two volumes, which concern events in Europe that Von Wickede is known to have witnessed, probably are to a large extent autobiographical, but it is obvious that his account of the Civil War is spurious.

For one thing, the text mentions by name many relatively minor figures encountered by the author in Denmark in 1848 or in Italy in 1860—places visited by Von Wickede during those years—but in America no one below the rank of general or cabinet member is so identified. Von Wickede never visited America, which probably explains why his hero could have fought along the Potomac River in September, 1861, at Belmont on the Mississippi in November, and then spent Christmas Eve at Chattanooga with Stonewall Jackson, when in fact the famous Confederate leader was in Winchester, Virginia, at the time. In February the author was supposed to have been one of the few to have escaped capture at Fort Donelson; in March he is alleged to have served under Morgan in Tennessee; and in April he fought at Shiloh. He also was supposed to have participated in the Seven Days' campaign before Richmond in June. Only one who had never encountered distances in America could be guilty of a plot such as this.

Yet it is obvious that Von Wickede did not invent everything concerning the Civil War, and "Landsknecht's" experiences bear a striking resemblance to the career of a well-known American soldier of fortune, General C. R. Wheat. Both had participated in expeditions to Latin America, both had served under Garibaldi, and both were mortally

[1] See the sketch on Julius von Wickede in *Allgemeine deutsche Biographie* (Leipzig, 1897), XLII, 318–19.

wounded during the Seven Days' campaign. Rob Wheat had settled in New Orleans, and it is significant that nearly all of "Landsknecht's" observations on southern society came from Louisiana, despite the assertion that most of the time he was fighting elsewhere. Both commanded outfits comprised mainly of Irish toughs, and both encountered among Union prisoners foreign officers they had known previously.

"Landsknecht" was persuaded to fight for the Confederacy by the son of a Louisiana planter whom he had known in Italy. Von Wickede and Wheat had both served in Italy, and it is possible, indeed probable, that it was from Wheat that Von Wickede learned what little he knew about the Civil War.[2]

[2] *Ein deutscher Landsknecht, passim;* Leo Wheat, "Memoir of Gen. C. R. Wheat, Commander of the Louisiana Tiger Battalion," *Southern Historical Society Papers,* XVII (Richmond, 1889), 47–59.

B

Analysis of Cavalry Operations in the American Civil War, with Special Reference to Raids on Communications

WESTERN THEATRE

by

CAPTAIN B. H. LIDDELL HART

(May, 1935)

I

Early in June 1862, Buell, with the Army of Ohio reinforced, was ordered to advance eastward from Corinth upon Chattanooga (200 miles distant), the gateway to the eastern, and main, part of the Confederacy. He was to repair the Memphis and Charleston railway as he advanced and use it as his line of supply. But the mere threat of Confederate raids upon this line, which ran parallel to the front, held him up. At the end of the month he was allowed to adopt a N.W. to S.W. line of supply, using Nashville as his advanced base. At the beginning of July Buell advanced to within 30 miles of Chattanooga, but was then paralyzed by two successive strokes. The first was by Forrest with 1400 cavalry who on July 9th moved out from Chattanooga and on the 13th descended upon and cut the Nashville-Chattanooga railroad at Murfreesborough, 90 miles behind the front and captured the garrison of 1700 men at a cost to himself of some 80 casualties. Buell's new line of supply was not repaired until July 28th. Secondly, on August 12, Morgan, sweeping further north, descended upon the Louisville-Nashville railway where it crossed the Cumberland River at Gallatin, 160 miles behind the front. He destroyed the bridge and tunnel, thus severing Buell's rearward link with his main base in Kentucky. Buell abandoned his offensive and fell back to Murfreesborough.

This paralysis of the Federal advance was followed up in September by Bragg with the main Confederate force. Bragg moved due north to Sparta, 60 miles to the E. of Murfreesborough; from Sparta he could either move W against Nashville or N against Louisville. The uncertainty of direction enabled him to slip past Buell's flank; thus he not only forced Buell to fall back hurriedly to protect Kentucky, but outstripped him in the race to Louisville. On September 16th Bragg reached Munfordville on the Louisville-Nashville railway, thus interposing between Buell and his base. He then, however, forfeited the opportunity he had gained.

2

Grant's First Advance, Overland, on Vicksburg in December 1862

Early in December, Grant, with nearly 40,000 men, advanced towards the Yallabusha (110 miles N. of Jackson), behind which lay the main Confederate force of 24,000 under Van Dorn; at the same time Sherman with 30,000 was to steam down the Mississippi against Vicksburg, where Pemberton had collected 12,000 Confederates.

Grant's advance was hamstrung by two simultaneous raids. A force of 3,500 cavalry under Van Dorn himself, starting on the 18th, passed round Grant's flank and on the 20th destroyed his secondary base of supply at Holly Springs (20 miles behind the front). At the same time, Forrest, with 2500 cavalry, was sent by Bragg for a westward stroke, (from Columbia, south of Nashville) of much longer range against the northern end of Grant's 180-mile life line—the Mobile and Ohio railway by which his supplies came from Columbus, Kentucky. The line and its bridges were destroyed over a 60-mile stretch between Jackson and Columbus, and this distant severance had the greater effect, making it impossible for Grant to replenish the supplies destroyed at Holly Springs, (Forrest inflicted a loss of 1500 and drew off 20,000 in chase of him). For over a week he was cut off from all communications from the North and was constrained to fall back to his starting point.

3

In April, 1863, Grierson, with three Federal Cavalry Regiments, rode due south from LaGrange, near Memphis, across the rear of the Confederate forces at Vicksburg, damaging the railroads and causing incessant alarms. He reached Baton Rouge on May 2nd having covered about 400 miles on an almost due North and South line in 16 days. At Jackson, the railway junction for Vicksburg, he had been within 40 miles of this place.

If the raid had little material effect it had a considerable moral effect on the Confederate commander, Pemberton, in distracting him while Grant was preparing his main manoeuvre, round the south of Vicksburg.

4

Campaign in Tennessee, 1863

During the first half of 1863 the Confederate Army under Bragg and the Federal Army under Rosecrans remained comparatively inactive, facing each other across a 25-mile interval, S. of Murfreesborough. That inactivity was due partly to the threat and effect, although more the former, of cavalry raids upon each other's communications.

Late in January, Bragg despatched a cavalry expedition under Wheeler to take up a position on the Cumberland River, far in the enemy's rear, and interrupt the passage of store-ships and transports. But on arrival they waited several days without sign of a target and then Wheeler insisted, despite Forrest's protests, on attempting an attack against Fort Donelson—which was recklessly launched and easily repulsed.

In April, Rosecrans organized a raid by a mule-mounted brigade against the Confederate depots in Georgia; the Round Mountain Iron-works, one of the most important Confederate factories of war material, was destroyed; but the mules were a poor lot and the force was rounded up and forced to surrender through Forrest's blend of bluff with superior mobility.

At the end of June Rosecrans (63,000) at last advanced, making a turning movement which Bragg (46,000) evaded by withdrawal to Chattanooga. No serious attempt was made by either to cut the other's rail communications during this phase. But in the next Rosecrans sought to throw his whole army across Bragg's. To mask this aim, he spread his cavalry over a 150-mile front along the Tennessee River, and deceived Bragg into thinking that the crossing would be made east of Chattanooga; Rosecrans crossed unopposed on the other flank, at the end of August. But he was too slow to prevent Bragg falling back southward, and setting a trap for him. Rosecrans emerged from the mountain belt in three main detachments spread over a 60-mile front, while Bragg lay centrally with a concentrated force, now strongly reinforced, which was nearly treble each of the invader's. But the very dispersion of the Federals and their wide front of approach bewildered and paralysed the Confederates, and Rosecrans was allowed several days to reconcentrate on his left centre at Chickamauga. At last, on September 18th, Bragg moved to envelop Rosecrans' left flank; he merely bent it back, but the strain upon the line then enabled his left, under Longstreet, to break the enemy's right. But the success proved barren, if costly, and the Federals withdrew safely to Chattanooga. In the battle, the Confederate cavalry had worked in narrow co-operation with the infantry, and there was no effective pursuit.

When back at Chattanooga, however, the Federal Army's communications were interrupted by Confederate cavalry raids, and it was in danger of collapse by starvation when Grant arrived to its relief, with ample troops not only to guard and improve the lines of supply but to renew the offensive. This, delivered in November, threw the Confederates back, but the Federal cavalry played a minor part and the enemy's retreat was never endangered.

In Sherman's 1864 advance from Chattanooga eastward upon Atlanta (130 miles), his starting point was 150 miles in front of his main base of supply at Nashville and 340 miles in front of his main base of supply at Louisville. Out of 180,000 troops, 80,000 had to be left to guard the communications and the occupied territory through which they ran. The main danger to this rear zone was offered by a few thousand Confederate cavalry under Forrest, who lay to the South. To counter it, a mobile force of 10,000 under Sturgis was formed and despatched at the end of May to disperse Forrest, who was then at Tupelo (S. of Corinth). Forrest had moved simultaneously, with 3,000 cavalry, against the rearmost sector of Sherman's communications—to ease the pressure on Atlanta, from which Sherman's forces were now barely thirty miles distant. He had hardly set out before he was called back to deal with Sturgis's expedition. He caught it at Brice's Cross Roads not far from Tupelo with its cavalry separated from the infantry, and in thick country that allowed him to cloak his own weakness. His dispersed and drove it back on Memphis, inflicting a loss of a quarter its strength (five times his own loss). The defeat had instant effects; it led Sherman to allot two fresh divisions, which had been intended for the attack on Mobile, to form a special striking force of 15,000 at Memphis to hunt down Forrest at all costs. (Sherman was only able to prosecute his own offensive meantime because of his previous care to build up a reserve of 20 days' supplies in cavalry-proof places close behind his front.) This force, if it did not succeed in cornering Forrest, at least held him in check, save for one daring raid into Memphis itself.

In the first week of July, when the Chattahoochee River was reached, Sherman used Stoneman's cavalry division to create the impression that he was searching for a crossing on the south flank, and thus drew off most of the enemy's cavalry, while he sent Garrard's cavalry division to secure a crossing 20 miles upstream on the north flank. He gained a bridgehead here with the cavalry, who were soon relieved by an infantry division, and also a midway bridgehead with an army corps—the possession of these two bridgeheads on the enemy's flank sufficing to loosen their grip on the river line.

In the next phase, the side-step onto the railway east of Atlanta, Sherman used his cavalry similarly—one part as the extension of his manoeuvring left wing, and the other part on the right wing to screen the ground from which he had moved.

Atlanta, and the Confederate army there, was supplied by three railways—one running E. to Augusta, one S.E. to Macon, one S.W. to Montgomery and Mobile. Sherman's general manoeuvre had placed him astride the first; a long-range raid from Tennessee by a small improvised force under Rousseau had made a temporary break in the second —at a point eighty miles from Atlanta, and now by a reverse side-step of his whole forces, Sherman came close to it at a point just below Atlanta. Simultaneously, he tried a pincer move with his cavalry against the third line, the central and so least accessible one—his idea was not to invest but to "draw their enemy out of Atlanta by threatening the railroad below," and strike at them while in motion. The right pincer (3,500 under McCook) duly reached the railway at Lovejoy's station (30 miles S. of Atlanta), and cut it,—if not very thoroughly. The left pincer (6,500 under Garrard), instead of fulfilling its primary mission, went straight for its secondary objective, Macon, with the idea of rescuing the Federals in the prison-camp there, and became entangled with the enemy.

Three weeks later, on September 18th, Sherman sent the larger half of his cavalry under Kilpatrick against the Macon railway—the orders being that "it was not a raid but a deliberate attack for the purpose of so disabling that (rail) road that the enemy will be unable to supply his army in Atlanta." Swinging south and then east, Kilpatrick cut the railway along a four-mile stretch near Jonesborough (25 miles below Atlanta), and then completed his circuit around the enemy's rear, arriving back on the 22nd. But the manoeuvre was better executed than the task of demolition, with the consequence that the enemy repaired the railway in two days instead of at least ten as Kilpatrick's report calculated.

On the 28th Sherman side-stepped his army and then swung it across the railway; this forced the enemy to abandon Atlanta, although they succeeded in evading his block by a skilled night retreat around it. The Federal Cavalry, poorly handled, did little to intercept them.

Sherman's delay to move with his main force earlier in the month was due partly to a menace to his supplies. For on August 10th Wheeler with the bulk of the Confederate cavalry had moved out on a long-range raid against Sherman's communications. On the 13th and 14th Wheeler made a series of slight cuts in the railway between Marietta and Dalton, but then moved off into East Tennessee, where he could have little effect on the main issue—while Sherman profited by the chance to take Hood off his guard with the manoeuvre onto his rear.

On September 2nd Atlanta fell into Sherman's hands, and he then projected the plan of advancing across Georgia to the Atlantic Coast. But on the 21st Forrest reappeared in Tennessee with a force of 4,500 from Mississippi, and on the 25th frightened into surrender the garrison of Athens, on the Nashville-Decatur line. This move threatened the main Nashville-Chattanooga line, and no less than 3 divisions were hurriedly ordered to support the protective troops. Grant wired Sherman that it would be "better to drive Forrest out of middle Tennessee as a first step" before attempting anything bigger. Although Forrest, for once, shrank from the risk of striking at Sherman's main line in face of such superior numbers, his raid wrecked 80 miles of the subsidiary line and captured or killed 3,300 Federals.

Forrest's raid was followed by Hood's step in moving the main Confederate forces past Sherman's flank, and making a progressive advance along the long Federal line of communication, with successive inward thrusts. In the first week of October the 24 miles of railway between Marietta and Dalton were destroyed—a break which took until the 28th to repair. These demolitions and the extending menace forced Sherman to come back with part of his forces, over a hundred miles from Atlanta; Hood evaded interception, and was compelled to avoid fighting as the morale of his troops had been impaired by their fruitless counter-attacks at Atlanta. Thus after reaching the neighbourhood of Chattanooga, the Confederates retired temporarily into Alabama to recuperate. The continued threat of their existence, however, caused the Federal Supreme Command to urge upon Sherman the advisability of postponing any further plans—and with them the chance of finishing the war—while this danger hovered on the horizon. It was only through Sherman's audacity in cutting loose from his communications, and marching across Georgia to the Atlantic, that this strategic paralysis was averted; and, even so, he had to leave two of his army corps, as a striking force, to make up a total of 70,000 troops under Thomas as an insurance against the menace of the 35,000 under Hood and Forrest. The force which on November 15th marched with Sherman to the Atlantic totalled 60,000.

Meantime, on October 16th, Forrest had set out with 3,000 cavalry from Corinth for a stroke against the great depot at Johnsonville, on the lower reaches of the Tennessee, whence a large part of the Federal supplies were brought by river for despatch thence by rail to Nashville. He succeeded in destroying it on the night of November 4th, under the impotent eyes of the guardian fort with its garrison of 2,000.

On his return Forrest was placed in command of all Hood's Cavalry, a total of 5,000 for the advance upon Nashville which the Confederate main force now attempted. With Forrest's Cavalry in the van, the Confederate army pushed past the west flank of the 1½ Federal Corps (20,000) under Schofield at Pulaski; his retreat thus threatened, he fell back towards Columbia on the Duck River. Forrest's cavalry arrived there first, on November 24th, but found the place held by the Federal fourth division which had just come up. Forrest was thus blocked until Schofield had safely withdrawn there. Hood did not come up until the 26th. Two days later Forrest succeeded in crossing the river on the left flank, to find Schofield again retiring. Forrest got across his line of retreat at Spring Hill, but the cavalry again proved too weak offensively, and the infantry too slow, and Hood missed his chance; thus Schofield made good his retreat to Franklin. Here Hood attacked him in position on the 30th and was bloodily repulsed. The cavalry were used in close extension of either wing and had no effect. Schofield then fell back on Nashville, followed up cautiously by the badly bruised Confederates. A stalemate ensued. During it a mixed detachment was sent off under Forrest to round up the small garrisons along the Nashville-Chattanooga railway, and collect supplies. Meantime, Hood foolishly waited while the Federals gathered strength.

On December 15th the much superior Federal Army opened an attack, forcing back the Confederate left, and leading Hood to take up a shorter line behind. The attack was here renewed next afternoon, but failed; meantime, however, the Federal cavalry under Wilson had been making a narrow move round the flank by steps, causing Hood to bend back and extend his line to check them. The stretching enabled the Federal infantry to pierce the line, whereupon the whole Confederate army dissolved in flight. Nevertheless, although Wilson was astride one road of retreat, the bulk of them slipped safely past down the parallel road only $1\frac{1}{2}$ miles away.

The general impression left by this analysis is that:—

1. *When acting in close co-operation with the army*, the mobile army proved ineffective in its offensive action—whether in driving home a stroke at the enemy's flank or immediate rear, or in pursuit. This may be explained by the difficulty it had in overcoming the fire-resistance of small bodies unless there was ample room to evade them by manoeuvre.

The best value of the cavalry seems to have been in seizing unoccupied points quickly, and holding them until relieved by infantry.

For reconnaissance, the value of the cavalry was not in proportion to its strength, the use of brigades and divisions rarely obtaining more information than that furnished by skilful patrole.

2. *When used independently*, for strokes against the enemy's communications, the mobile arm was occasionally of great effect, if more often negligible. The determining factors in the difference seem to have been:—

i) The choice of the target.

ii) The skill of the leader in avoiding obstruction.

iii) The thoroughness of the troops in the task of destruction.

Apart from these factors, the effect seems to have been greatest when executed in conjunction with action by the main force, and when the enemy's force was on the move. Long-range moves seem to have been more effective than close-range.

Cutting Communications

In the planning of any stroke at the enemy's communications, either by manoeuvre round his flank or by rapid penetration of a breach in his front, the question will arise as to the most effective point of aim—whether it should be directed against the immediate rear of the opposing force, or further back. Some guidance on the question can be obtained from analysis of cavalry raids carried out in the past, especially in the more recent wars since railways came into use. While such cavalry raids had more limited potentialities than an inroad of modern mechanized forces, this difference emphasises rather than detracts from the significance of the evidence which they provide. Making the necessary adjustment, the following deductions can be drawn—

In general, the nearer to the force that the cut is made, the *more immediate* the effect; the nearer to the base, the *greater* the effect. In either case, the effect is much greater and more quickly felt if made against a force that is in motion, and in course of carrying out an operation, than against a force that is stationary.

In deciding the direction of a mobile stroke, much depends on the strategic position and supply conditions of the enemy forces, i.e., the number of their lines of supply, the possibility of adopting alternative lines of supply, the amount of supplies likely to be accumulated in advanced depots close behind their front. After these factors have been considered, they should be re-considered in the light of the accessibility of the various possible objectives, i.e., the distance, the natural obstacles, and the opposition likely to be met. In general the longer the distance that has to be covered, the greater the ratio of natural obstacles, but the less the ratio of opposition.

Thus, unless the natural obstacles are very severe, or the enemy has unusual independence of supplies from base, more success and more effect is to be expected from cutting his communications as far back as possible. A further consideration is that while a stroke close in rear of the enemy force may have more effect on the minds of the enemy troops, a stroke far back tends to have more effect on the mind of the enemy commander.

Cavalry raids in the past often forfeited their effect by lack of care in carrying out the demolition side of their task. As a result the prospective value of mobile raids on communications has been unduly discounted. It is apt to be forgotten that the flow of supplies may be interrupted not only by demolitions on the route, but by actual or threatened interception of trains and lorry convoys. The latter form of interruption is increased in potentiality by the development of mechanized forces (because of their fluidity).

Index

[*Note:* Individual battles are listed alphabetically under "Battles, campaigns, and sieges."]